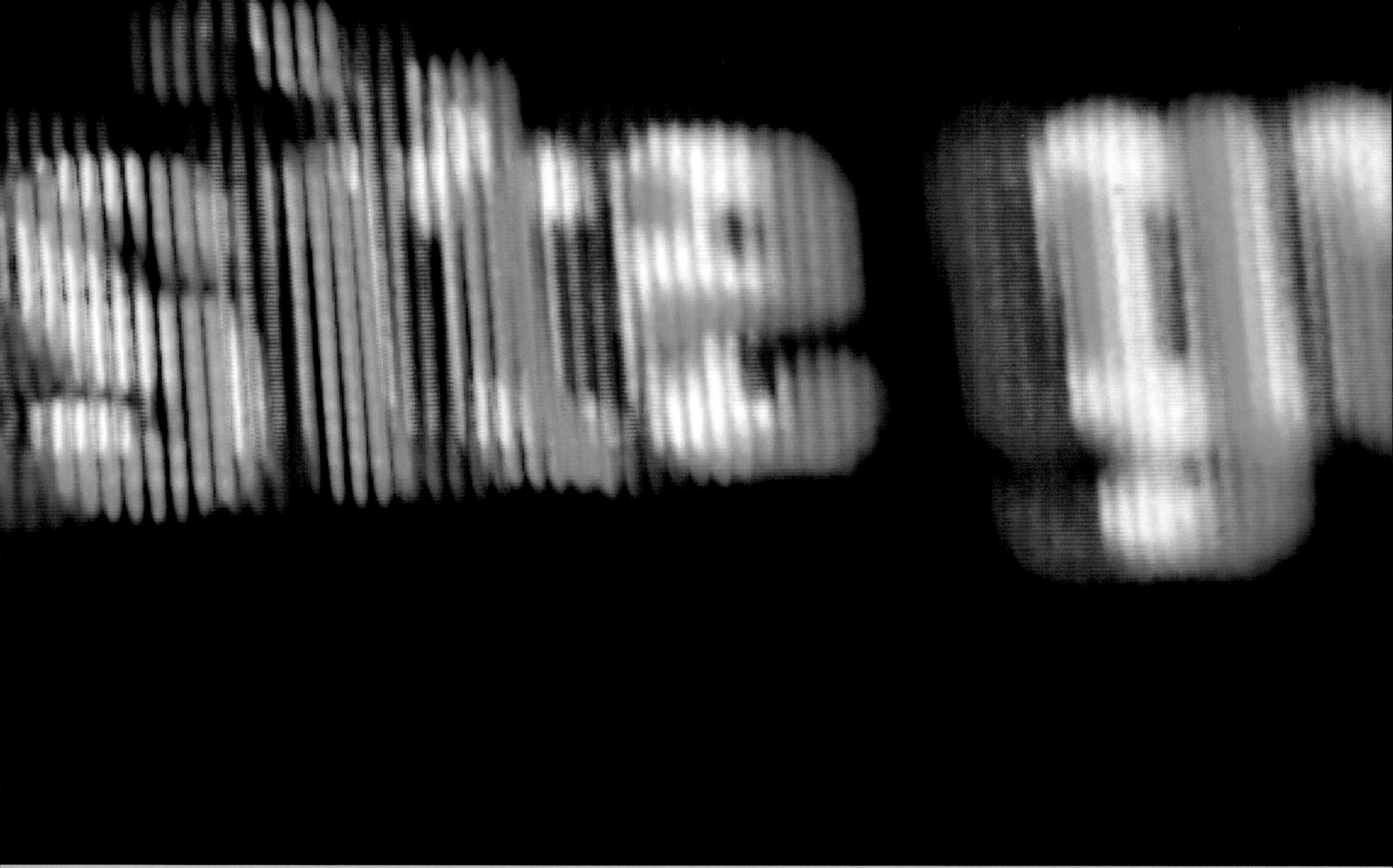

Website Graphics

The best of global site design

by the editors of Mediamatic / Willem Velthoven, Liesbeth den Boer, Geert-Jan Strengholt

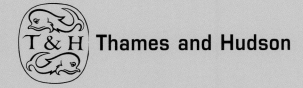

Thames and Hudson

Website Graphics / Tab

Copyright

First published in Great Britain in 1997 by Thames and Hudson Ltd, London
First published in the United States of America in hardcover in 1997 by Thames and Hudson Inc.,
500 Fifth Avenue, New York, New York 10110

© 1997 BIS Publishers

British Library Cataloguing-in-Publication Data

A catalogue record for this book is available from the British Library

ISBN 0-500-01788-3

Library of Congress Catalog Card Number 97-60326

Printed and bound in Belgium

e of Contents

Colophon

Editors
Liesbeth den Boer, Geert J. Strengholt, Willem Velthoven (Mediamatic, Amsterdam)

Editorial Production
Mediamatic, Amsterdam / Liesbeth den Boer, Dennis A. Kramer, Geert J. Strengholt

Final Editing
Peter Davies

Selection
The selection of sites has been made by the editors in close co-operation with the contributors

Contributors
James Boekbinder / j.boekbinder@inter.nl.net, Max Bruinsma / maxb@xs4all.nl, Adam Eeuwens / fluxus@earthlink.net, Sophie Greenfield / sophie@mmcorp.com, Clement Mok / clement@studioarchetype.com, Giles Rollestone / giles@urban.demon.co.uk, Jorinde Seijdel / seijdel@xs4all.nl, Nathan Shedroff / nathan@nathan.com, Mari Soppela / ano@xs4all.nl, Geert J. Strengholt / geertjan@mediamatic.nl, Willem Velthoven / willem@mediamatic.nl

Design
Koeweiden Postma Associates, Amsterdam

Translations
Peter Davies, Olivier&Wylie

Thanks to
Sander Kessels, Rick Prelinger, Dick Rijken, David Siegel, Remco Vlaanderen, Staff Mediamatic

Preface

Clement Mok / Studio Archetype / Identity and Information Architects

We – all of us – are living through a media revolution, as computing technology changes everything around us. It is chaotic, it is complicated, and many people find it uncomfortable. The challenge facing designers working with new media is not about shifting paradigms, re-engineering, or 'being digital'. It is about using design to find order and opportunity in the disorder generated by the computing medium. It is also about the ability of people to adjust to change, a decisive factor in the acceptance of any new technology. People adopt ideas when social, personal, and financial trends converge – a confluence that may seem random but usually happens 'by design'. Design, in its broadest sense, is the enabler of the digital era – it is a process that creates order out of chaos and tailors technology to the aims of business purposes. Design means being good, not just looking good.

Designers and businesses have to work now in the computing medium – a medium with a particularly stimulating effect on the disciplines of identity design, information design, and interactivity design.

Computing's essential function of processing is not easy to grasp. However, paradoxically it embodies the shift that business and industry need to make. The pay-off will not only come from focusing on an end result, but also from paying close attention to the way things are done.

The computing medium is vastly different from all others. Its extraordinary transformational behaviour and powers make any attempt to label it futile. People who work directly with the computing medium know that making assumptions about where it will lead is a waste of time and may result in unsound business decisions. What is really different about computing is not how it gets us from point A to point B, but how it has merged point A with point B.

As printed media, broadcasting, and computing are transforming and merging, the same is happening to the industries and professions using them. The more technology changes goods and services, the more they will in turn change our lives. And, the more our lives change, the more we demand that businesses respond with appropriate goods and services. The proliferation of digital technology is resulting in a new two-way relationship between business and consumers.

By decentralising access to information and promoting individual empowerment, digital technology is wreaking havoc on established business conventions and making companies behave in unpredictable ways. Technological changes are having such a fast impact that individuals and businesses scarcely have the time to comprehend them. Yet people who disregard technological megaleaps are likely to end up feeling out of touch. Worse, once a person falls behind in the endless race to know and understand new technology, it takes tremendous determination and stamina to catch up. The way to adapt to the pace of change is to be constantly aware of new developments, but it is time-consuming, difficult, and frightening to try. The only way we have of judging the usefulness of the results of this spreading and merging is through the application of design disciplines.

Interactivity and multimedia design may seem complex and difficult to master, but the truth of the matter is that interactivity is a social science, not rocket science. The computing medium is really a means to an end, and that end is engaging people with the forms of expression made possible by computing. At the heart of all the talk about the virtual world, connectivity, and the tremendous amount of information available is people's desire for the ultimate interaction: social interaction. A designer has an important responsibility to keep in mind that people need to communicate and express themselves. A designer's work must always be focused on the people who will experience the interactivity and on what is appropriate for that particular community; the technology employed is always a secondary consideration. The ultimate task of every designer is to create ways for people to communicate with each other and share common interests.

About Website Graphics

Liesbeth den Boer, Geert J. Strengholt, Willem Velthoven

With the World Wide Web consisting of about 50 million pages and a growth rate of 10% each month, it seems presumptuous to pretend that you have seen all there is to see on the Web. Looking at Yahoo's Top 10 of the Web or David Siegel's High Five awards makes you realise once more how fast today's winners are replaced by tomorrow's innovators. So from the start it has been our intention to gather poignant examples of what is state-of-the-art at this point in time.

So what can you expect from a book called 'Website Graphics: The Best of Global Site Design'? How should a book capture what is essentially dynamic and ephemeral, subject to constant change and development? Let us explore some of the reflections that played a role in the making of this book.

First and foremost Website Graphics is a book about visual/ graphic design for Web pages meant to be displayed on the computer screen. Graphics for the Web feature much illustration work designed with any kind of regular authoring software. However, we felt that its main challenge lies in practising graphic design and layout within the confines and limitations set by HTML and Web browsers, as well as in searching for new options and possibilities along the way. Consequently we considered sites in which visual design was based solely on

PhotoShop and the likes to fall short of these criteria. Furthermore conventions from a centuries-old graphic design tradition do not necessarily apply to the range of new challenges posed by multimedia and user interaction. An important element for Web designers therefore is the visual clarity of their interaction design — the navigation devices, the choice of metaphors — but also the visual transitions from page to page. The element of time — engaging and entertaining the users as they navigate through a site — poses a whole new challenge to designers. None of this, however, can be viewed separately from its context, the goals and aspirations formulated for a particular website. Since each site is made up of a number of disparate pages, it is the context, the general concept that gives meaning to them as a whole. In the end this is what makes a website. This chosen concept and the visual design that conveys or carries it constituted a further step in our evaluation of pre-selected sites.

Throughout the book sites have been grouped according to six main categories, defining a general 'raison d'etre' for the chosen sites. Obviously each category, whether it is On-line Commerce or Magazines, presents its own practical demands as well as its own design aesthetics. As is the case when evaluating graphic design in print, an important part of our selection process involved checking the original function of a website – its mission as it were – with regard to how it is realised visually by the designers in the context they have created.

Ultimately 'Website Graphics' does not present an easy 'how-to...', but simply a wide variety of solutions developed by designers and artists while hacking their way into uncharted territory. The consistency in their approach — the decision not to stop at designing a 'facade' for their site but to develop an overall concept from which the design follows naturally — has been an important criterion in our selection. We are confident that we have found some stunning examples, and hope that you will use this book for some 'live' excursions on the Web to experience the richness and depth of these sites for yourself.

Designing senses – a proposal for an approach to interactive design

Willem Velthoven

This article is about the design of interactive media. The most important step in each design process is the formulation of the design problem – asking the right questions. As we all seem to agree by now, interactive media is a new discipline of design. If this actually is the case, it should also be possible to formulate new design problems. We will have to ask new questions.

There is one new question which applies to the entire process of design of an interactive project, from concept and editing to visual design and technique. Asking it could even affect decisions on the financing and the commercial possibilities of a project.

It is an astonishingly simple question: how do I perceive the user? Asking ourselves this question certainly helps to clarify matters at all stages of the development process, whether the project is an interactive work of art, a word processor, a PR website, a game, or an on-line shopping mall.

What do I perceive? What do I want to perceive? What are my senses? and How can I act on what I perceive? become questions which logically follow.

Warning Just for the record: the question about perception is a new question, which does not replace, but complements the old questions. The interactive media has many similar properties to old media, with one more additional property: it changes as a function of its perception of its users. So all the design problems of the old media are still fully applicable. Only the solutions will change.

Therefore, this article is emphatically not intended to be a proposal for a comprehensive design method. It is meant as an essential addition. What other questions need to be asked greatly depends on the project at hand. You can draw on a variety of disciplines and sources: architecture, services, opera, TV games, graphic design, psychoanalysis, industrial design, magazines, amusement parks, film, ergonomics, soap operas, funfairs, telephone, restaurants, peep shows. Each of these has its own patterns and accomplishments.

Some of the old disciplines are already interactive, because they work with people. These are very instructive; they have built up knowledge on perception of the user and on how to respond adequately to what they perceive.

A Misunderstanding People often think that the unique characteristic of interactive media is that the users themselves can compile their own programme. Basically, this is right. The users make their choices and determine what will happen. From this point of view, the computer is a tool with which a certain goal can be reached. User perception is also essential for the functional design of interactive equipment.

In my view, the computer is a medium, one whose enormous cultural and commercial potential will only be fully realised when the medium's perception of the user becomes a vital element in the design. Understanding that will identify the new design challenges of this medium.

The senses of the computer Perception is a matter of the senses. It is an interpretation of stimuli from the environment conveyed through the senses. The senses of today's computers are indeed very primitive and passive. In fact so passive that, at face value, it is ludicrous to call them senses. I would therefore rather call them sensors.

At this moment, virtually all personal computers have two standard sensors: the keyboard and a pointing device with one or two buttons (usually a mouse). These are the only two sensors available by which the designer can learn something about the user.

We can complement our computers with various other sensors, such as a microphone and video camera. These sensors are insufficiently widespread for designers to be able to use them in standard applications for a large public. Moreover, the technical possibilities for interpreting the signals from these sensors are still so limited that I will not deal with them in this article.

A variety of sensors has been developed for special systems, such as process control or surveillance of buildings. The most fascinating explorations in the field of new senses for the computer are taking place in the visual arts. Artists who use the computer as a medium often come up with very inspired ways of perceiving users in their installations, but those will not be dealt with here either.

The intention of my proposal is to treat the commonplace keyboard, and, in particular, the mouse, as senses. They are the user's operating devices; however, they cannot function as such unless this function is directly supported by the application. There is, in fact, no question of direct operation. This way of thinking is also applicable to any other sensor that can be connected to a computer.

The keyboard The keyboard is the computer's most specialised sensor. It can feel when its keys are being pressed, but it can hardly be called an organ of touch. The use of the keyboard is very precisely defined. It can be used to feed in text and numbers which have a certain meaning, depending on the context. The keyboard mainly plays a role in the use of the computer as a tool. Short cuts are possible in the operation of this tool; known key combinations which have an agreed function. The user can also choose between options offered on the screen, such as the menus in MS-Dos. Nowadays, the mouse is used for this.

The mouse The mouse is interesting. You can use it to point to things on the monitor. Apart from accurately pointing to something on the screen, the movement of the mouse can also be registered. Games often make use of this: speed and direction of the movement are essential here, and the cursor is often dropped from the screen. In such cases, the joystick is a better sensor. For the user, the mouse and the joystick are more direct and intuitive operating instruments, which makes them much more useful sensors for the designer. It is for good reason that the mouse is intensively used in nearly all interactive programmes.

<u>Sensor</u> + <u>Interface</u> + <u>Sense</u> **A sensor is still not a sense; to perceive the user in a useful manner, we have to be able to interpret the stimuli registered by our sensors. This is accomplished by creating a context which invites the user to make use of the mouse or keyboard. This context is the interface. The user is offered various options on the screen, to which he obediently responds by operating the sensors.**

Imagine a screen displaying the following elements: the text 'Would you like to see more text?' and two clearly recognisable buttons with, respectively, the words 'Yes' and 'No'.

Such a situation can certainly be understood as a moment of choice for the user. And this is basically right; however, it should not be assumed that the user decides what is actually going to happen after he clicks his mouse at one of the buttons. The only action that the user can take is to click. We register this click, and, via the context, interpret it as a perception of the user's wish. The user's control over the situation is only apparent, and totally depends on what happens after the click. Say that the user clicks at 'Yes'. If the rest of the text then follows, the user would appear to be in control of the process. The system does what the user expected.

If, after the click, the text 'Unfortunately the article is finished' appears, it turns out that the user has no control at all. As designers of the system, we respond to the user. Our perception of the user enables us to do so. We have designed this perception ourselves, by asking the question and offering a number of options.

Imagine the following question: 'What is your opinion of the article so far?' Depending on your choice from the answers: 'Interesting', 'Tedious', and 'Superfluous', I can decide to continue in various ways.

As a reader, you control our interaction by deciding whether to read on or not. As the writer/designer of an interactive system, I can control the interaction by incorporating moments of perception and acting on what I have perceived. I can adjust my text to you, the reader, to make it more interesting for you, to inform you more specifically, to convince you better. I can even make you laugh or tease you.

As a partner in conversation, I observe you and respond to you. If I do this well, you will listen to me and consider my point of view. This is an example of the simplest ways to perceive a user. It is a kind of perception which is only possible with the use of an interactive medium. This text is written for a book, so I have no idea whether you are still reading. Perhaps you are already looking at the pictures further on. That is your own choice as the user of my book. There is no interaction. I cannot perceive you.

Perhaps you would like to do me a favour now and send an e-mail to senses@mediamatic.nl, to let me know whether you are still reading and what you think of it? I would be very grateful. But even if you did, I still could not do anything about our interaction. My text has already been written and printed, the same for everyone.

As the user of the book, you have all the options you could wish for. You can leaf through it, put it aside, decide to read Nathan Shedroff's or Clement Mok's article, reread my article, or whatever. These choices have nothing to do with interactive media. Many interactive programmes and websites offer their users little more choice than you, as the user of this book, have at this moment. Their makers only ask the user the most obvious questions, such as: Do you wish to return to the homepage? Would you like to order this product? Would you like to see our corporate profile? Which stock market quotations would you like to see? The users are being perceived, but the perceptions are trivial. Such environments are not really interactive, they are only navigable. The users can make a choice, but the makers of those environments themselves are not making any choices in response.

It is because they think in terms of user options and they do not grasp that they are designing senses. So they don't realise that they have the option to actively participate in the interaction. Of course, a website or CD-ROM has to be properly navigable. After all, the user cannot leaf through it like a book. Users also have to be able to make choices themselves. This kind of trivial perception is certainly important, and the user has to be offered a well-organised environment. Navigation can in fact often be further enhanced by the designer asking himself the questions: 'How can I best perceive the wishes of the user?' and 'How can I best respond to what I perceive?'

But navigation is only half the job. The potential of interactive media can be found in interaction based on intelligent user perception.

Other ways of perceiving the user The above examples are very simple and obvious. There are many interactive programmes which make excellent use of user perception. Good computer games, for example. Computer games rarely offer the user a clear choice. The progress of the game depends totally on the player's actions. On the basis of her actions, the player is offered new challenges and rewards. In a well-designed game, these are meticulously balanced. The game adjusts itself to the player's agility. If a player is good, she will easily overcome the first challenges and then, just before she becomes bored, the level is increased so that she has to try harder and be challenged again. As the player becomes better, this process repeats itself until the highest level is reached. With a good game, this could take a long time.

Websites become extremely fertile grounds for the complex art of designing senses. Not only can designers make choices on the basis of the individual actions of a user visiting the site, but they can also store their perceptions of each user in a database, so that the next time a visitor calls, he will be offered a better individual response – tailor-made service. And if designers also communicate with this visitor via other media, they can then incorporate knowledge from those sources into the system and put it to good use. This results in better service for the client the next time they visit the site.

These possibilities, especially the latter ones, are now still in their infancy and require particular refinement in the art of perception. In the next few years, the design of appropriate senses and the discovery of intelligent, effective and indeed, also ethical ways of dealing with the results, will burgeon and become crucial in the development of the interactive media.

Recipe for a successful website

Nathan Shedroff / Creative Director at vivid studios

Listen up, this one is a no-brainer. Building a successful website is as simple as an Easy-Bake Oven™. Although it is a lot of hard work, it is not very difficult to understand. The directions are clear, so here is a list of six basic ingredients: Content, Organisation and Navigation, Visual Design, Performance, Compatibility, Interactivity.

Each of these ingredients is important and none of them can be left out. Would you leave out sugar in a cake recipe? Would you bake bread without yeast? Of course not, but that is what 95% of the websites on the Internet are doing — even the commercial sites, where it is even more important. A successful website might be able to get by with only five of these ingredients — if they are exceptionally strong and well-crafted — but you cannot expect a site to attract diners unless all six courses are served, especially as the competition in the market heats up.

Content For the first ingredient, you will need plenty of content, and, as with caviar, only the best will do. Anything less is just fish eggs. High-quality, interesting content can go a long way. You do not even need that much if it is good, but it is critical to understand and practice this. Just copying text and images onto a server and making it available is not enough. Most people will not stay around to finish a meal that is not tasty to start with. The sites that have good content are the ones that make you laugh, think, get upset, become motivated, be more informed, and, most importantly, come back for more.

When you make a salad, how fresh are the ingredients? Do you use week-old lettuce, month-old tomatoes or ancient cucumbers? Why, then, do people assume that websurfers want to devour out-of-date content that is stale and uninteresting? Granted, some content requires a certain age, and can last forever while being just as appealing as when it was fresh. Unless you own content like Shakespeare, Orwell, or Zen proverbs (and even these pass into the public domain), do not expect to make a living off tired material. Resign yourself to preparing fresh content daily, weekly, or even hourly if appropriate.

Publishers often chant the mantra 'Content is King' with the fervour of a religious convert. They talk to each other at conventions about how they have more expertise on content than anyone else in the industry — and they are right. However, content is not enough. Most of these publishers are so busy convincing themselves that it is the key to successful interactive media that they can see no further than putting their existing content onto the Net without the slightest change to address the medium. Newspapers have shown themselves to be particularly adept at this. They put their news on the Web and cannot figure out why people do not register for their site, let alone subscribe and pay money. What they forget is that the term 'Interactive Media' starts with the word 'Interactive' and that they know less than most about creating interactive experiences.

Lastly, too many sites try to address everyone by serving up a bland blend of content. By trying to be 'ubiquitous' or 'objective', they end up creating a site with no personality and no flavour, that ultimately appeals to no one. Objectivity does not exist and your voice, your point of view, is exactly what people will come to your site for.

Organisation and Navigation Next, you will need a generous amount of organisation and clarity in your site. To begin with, map out everything you have to present: every piece of content you envision and every interaction. Mix well and separate into

different arrangements until you find one that is more successful than the others in meeting your objectives. Leave enough
time to experiment with organisations and by all means, stay
away from over-ambitious metaphors. Nothing confuses audiences more than trying to navigate a site based around a poorly
matched and ridiculously implemented analogy which is funda-
mentally inapplicable to interactive media.

Navigation is more than merely telling people where they can go.
It is the artful setting of context which allows people to know
what to expect, what to do, and even, to some extent, how to
do it. This is called a cognitive model and represents everything
people understand and remember about your site when it is not
actually in front of them. If your audience has to ask too many
tough questions about what they are to do and where they can
go within your site, you can be sure they will not stay around
for long.

Be sure that the navigation in your site allows your audience
easy access to its breadth and depth. Do not force them to
return to the homepage every time they need to backtrack or
access a different portion of your site. The bigger and more
varied your site, the more important this is. Elements of good
navigation include giving your audience the ability to navigate in
many ways. Can they get around without going to a 'map' or
back to the homepage? Can they distinguish how deep they are
in a site and in which section? If not, your site's organisation is
still half-baked and needs more time in the oven.

Now, do not confuse a site's organisation, its information
design, with the representation of its organisation or its visual
design. How a site looks is important, but the representation is
ultimately not as important as its organisation. Do not try to
rush this process. It may not be glamorous and it may not look
as if you are getting anywhere, but you are laying the ground-
work for the future of your site. Good meals are not simply
thrown together. They are the result of careful planning.

Visual Design While many meals are impressive to look at,
once tasted, they can leave a lot to be desired. Meals should
always look good, but not at the expense of how they taste and
how nutritious they are. A beautifully decorated website entices
people to dine, but if your audience 'bites' into it and is not
rewarded with something wonderful, you cannot blame them for
branding you 'unappetising'.

While too many sites look but do not 'taste' marvellous, just the
opposite is often the problem. There are many sites — even
from respected companies — which look so amateurish that you
wonder whether the CEO's kids designed then. These are often
unoriginal, always inappropriate and send the message that
quality is not very important. Not everything needs look trendy,
hip, or be on the cutting edge to work, but neither should it look
as if it was deep frozen three decades ago and recently
defrosted. Hire an experienced professional who is capable of
helping you communicate visually — something few people are
taught to do well — and whatever you do, do not try to dictate
your favourite colour to them!

On the other hand, do not let them push you around. If they are
taking you out on an uncomfortable limb which you know just is
not right for your company, say so. At the very least follow your
company's identity standards. Use the correct version of the
logo, colours, and typefaces, and involve those in charge of your
'brand'. If your company has no identity standards and you do
not know what your brand is, then that says it all there. You do
not need a binder-thick identity manual, but even the smallest
company should have a few rules about what is and is not
appropriate for its company's image — if for no other reason,
then for consistency. Consistency may be a bit boring at times,
but it is what great companies are built on.

As for a brand – simply put, this is the experience people have
when they deal with your company. Previously brands were
mostly described and managed by visuals, in print, on television

or on packaging. But brands have always been about the interaction between a company and its customers. Now, guess what is going to communicate and extend a brand more on-line: is it faithfully replicating the logotype and colours, or finding ways of creating innovative interactions that allow customers to experience high levels of service on-line? Wrong. The correct answer is both, but if you had to pick one, the latter is far more important.

Performance Do you know that feeling you get when you are told by the maitre-d' of a restaurant that it will be 50 minutes before you can get a table? That is how your customers feel when surfing your site at 14.4 k and it takes more than a minute to download your homepage. The result is the same: they will leave and probably never come back. Now, while some may be able to get by with the swanky patronage of the 'I've got plenty of time to wait' set, I doubt whether you and your customers fall into that category. You should get used to the trade-off between speed and elaboration. Just because something looks great on a T1 line, it does not mean it is worth waiting for over a 14.4 k connection.

The first thing you should do is to determine who your audience is: are they surfing at T1 speed? ISDN? 28.8? 14.4? Less? Many people do. This is even more compounded by on-line services like America Online or overseas connections. Are you hoping to attract an international following? Then count on half the performance your domestic customers get. I know this is disappointing and throws a wrench into your plans for an incredible site, but you will have to get used to it. You have no recourse until the Net is capable of more bandwidth and your customers have better wiring.

What does this mean? You will need to count the size of all the graphic elements on your page to get a realistic estimate. Assume that any total page size (the total size of all elements on a page) equals (roughly) the time in seconds it takes to transmit it across the Net. Times vary greatly due to server loads, network traffic, destination, noise, and about fifteen other issues, but this is a good measure, based on timed experience and not simply on theoretical calculations. For example, if your homepage adds up to 30K, then you can be sure it will take up to 30 seconds on average to download to your customer. If you have not actually been on a 14.4 connection for some time and have not experienced what 30 seconds feels like, waiting for a page to download, perhaps you should. It is worse than sitting through a commercial break while you wait for an episode of Star Trek to continue.

Compatibility While not every restaurant may accept American Express, you cannot afford not to. If your audience cannot shop, see, eat, or visit your site without downloading a browser they may not have and may not even be able to use, your audience will be smaller than it might otherwise be, and you will be short-changing yourself in the process. Realistically there are in 1997 probably only three browsers you will need to watch and engineer for: Netscape Navigator, Microsoft Explorer, and Spyglass. The latter is only important in that the most adept foreign language browsers in the world are currently based on Spyglass, although this will undoubtedly change.

Worst of all are those sites that have been duped into promoting one company's browser over another by making a deal with one of the two devils in this business, Netscape and Microsoft. What they are getting in return from supporting only one of these browsers over the other is a mystery to me, but I am certain that it is not worth the loss of content and participation from people without that browser on hand. It is hard enough to get people to stop by and come back again on the Net, but to consciously exclude people from entering your site smacks of an ignorance and exclusivity not witnessed since country clubs and private golf courses were allowed to exclude minorities. Very unfashionable. Very gauche.

Also, just because there is a new version of a browser on the market doesn't mean your customers are using it yet, or ever will. Most new browsers crash so frequently that your audience may be using an older version out of self-preservation. If you tell them they are wrong and out-of-date, you misunderstand something very important about customer service and you deserve to fail. Building inclusive, compatible systems is not easy. But this medium is anything but easy.

The most savvy of these sites automatically serve up the right version of pages based on the type of browser the request came from. This 'smart serving' or 'smart swapping' distinguishes a sophisticated website that cares about its audience from one that cannot or will not care about its customers, or is too slow-witted to realise the difference.

Lastly, your sites need to be compatible with all the computer platforms your customers use — this means Windows, Macintosh and UNIX machines — if your want their business. You should definitely post several versions of downloadable files so that Macintosh, Windows and UNIX users can hear that sound file, see that video clip, and decompress that document.

Interactivity I have a friend who chooses restaurants based on their ambience. In Sterling's own words, 'If I only wanted good food, I'd stay home and cook it myself.' A restaurant's appeal is based on more than the quality of its food, at least if you go to dine rather than just to eat. Interaction to a website is what ambience is to a restaurant. It is probably the most important aspect of websites.

Building interesting, valuable experiences — in other words, interactivity — is what interactive media are all about. This medium is so new that it is difficult to find good examples, but believe me, it is what you have to go for. If you care about attracting an audience, keeping them, and having them return, give them something to do that is useful, personal, and fun. There are six major components of interactivity: Feedback,

Control, Creativity, Productivity, Communications, Adaptivity. But how do these translate into activities on the Internet? Here are just a few examples of interactive experiences already being built: on-line Customer-Service-like answers to frequently asked questions, customer representative contact, real-time accessibility of service info, automated e-mail product/info updates, discussions about products with other users, customer communities and forums. You should build as many of these into your sites as you can, particularly anything that allows communications and adaptive (or customised) experiences, as these provide the most valuable experiences. Unfortunately, there are no off-the-shelf tools for these experiences, and no recipes to follow. So they require invention, which is even more time and money consuming, but they are well worth it.

Feedback & Control Any experience that allows the audience (your customers) to control it, is a good thing. Of course, if they are not interested in taking the initiative, you have to be ready with an alternative, but if they want to take control, turn over the reins to them. This will become much more important as the technology of the Net evolves with Java, Shockwave™, etc. Remember, if all your audience can do is to sit back and watch, they will probably turn off their computer and go and watch television — or at least, go to another site. Give them a chance to control what they see, do and say. Let them know what is going on, so that they know where they are and what is happening.

Would you go to a restaurant where you had no say in the food you ate or when it was served? Of course not, unless you did not value either your taste buds or your time. Neither will your audience.

Creativity & Productivity Would you believe it, these are really the same thing. They both have to do with creating experiences that allow the audience to 'do' or 'make' something at your site. That is what humans are good at: creating things, whether for themselves or for others. If only a few people have dropped in or returned, this may be because there is nothing to do at your site but read.

There may still not be many good examples, but there are a few. Some are frivolous and fun, others are more useful and productive. All point the way to an Internet that prods people into participating. Do not let anyone tell you that people are not ready to participate or that they do not have the skills to cook up their own content. People do this every day. They work, play, talk, share, and dream, and they are interested in doing all these things on-line as well as in their realspace lives.

Communications What do people love doing the most — OK, perhaps second to eating? Why, talking of course. People love to talk, whatever they may tell you. They may not like talking in public or to large groups, but everyone basically likes to share their thoughts with someone. Telecommunications companies make so much money because humans just love to talk.

Anything you can do to allow your audience to talk to others, listen, identify themselves, share things, and tell their own stories, will make your site more successful and could be the beginning of building a community. It may be as simple as creating or linking to discussion groups, bulletin boards, IRC channels, or merely giving visitors feedback forms and e-mail access to you or each other.

This is actually quite easy. Instead of developing complex ways for people to talk to a machine, simply provide a conduit for people to talk to each other. The conversation will be richer and the overhead simpler.

Adaptivity Lastly, the most valuable interactive experiences are the adaptive ones. This means that they change for each member of the audience in order to meet their specific needs, interests, skills, and behaviour. This is certainly not easy, but

any unique experiences you can build up for your audiences will seem more interactive. Any way in which your experiences can respond to time and place (theirs and yours) will also add to the interactivity.

Where are your customers? If they come to you from Hong Kong there must be something you would rather tell them than if they came from Albania? Or from Paris? If not, then maybe you should take another look at your business. If so, then send them different pages based on their domain extension. Does it seem like they are having trouble finding something? Then, ask them if they need any help and offer it. Does it look like they know exactly what they are looking for? Then, by all means, keep out of their way and let them speed along.

While some of the first truly adaptive experiences may have been scavenger hunts, there is now a wealth of individualised, personalised content and interactions on the Web: everything from banking to news. These companies are finding that serving people as individuals not only makes for a good site, but also for good business.

For these last issues, you are on your own. This is where you need to be creative, ingenious, and forward-thinking. What the Net and Web will become is probably quite unlike what they are now, and the only way from here to there is by daring to create interesting experiences and innovative ideas.If you cannot handle that heat, get out of the kitchen now and look for a more stable, well-understood medium, like television or magazines. However, if you are not averse to a little challenge — well all right, a big challenge — the kitchen is the place for you. You will need plenty of ingredients (like fresh content), some tried-and-true tools (like PhotoShop™), and a lot of old-fashioned ingenuity. Oh, and a dash of garlic never hurts.

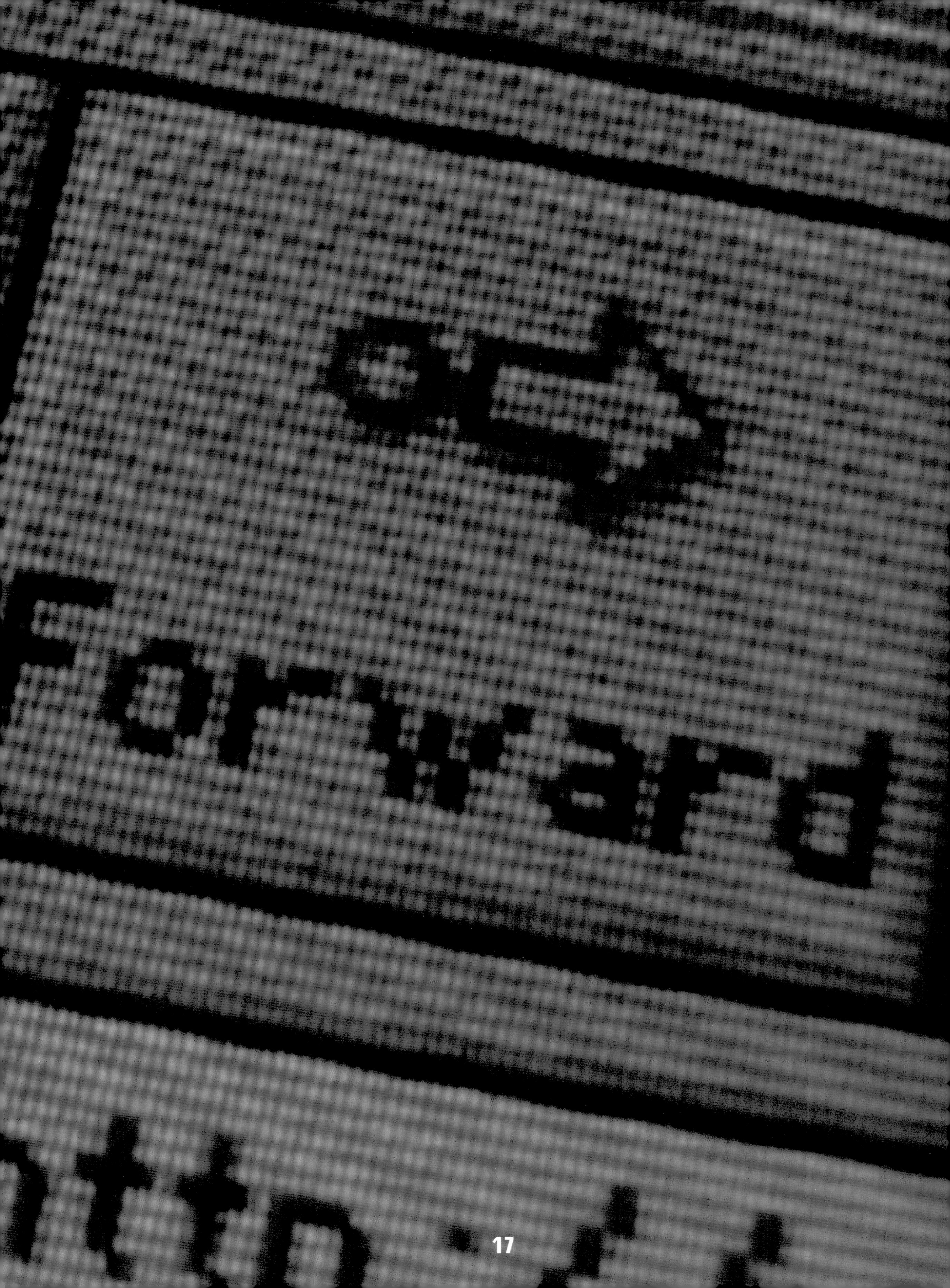
Forward

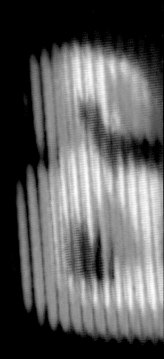

One of the best challenges to the age-old autonomy
of the artwork is the World Wide Web used by
artists. I have seen signed copies of videotapes and
even computer diskettes bearing the signature of
an artist, but a website cannot possibly function as
an original, unique and irreplaceable work of art.
Unless you define these terms in a different way. It
has been argued that 'art' in on-line artworks does
not depend on the visible result, but on the invisible
intricacies of the algorithms that direct the cathode
rays behind your screen. They who master these
indeed unique combinations of formulae are the
true artists of our times. On the other hand this
way of defining the new artistic realm in digital
environments may be stressing the old criterion of
craftsmanship too much. What about ideas?
Viewing a large sample of artworks on the World
Wide Web, it is striking that this new medium is so
often used in a nostalgic and melancholy way! Why

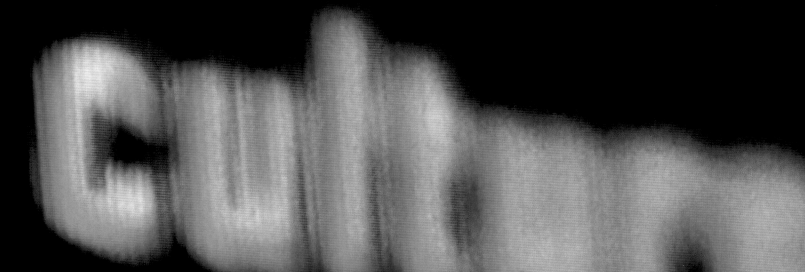

would one find so many old photographs on the Web, and so many images that seem to be almost withered with age? So many thoughts about lost childhood or a vanished past? Maybe this reflects the other aspect of the World Wide Web that links everybody to everyone: one sits alone behind a screen and a keyboard, trying to make connections between old memories and a world that sometimes seems to be so disconnected...

Maybe it has to do with the reflective character of working with the medium. There is one thing you cannot do in hypermedia: improvise with the material with the same directness as in paint or raw material. Artists who want to show something on the Web need to be very disciplined editorial designers as well. And many artists cannot exert control: for example, they may ask you to change the settings and typefaces on your browser. However, if you do not do this, you may view

something rather different than the artist him- or herself had in mind. So what else can they do but adjust themselves to the conventions of the medium and try to tell their own stories within these still narrow confines? Many artistic websites function in this way. They are often visually stronger than most sites and use the same structural routines: main page, indexes, sections, interlinked series of images and texts. These are all kept together by a navigation system that consists of toolbars, pictograms and buttons. It is very rare to see a site like that of Debra Solomon, who has created one screen which can be navigated. This screen is an abstract room which apparently has no boundaries, just directions. Ironically, this kind of work comes very close to the most autonomous art of all times, abstract art.

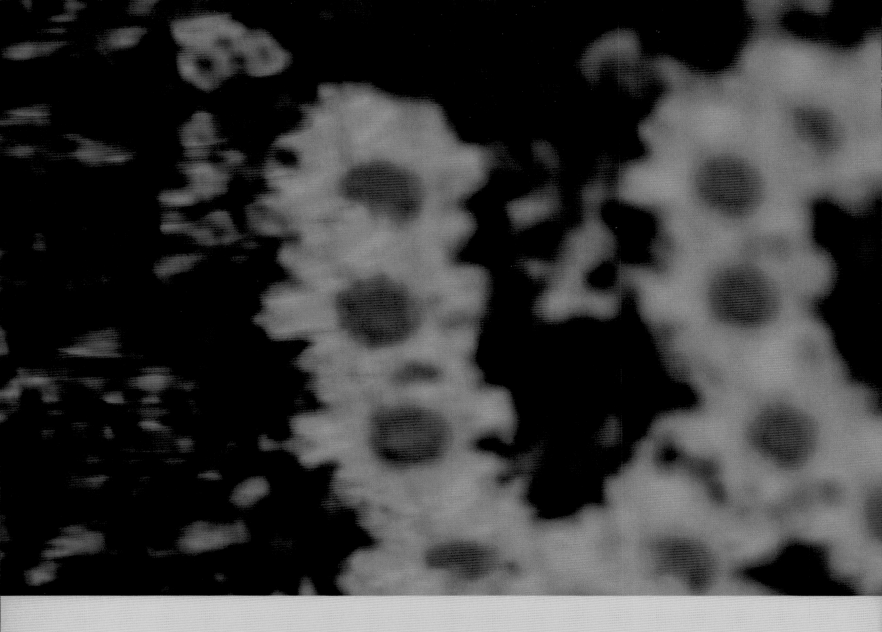

LOVE

http://www.adaweb.com/~GroupZ/LOVE/

DESIGNER Group Z / YEAR OF DESIGN 1995 / PLACE OF DESIGN Ronse, Belgium / COPYRIGHT OWNER Michaël Samyn / DESIGN COMPANY Group Z / SCREEN DESIGN Paul O'Paradis / ANIMATION/GRAPHICS Michel Dewulf / INTERACTION DESIGN Andre Courtier / PRODUCTION Isabelle Z / EDITOR Eric Steyns / CONTRIBUTORS Dirk Desmet, Lies Vermeulen, Lodewijk Johannes, Vergote & Vanmaele / SOFTWARE USED mpc: Programmers File Editor, Aldus Photostyler, CorelDraw, Netscape Navigator 2.0 / DESIGN PLATFORMS mpc: 100%

1

The introduction page is a clear indication of the contents of the rest of the site; it is about the sweetness of love — with an occasional bitter taste to keep lovers alert.

The LOVE site is a project by the Belgian artist and webdesigner Michaël Samyn together with Group Z. It is meant, as they say, to be 'about love in general, not about some preference or another. We wanted this to be said because we want you to know that in our work we never try to take anything for granted.' Still, there are some idiosyncrasies, for instance the heterosexual approach to love, for which the makers more or less apologise — it just happens to be their own experience of love. Samyn's personal experience is at the root of at least one of the seven series of which the site consists: entitled Forever Young, this series shows pictures, drawings, quotes from letters, and other souvenirs of (girl)friends he had in his youth. The other series all offer different viewpoints on this thing called love, from the daisy-pulling insecurity of the love-dazed adolescent, to the horrifying quotes from the oeuvre of the Marquis De Sade. LOVE is a kind of game, like many of the designs of Samyn. The site is structured with frames and Java script in such a way that one can browse from any given page into five directions,

without knowing what will come next. Clicking a hotspot in the image itself will bring up the next in the same series of five similar pictures, while clicking in the margins will take you to another series. In this way the reader should be able to access all 49 pages easily, but from time to time the interface has a kind of 'bug' that brings you back to where you started. 'Like in real life, LOVE sometimes stops when you don't expect it to.' The graphic design of the site is in line with the sweetness of its content: daisies and more daisies. A ring of colourful flowers surrounds the actual images that keep coming up within this framework. For some images the viewer must scroll within the frame. In the case of the third series, called Romance, this is used to create something of a shock effect. The fourth series is actually one interactive page, which you can fill in 'like an old tree in which you can carve your name and the name of the one you love.'

Max Bruinsma

The starting image for the game of LOVE, giving an overview of the structure of the site and the intentions of the designers. It is on this page that the reader will involuntarily start to explore the site.

The first series is called 'She Loves Me', after the game in which you count your chances by pulling the petals off a flower. When the petals have all disappeared, clicking the flower's center will bring up an e-mail page in which you are invited to send a letter to your beloved.

Forever Young is part of a project Michaël Samyn is working on called 'Temporal Insanity', about his teen years. The five screens show pictures, drawings, quotes from letters and other souvenirs of (girl)friends Samyn had in that period of his life.

The third series, called 'Romance', starts with some of the ultimate clichés of romantic love in text and image. When you go to the bottom of these pages, it becomes clear that love is not just a matter of pretty words in pristine landscapes.

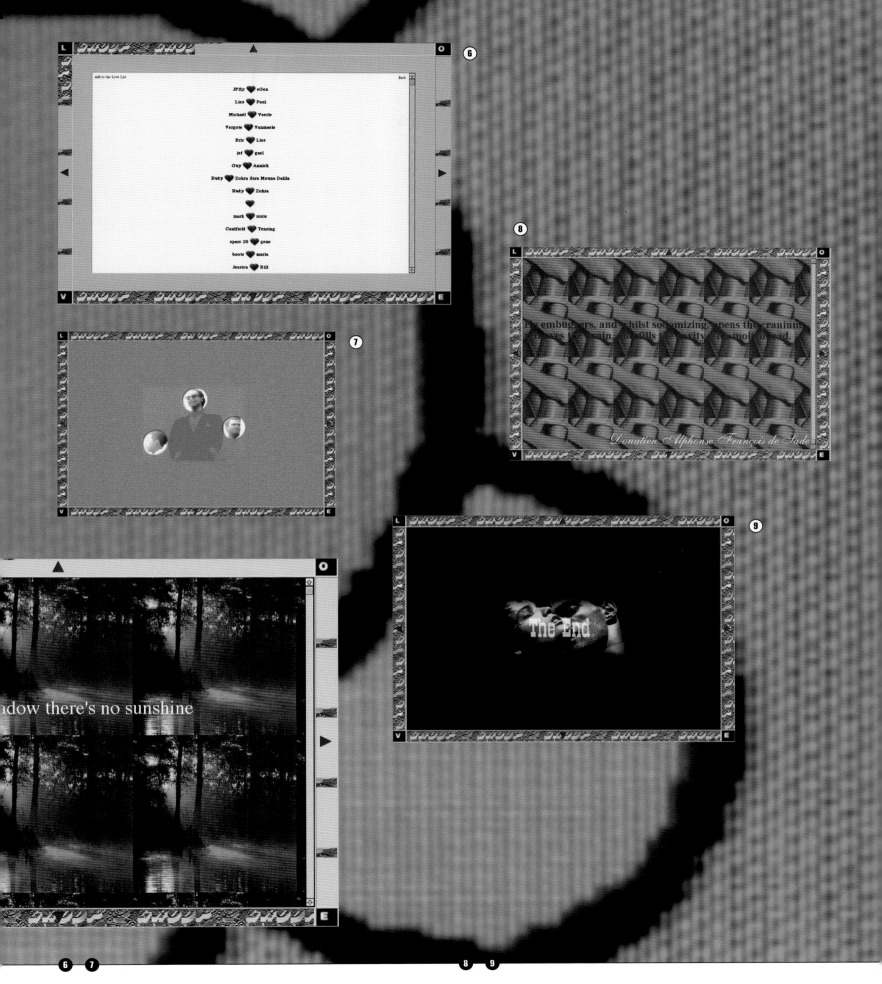

The fourth series is actually one page, repeated four times on the site. The Love List is a list of names of people who love each other and have answered the invitation to add their own love to the site. It has already become very long.

In 'Three, the One and Only' five different threesomes are depicted, leaving it to the viewer to decide whether the message is 'Three is a crowd', or Bing Crosby's 'Why can't we go on as three?'

Sade is the name of the sixth series, which consists of memorable quotes by the notorious nobleman from eighteenth century France. In any other context than this the background of entangled body parts would be considered innocently romantic.

Like in a film, the final sequence shows a picture of two lovers, together at last. As soon as the image is complete, the end title appears.

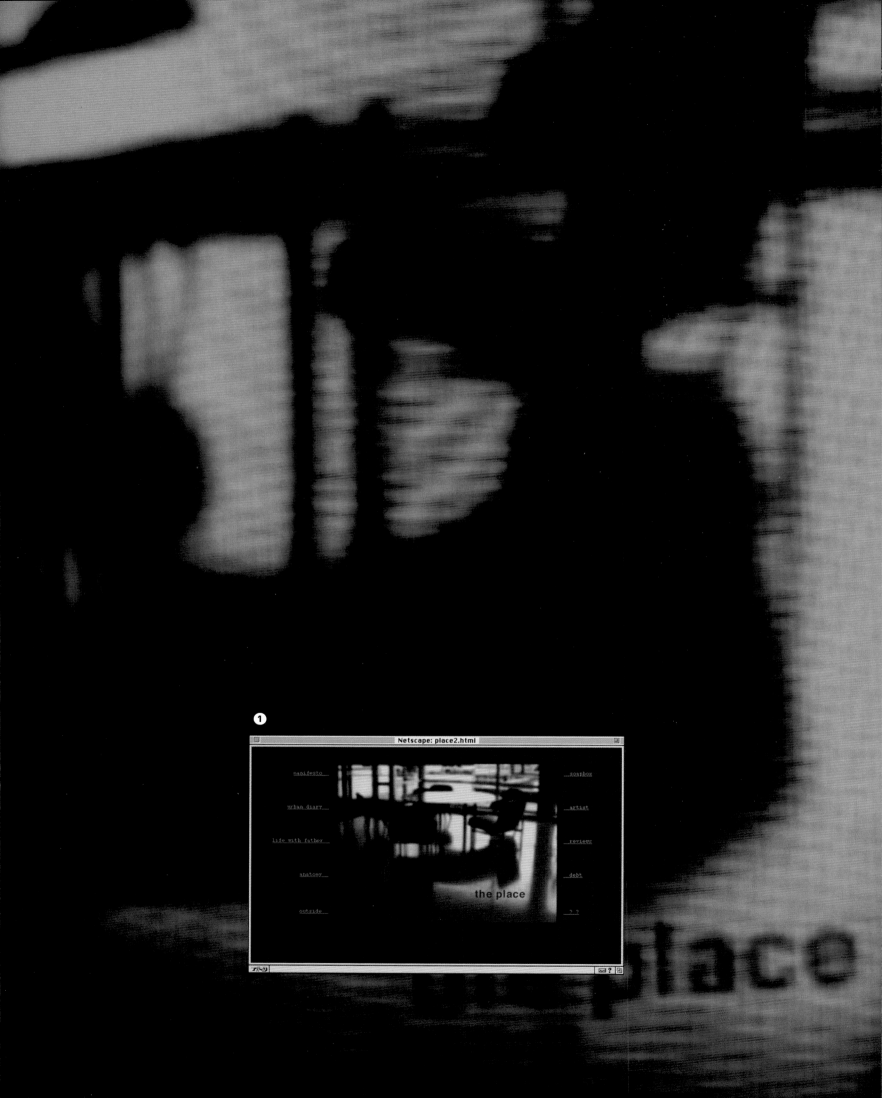

The Place

http://gertrude.art.uiuc.edu/ludgate/

DESIGNER Joseph Squier / YEAR OF DESIGN 1994 / PLACE OF DESIGN Champaign, USA / COPYRIGHT OWNER Joseph Squier / SCREEN DESIGN, ANIMATION/GRAPHICS, INTERACTION DESIGN Joseph Squier / PRODUCTION Joseph Squier / EDITOR Joseph Squier / AWARDS PC Magazine Top 100 Web Sites / SOFTWARE USED Mac: Adobe Photoshop / DESIGN PLATFORMS Mac: 100%

The Place was created by artist, educator, curator and writer Joseph Squier as an evolving repository of his work, made specifically for distribution on the Web. It contains ten parts, all present as links on the gateway page, surrounding an image of an empty table with chairs around it. The image on the opening page is an appropriate one: The Place is conspicuously devoid of anything that might distract from Squier's work.

It is a very simply structured site, a suitably empty and quiet environment for viewing and reading these pieces, which often contain pages consisting of a single or a few images and words. The opening pages of some of the more extensive areas make a distinction between 'first visitors' and others, giving the option to read the pieces in a linear or non-linear fashion. Most of the sections contain brief introductory texts about the contents. The simplicity of the site is a reflection of the faith the artist has in the power (especially the visual power) of his work: these pieces have been accorded a place in this virtual gallery, like visual art work in real-life settings.

Very concise texts form a connecting thread in Life with Father, a thirty-page, illustrated memoir of the artist's life with his extremely violent father, beginning with Squier's earliest memory of him at the age of three. Read in linear fashion, these pages are an understated chronicle of the artist's experiences with, feelings about and understanding of his father. The eight pages of An Urban Diary — scrawled, typed, scotch-taped and crumpled together — chronicle the thoughts of an anonymous urban citizen. All of the plastic qualities of these materials are evoked to the fullest: torn-off calendar pages unfold when clicked; circled numbers evoke dark pages framing large, high-density images, sometimes accompanied by minimal texts of a few words. Anatomy is an exploration of the expressiveness of the human body. The Soapbox contains a selection of Squier's essays. There is also a brief portrait of the artist himself, a page of reviews and a page of credits.

The anonymous table on the opening page perfectly embodies the public privacy of The Place: a 'room of one's own' for us to study the artist's work and ideas.

James Boekbinder

❶

The entrance to The Place is a perfect embodiment of its 'public privacy':
a public place to be alone with works of art.

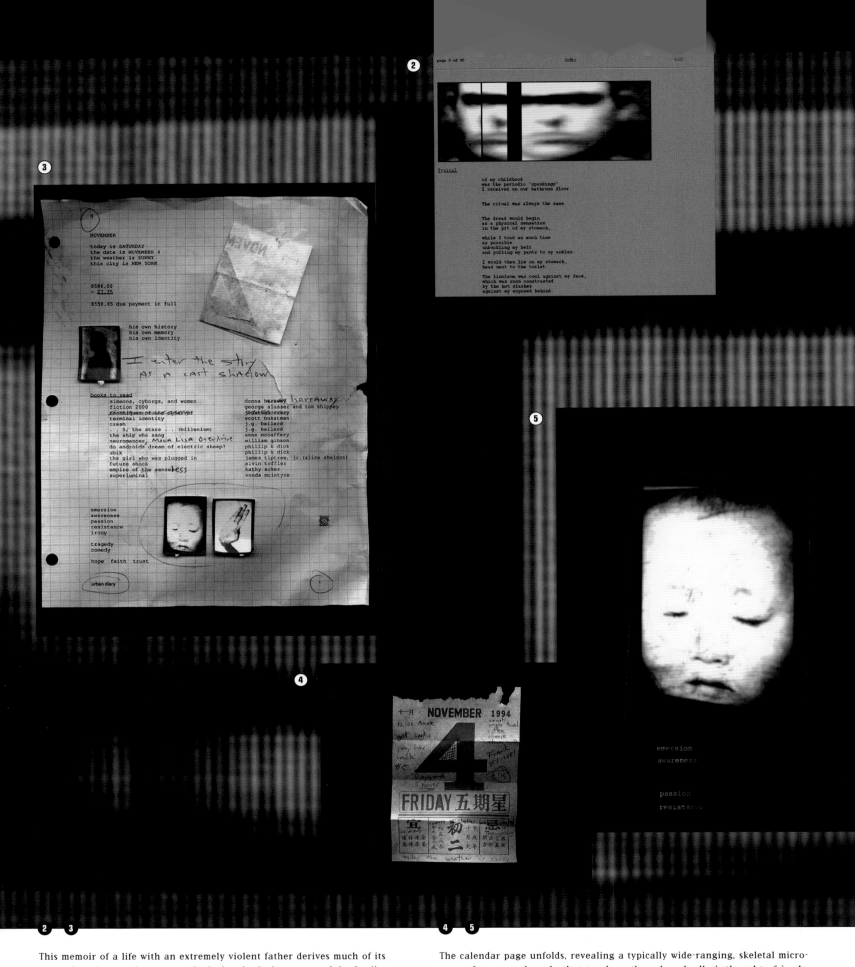

This memoir of a life with an extremely violent father derives much of its power from images that suggest both the physical presence of the family members and their mental and emotional evolution.

The anonymous Urban Diary dweller contains whole skeletons of days, with the many sub-hierarchies of lesser and greater needs and thoughts compressed into a pasted-up collage of sparsely-worded lists, photos and scraps of various kinds. Note the cross-off list of 'books to be read'.

The calendar page unfolds, revealing a typically wide-ranging, skeletal micro-cosm of traces and marks that touch on the urban dweller's thoughts, friends, mundane tasks and deeper aspirations. Clicking anywhere on the pages of the diary allows us to leaf backwards and forwards.

The image at the bottom of the first page leads to this page, composed of two images and four thoughts: immersion, awareness, passion, resistance.

The second page moves into the deeper thoughts exercising the urban dweller's mind. Many of these center around our relationship to our bodies.

Clicking the frontal collage on page 2 brings us to this back view, again accompanied by a conceptual list. Anatomy and the body are recurring themes throughout the site.

A sense of struggle pervades the diary, which for all its sparseness is a remarkably complete document of the many aspirations, mundane and profound, that make up a day.

Composition from the third page, devoted to 'desire' and 'discipline'. Note the graceful turning movement described by the repeated images of the female figure, distributed through the window panes.

A composition from 'Anatomy' speaks for itself. A dorsal view also appears as one of the first images in Life with Father, where it is used to convey the imposing physical power of the artist's athletic father.

Poem✳Navigator
http://www.khm.de/~merel

DESIGNER Merel Mirage, Chris Ganter / CLIENT Stedelijk Museum Amsterdam / YEAR OF DESIGN 1996 / PLACE OF DESIGN Cologne, Germany / COPYRIGHT OWNER Merel Mirage / SCREEN DESIGN, ANIMATION/GRAPHICS, INTERACTION DESIGN Merel Mirage / PRODUCTION Merel Mirage / CONTRIBUTORS Chris Ganter, Detlef Frenken, Dana Linsen / AWARDS Selected for the 'Digital Salon' website exhibition in New York. Selected for the 'Sydney Biennale' / SOFTWARE USED Mac: Adobe Photoshop, sgi: HTML, CGI Scripts, Image Map / DESIGN PLATFORMS Mac: 50%, sgi: 50%

1

A short introduction sets the context for the project; clicking the poem will take you in.

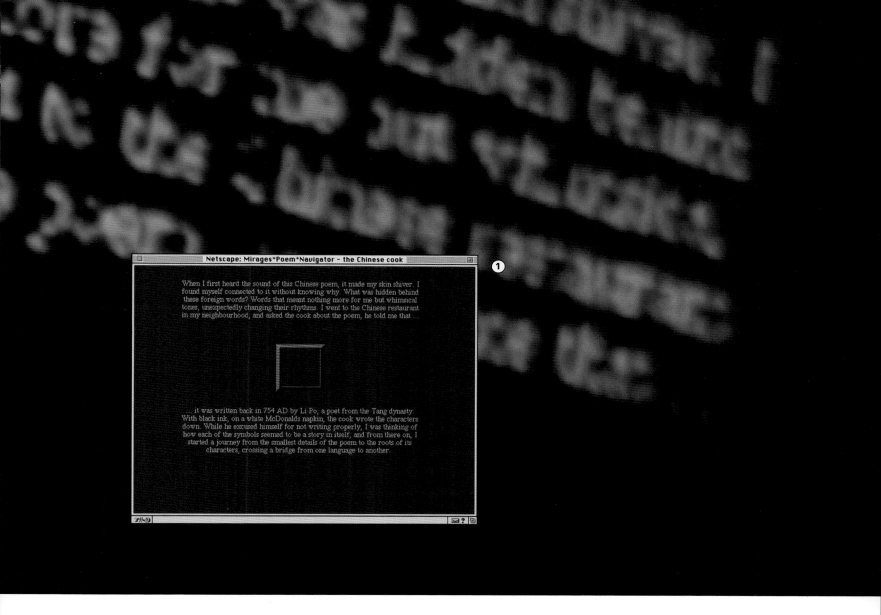

In 1996 media-artist Merel Mirage was invited to participate in the on-line section of 'Under Capricorn – The World Over', a dual exhibition in the Stedelijk Museum of Amsterdam and the Wellington Art Gallery in New Zealand. Her project, entitled Poem*Navigator, was presented on the exhibition website that connected the two physical exhibition spaces.

The starting-point for this relatively small but intricate web-project was an 8th century Chinese poem by Li Po called Spring Thoughts. The sound of the poem tickled the artist's imagination, but translation at first seemed to break the spell. Wondering about her initial interest, she decided to explore the poem further, to uncover where it came from and what it actually meant. Like the proverbial grain of sand the poem turned out to encompass an entire world of stories, references and suggestions within its six verses. This journey of discovery is recreated here for the user to explore and re-experience by offering an interface, a tool to navigate the various aspects and levels of meaning within the poem.

After a short introductory page the Chinese version of the poem is presented in an almost matrix-like layout, accompanied by an English translation. From here it is possible to examine the whole poem in Chinese, each verse separately or even the individual pictograms. Some pages provide clear explanations and interpretations of the verses, while others show the origins of the Chinese pictograms and their associated meanings.

All pages are bathed in luscious Chinese red, on which the pictograms stand out because they have been given a slight drop-shadow. Through clever use of tables and borders the poem is framed in an almost architectural setting. Navigational options are clear throughout the site, always allowing viewers to travel 'any way the wind blows'. Without much effort readers will discover that they are not only able to read through the poem in a linear fashion, but also delve into various levels of meaning and information. Clicking the poem takes you to the verses, which give access to the pictograms, and in their turn the pictograms to their origins...

The navigational focus is also an interesting formal play on the geographical references made in the poem, where physical distance is contrasted with spiritual proximity. In a sense Poem*Navigator epitomises the way the World Wide Web plays tricks upon our notions of (cultural) separation and distance, of the exotic and the familiar, of global and local culture.

Geert J. Strengholt

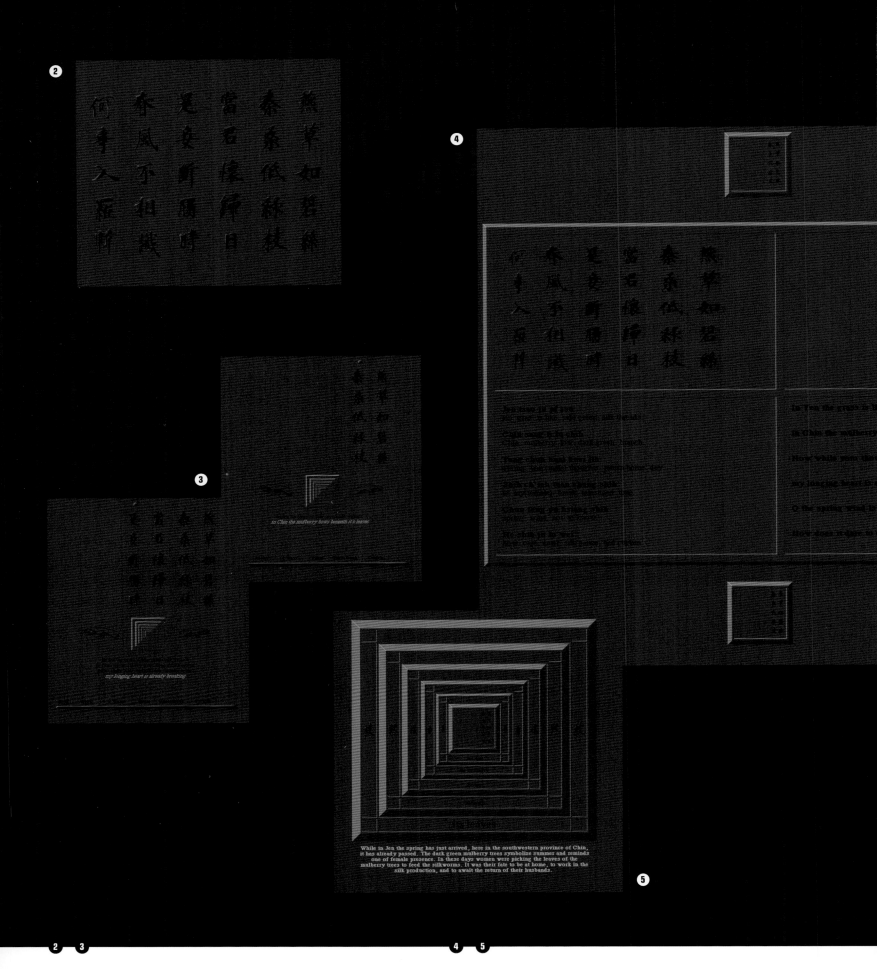

This page presents the complete Chinese version of the poem. Through an image-map each single pictogram links to a page containing more detailed information on its history and associations.

In this section you can read through the poem line by line; clicking the hands will show the way. Note that Chinese is read from top to bottom and from right to left. Lines read in the Chinese text become bold and are then shadowed to set them apart from lines still to be read. Clicking the pyramid in the center will allow you to explore a verse in detail.

In this matrix-like construction, called Two Ways, four versions of the poem — as pictograms, in the Chinese language, in a literal English and a poetic translation — are placed side by side, exposing the process and problems of translation. A host of juxtapositions are brought into play such as a literal versus poetic translation, image versus text, and east versus west.

An elaborate play of nested tables and borders results in a cascading, architectural shape. Like an inverse matrix it splits up one verse of the poem into segments corresponding with pictograms. A short interpretative text, added below, explores the meaning of the verse in an associative way.

6

Three examples from the extensive collection of pictograms that make up the poem. A short text explains their associated meanings. At the bottom a complete line gives access to other pictograms in the same verse. As is the case in other pages, borderless tables determine the general layout here.

7

After all the grandeur of poetry and pictograms a modest 'film scroll', constructed by using a forms trick, provides the credits for this project.

31

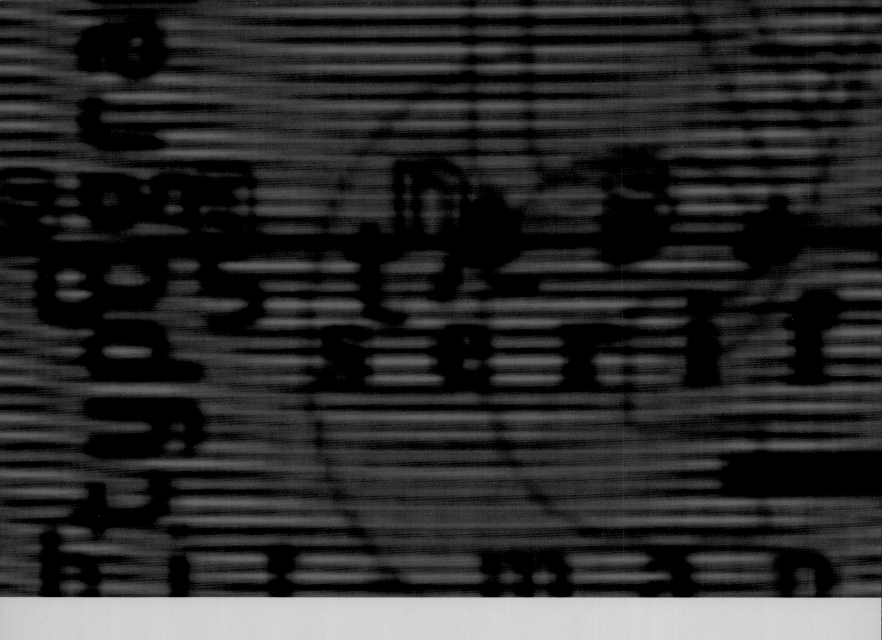

typoGRAPHIC

http://www.razorfish.com/bluedot/typo/

DESIGNER Alex Smith, Craig M. Kanarick, Stephen Turbek / YEAR OF DESIGN 1996 / PLACE OF DESIGN New York, USA / COPYRIGHT OWNER Razorfish Inc. / DESIGN COMPANY Razorfish Inc. / SCREEN DESIGN, ANIMATION/GRAPHICS, INTERACTION DESIGN, SOUND DESIGN Alex Smith, Craig M. Kanarick, Stephen Turbek, Oz Lubling / PRODUCTION Alex Smith, Craig M. Kanarick, Stephen Turbek, Oz Lubling / EDITORS Alex Smith, Craig M. Kanarick, Stephen Turbek, Oz Lubling / SOFTWARE USED Mac: Adobe Photoshop, Adobe Illustrator, Netscape, SoundEdit, Suitcase; mpc: Adobe Photoshop, Cafe, other: Java C, Emacs / DESIGN PLATFORMS Mac: 65%; mpc: 25%; other: 10%

1

The homepage reflects the general layout of the site and sets the tone for its design: stern modernist typography, strong black lines to structure the interface and a playful juggling with type in the margins.

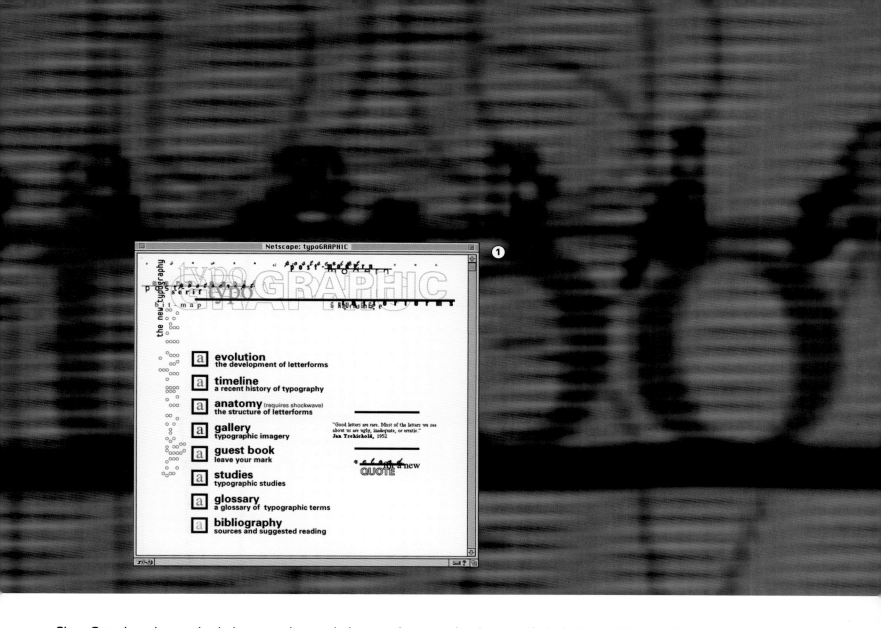

Since Gutenberg invented printing, countless variations on the alphabet have been designed. How all these different letter families are related to each other, and how they can be put to their best use, is shown in a simple but delightful way in typoGRAPHIC, a project on the Razorfish site. It is a short introduction to the history of type and it illustrates a few basic aspects of typography. You can play around with a given text to study the effects of spacing or compare serif and sans-serif type. These practical examples can be found in the seven departments of typoGRAPHIC, along with a pocket dictionary of typographic terminology in the Glossary and a Bibliography, which not only suggests books for further reading, but is also linked to other typographic sites on the World Wide Web.

A very interesting corner of the site is the Gallery. Here we find access to fifteen different typefaces, information on their makers and a typographical interpretation of the atmosphere and 'feel' of the font, by the designers themselves or by other typographers. The inspired images take some time to download, but it is well worth the effort. The Evolution section compares letter forms from Ancient Egyptian, Hebrew, Greek and Latin; the Timeline is a clickable graphic which functions as a concise encyclopaedia of type designers; and in Anatomy you can put different weights of the same letter on top of each other to see

in what way their design is different. More practical examples regarding the relationship between text and image, text as image, legibility and meanings, along with a demonstration of a number of possibilities of 'dynamic' typography on the Web, can be found in the Studies department.

Typographically the site itself is of course well laid out. The design pays homage to the now classical tradition of modernist typography, with its restrained combination of heading JPEGs, frames and a well balanced use of default text. One problem, not addressed in typoGRAPHIC, is that most of the existing type fonts have been designed for a much greater resolution than your average monitor can offer. This becomes apparent in the Gallery, where the alphabets tend to hover on the verge of dissolving into a sea of pixels. However beautifully this may have been designed, it would have been appropriate to explore this issue in more detail.

Nevertheless, typoGRAPHIC works fine as a 'birds-eye' view on the basics of this age-old craft. It is an enticing mix of entertainment and information, well structured and exploiting the display possibilities of advanced HTML to the full.

Max Bruinsma

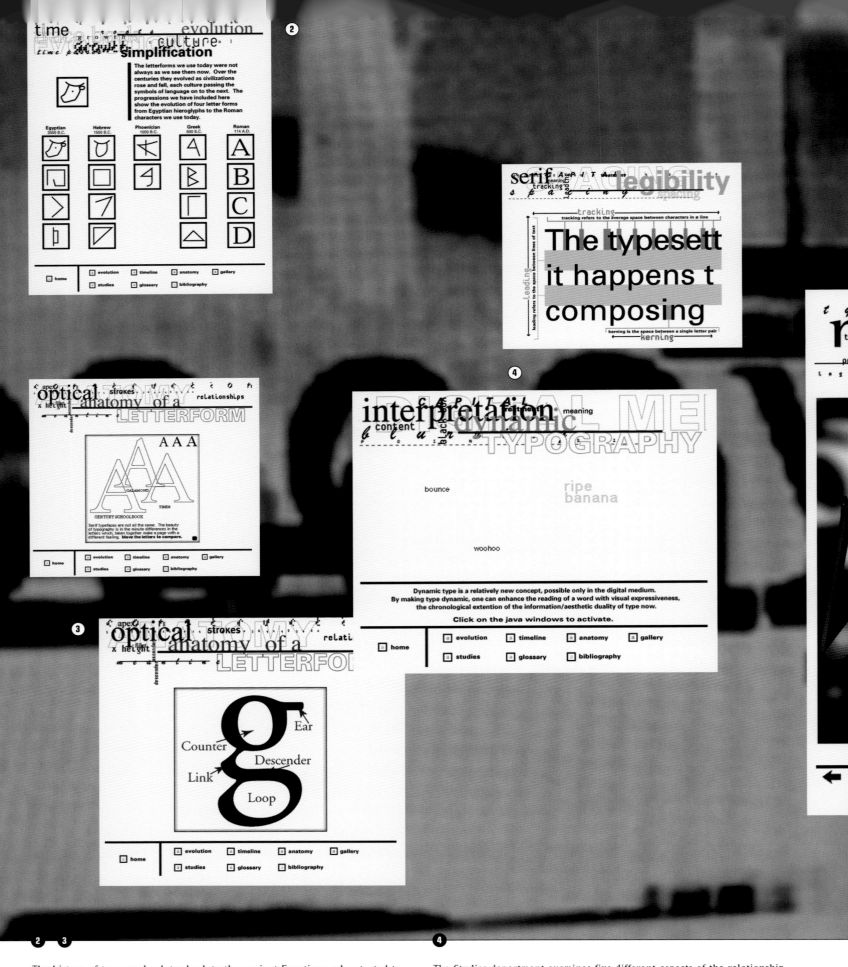

2

The history of typography dates back to the ancient Egyptians, who started to use images as signs for specific words and sounds. Our letter 'A' finds its roots in their hieroglyph of an abstracted cow's head. The 'A' as we know it was designed by the ancient Romans. On this page different letters and the stages of their development are compared.

On the Anatomy page you can play around with a given text to study the effects of spacing, you can put different weights of the same letter on top of each other to see how they are designed differently, and you can compare serif and sans-serif type.

The Studies department examines five different aspects of the relationship between typography and image. In Dynamic three examples are given of the possibilities of movement and sound with typography in multimedia environments like the Web.

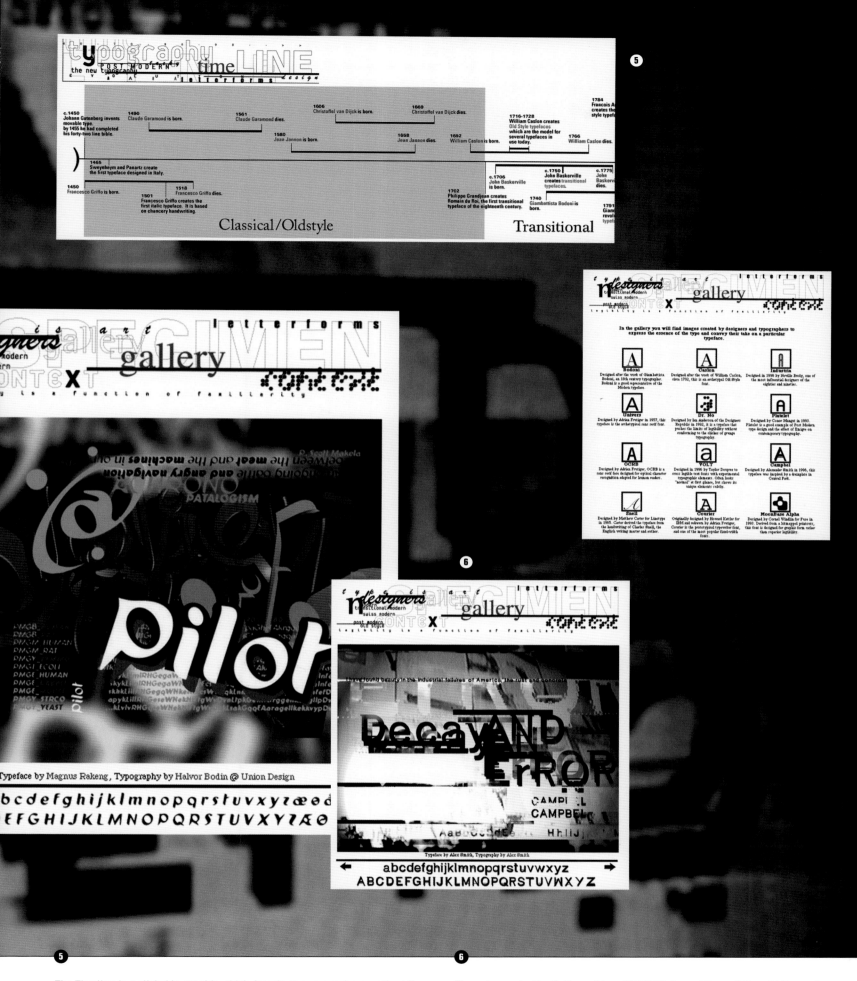

5

6

The Timeline is a clickable graphic which functions as a concise encyclopedia of type designers and typefaces.

The entrance to the Gallery of typoGRAPHIC shows fifteen different 'A's, each linked to a page in which this typeface is used in a collage of type and image. The resulting pictures are accompanied by a complete alphabet and concise information on their makers.

❶

Netscape: ESPRIT

The search for differences
or fundamental contrasts

esprit.domain

between the phenomena
of organic and inorganic,
of animate and inanimate
things, has occupied many
minds, while the search for
community of principles or
essential similitudes has
been pursued by few...

D'Arcy Thompson *On Growth and
Form* (1961)

.editor

.directory

.portfolio

.gallery

.editorials

.history

.alumni

.credits

.staff

.links

Home   Go

Espritdomain

http://www2.espritdomain.com/esprit/setup/base.html

Esprit is the acronym for 'Electronic Stills Photography at the Rochester Institute of Technology'. The acronym, like the site, impresses with its succinct elegance.

In its early days, Esprit was a printed magazine which used the latest digital print technology in its production. Over the last seven years the publication has evolved substantially. In 1994 the RIT decided that in order to maintain its aims of being at the forefront of experimentation in all aspects of visual communication, design and technology, it had better address the digital realm. Esprit was launched on the Internet in 1994 and is now also printed as a limited edition folio of photography. Throughout the site you are reminded of the abiding principles behind its design. The site acts as the RIT's manifesto as much as its showcase. Esprit impresses because it has more than simply repackaged itself; it has reinvented itself in order to exploit the digital domain. This is best expressed in Esprit's combination of interactive functionality and customised graphic elements which structure the content. Esprit uses specific systems for organising information and navigation; non-linear indexes or mapping devices, such as the main site map, and dynamic, three-dimensional visualisations of content such as the Gallery navigation interface. This 3-D version is created with 'VRML', a Virtual Reality Mark-up Language, which allows the user to manipulate three-dimensional graphics live on-line. The use of such techniques, combined with the development of a graphic vocabulary to house the content, allows Esprit to transform itself into an autonomous on-line publication.

The Nautilus shell serves as a powerful graphic and metaphoric structure for the Esprit website. From the homepage through to the portfolio, the shell's structural skeleton is incorporated into page layouts in various ways. In the History section of Esprit, the 'architectural blueprint' of the shell is not merely used as a background texture; it also plays a structural role within the page layout, the body of text shaping itself around the shell's outer edge. In other sections of the site, menus and headings curve and arc across the pages, echoing the same spiralling form.

Overall, the site is characterised by uniformity and clarity, achieved by using restrained colours and simple lower-case, sans-serif headings. In many ways the design is an exercise in moderation. The strengths of this site lie in its graphic clarity and the close connection between its design and content.

Sophie Greenfield

❶

The blue grey Nautilus shell, the central motif of this site, spirals into the background colour of the home page with the site section headings arching around its form. The two frames at the bottom of the page are high and low resolution navigation devices. They give short cuts to all the main sections within the site as well as to e-mail, page reload, and forward and back buttons.

This detailed site map provides a quick and comprehensive guide to the entire site. Every element of the map has a direct link to a relevant page. The main section headings center around a nine-pointed star and the rest of the information radiates from this focal point. Surprisingly, all of the students listed have a specific link to a page featuring samples from their portfolios.

'Filter' is one of the many images featured in the student portfolio project, where key words such as 'virus' and 'binary' are used as inspirations for digital imagery. The illustrations are represented as horizontal and vertical blocks, integrating the scattered words to create pages with appealing clarity.

In this section of the site you are presented with background information about the inspiration behind the students' work. The various paragraphs are held in neat blocks by the key lines running from the illustrations featured on the page.

An X-ray cross-section of the Nautilus shell forms the backdrop and structural template for the History section. Clicking on the range of dates presents you with a series of texts which are shaped to complement the shell's form. The repeated use of this central motif creates a sense of unity and interconnection between the pages in the site.

esprit.history.1994

esprit

Medium Under Mind - Manifesto

Staff

esprit.gallery

HTML

VRML

esprit.gallery

sprit.gallery.young lim chung

Illusion

C Print
©1996

Before you enter the Gallery, you can choose whether you want to view it in a two- or three-dimensional version. This image map is a condensed representation of the graphical user interfaces found in the two different visualisations of the Gallery.

This graphic device acts as the main menu for the two-dimensional version of the on-line Gallery. Every student on the course is represented at the end of each of the spokes in this spiral menu.

Students featured in the Gallery show between two and five illustrative photographs which represent their style and work. Some of the work is accompanied by soundtracks, but in most cases it is simply presented as a column of thumbnails to choose from. 'Source' provides further information about the work and inspiration of the students.

The Staff section is put together as a collection of black and white, hand-written pages featuring portraits of each individual member. In this example, the designer has composed a collaged, layered page where the HTML tags formatting the text are faintly visible.

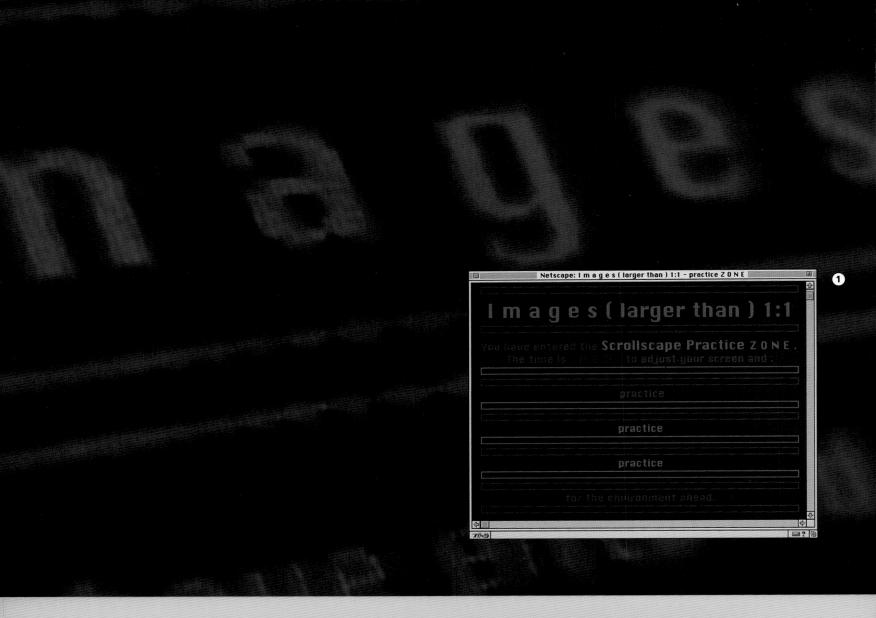

Netscape: I m a g e s (larger than) 1:1 - practice Z O N E

I m a g e s (larger than) 1:1

You have entered the **Scrollscape Practice** Z O N E .
The time is [ ] to adjust your screen and [ ]

practice

practice

practice

for the environment ahead.

Images (larger than) 1:1

http://www.xs4all.nl/~dsolomon

DESIGNER Debra Solomon / YEAR OF DESIGN 1996 / PLACE OF DESIGN Amsterdam, The Netherlands / COPYRIGHT OWNER Debra Solomon / SCREEN DESIGN, ANIMATION/GRAPHICS, INTERACTION DESIGN Debra Solomon / PRODUCTION Debra Solomon / EDITOR Debra Solomon / AWARDS NPS Cultuur Prijs Nomination / SOFTWARE USED Mac: BBEdit 3.5 & 4.0, Live Picture, GifBuilder, English_Text-to-Speech Software, Life Forms Software, Color FindeR, Adobe Photoshop 3.0, Netscape / DESIGN PLATFORMS Mac: 100%

1

The beginning of the Scrollscape Practice Zone. If you click on 'adjust your screen', the picture moves teasingly upwards, but nothing actually changes. By clicking on 'practice', you enter the 'scrollscape'. At the bottom your mission is stated.

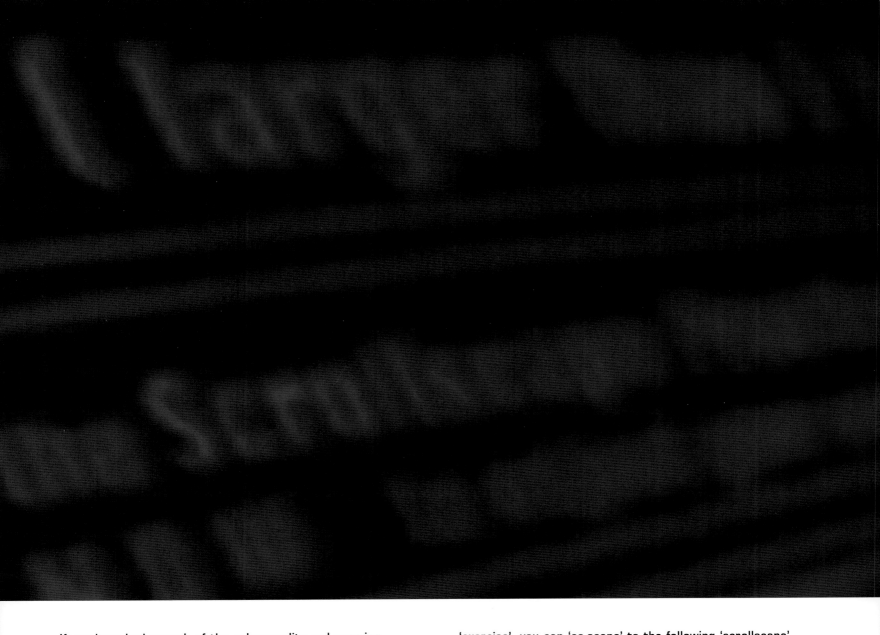

If you have had enough of the ephemerality and seeming-temptations of the Web you should check out Images (larger than) 1:1. In a highly original way Debra Solomon explores the limitations of the Web and the computer screen by skilfully inflating or enlarging the conventions of webdesign and navigation. Upon entering her site you are initiated by the Scrollscape Practice Zone, where you can experience the physical dimension of images and borders of the screen by doing some massive scrolling both in a vertical and horizontal direction. You realise that there are no separate webpages here, but that you are gauging a large area, a digital landscape, which manifests itself bit by bit. The monitor can only show a fragment of the whole 'scrollscape', which consists of text lines, grids and compositions of blocks against a blue background, rudimentary and code-like, as if it refers to the concealed interior of the Web. The exciting, sometimes teasing act of scrolling makes you realise how rigid our way of dealing with the Web usually (still) is. You would wish that you could go swiftly through the area in a criss-cross way. However, in order to move in a non-linear way, the image has to be scanned blind with the mouse in order to simply discover what is clickable. Sooner or later a 3-D image of two human figures passes by – smaller than 1:1 – or fragments of an enlarged version which does not fit within the confines of the screen. Once you are satisfied with the results of your

'exercise', you can 'ee-scape' to the following 'scrollscape'. At the beginning of the next 'scrollscape' there are statements about the concept of the site. However, most of them have been crossed out and require scrolling up and down in a 'dragging' way. There is nothing left but to let yourself slide down into the 'scrollscape'. You will encounter shining, gigantic buttons, like monuments in a desolate landscape, which challenge you to click. Each button shows a photographic detail of a face or other body parts, whose scale does not bear any relation to that of the computer screen: images (larger than) 1:1. This rather subjective aspect of the site finally ends up at an ordered archive of tiny photos, where the images also available through the buttons have been stored.

Everything on Images (larger than) 1:1 seems to be out of proportion, but it depends on what your criteria are. The rules which control design, images and sight within the Web are arbitrary rules outside of it. Solomon tackles all these protocols in a slightly ironic way, making you become aware of the small window and frames of your computer screen. However, at the same time you can catch glimpses of surprising vistas – definitely a mind-broadening experience.

Jorinde Seijdel

41

The 3-D image eventually encountered, accompanied by a fragment of its inflated version. The grids in the background reinforce the sense of spaciousness of the site.

Strewn across the 'scrollscape' are red blinking elements, texts or blocks. A number of them — though which you will have to find out for yourself — can take you to a different location. Most do not have any special function and seem to refer to the meaningless use of blinking effects on the Web. By clicking on 'ee-scape' you get to the 'real scrollscape'.

The introduction of the 'scrollscape' for experienced scrollers. Upon reloading the page the text is sometimes briefly legible.

Two of the buttons which loom up when scrolling horizontally and vertically. Here in particular the different dimensions of the buttons and their apparent disorder evoke a suggestion of space.

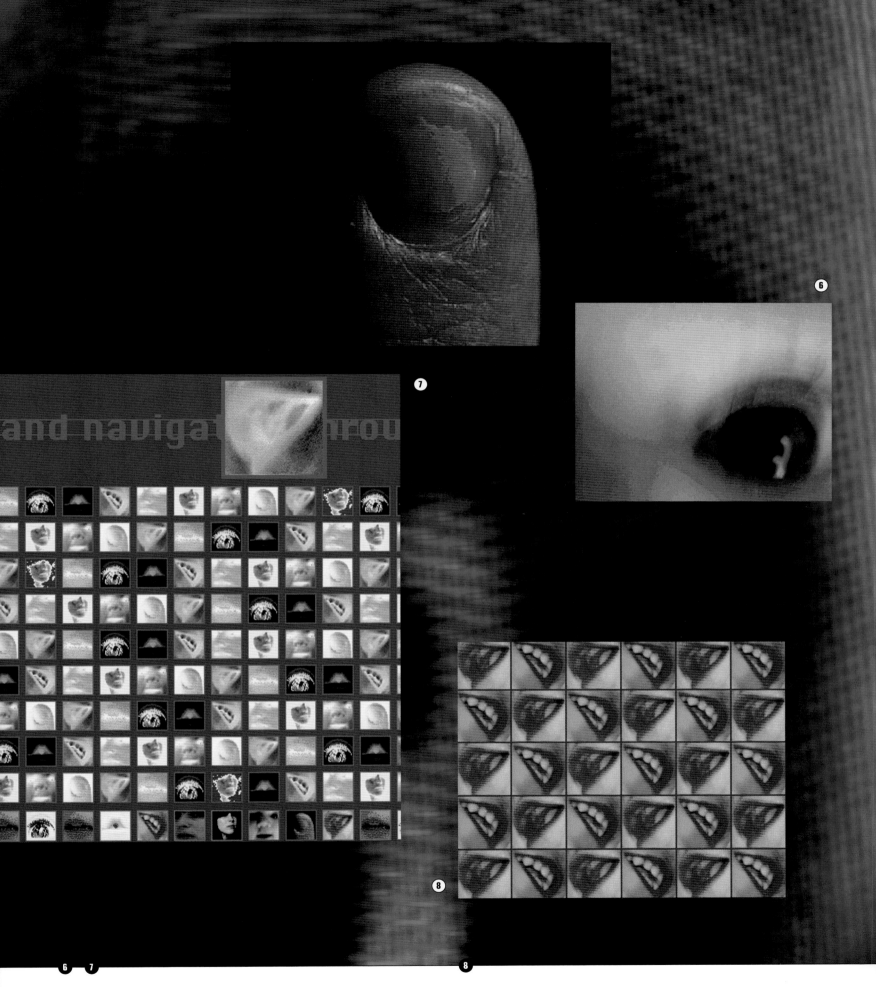

When clicking on a button this larger-than-life finger or eye appears. A reduced version can also be found in the image archives. Since you only see enlarged details, you have a feeling that you are scanning a gigantic and alien body.

Part of the index functions as an archive which offers an unexpectedly intimate dimension to the site. This archive is structured according to a repeating series of nine images, that displays moving and flickering patterns.

These rather sardonic mouths appear frequently...

this wide

Netscape: E N T R O P Y 8 . C O M

①

Entropy8
http://www.entropy8.com

DESIGNER Auriea Harvey / YEAR OF DESIGN 1996 / PLACE OF DESIGN New York, USA / COPYRIGHT OWNER Entropy8 Digital Arts / DESIGN COMPANY Entropy8 Digital Arts / SCREEN DESIGN, ANIMATION/GRAPHICS, INTERACTION DESIGN, SOUND DESIGN Auriea Harvey / PRODUCTION Auriea Harvey / EDITOR Auriea Harvey / AWARDS Cool Site of the Day - June 29 1996, Prophet Communications' Iconoclast Web Design Contest (first annual winner), Fractal Design Digital Art Awards - Third place, The High Five Award for Excellence in Site Design, The IPPA Award for Design Excellence / SOFTWARE USED Mac: Adobe Photoshop, Fractal Design Painter, Strata Studio Pro, GifBuilder, Adobe Illustrator, Adobe Premiere / DESIGN PLATFORMS Mac: 100%

Entropy8 was produced and designed by Auriea Harvey. It is a particularly densely woven website with rich content and complex, layered graphics. The site has won a slew of awards in recognition of its accomplished design.

When you enter the site you are greeted with an opening splash sequence which brings you to the welcome page. Once you follow the initial procedure indicated here you are viewing the site as the designer intended.

Entropy8's navigation device is like a strip of 35mm film with richly textured images in each frame. From this device you immediately deduce that the site is divided into six main sections. As you explore, you find that each page is as densely layered as the next. The 'Hallucinations' section is particularly lavish with three different animations displayed on one page: a deconstructed cube above the 'Portraits' heading; a blinking eye beside the word 'Ephemera'; and a jagged, animated line originating in the word 'Angst' at the base of the page. In this section, Harvey uses illustrative typefaces reminiscent of Sanskrit engraved into the textured surface of the page. Small sparkling animations are used throughout the pages to heighten the sensual quality of the graphics.

'The 'Family Project' section has a more restrained graphic quality and features a scrolling gallery of candid portraits of Harvey's family members. As a portrait is selected, a small caption flashes up beneath, prompting the viewer with 'my sister' or 'my mother' as appropriate. Fleeting details like these give the work a crafted, quality feel. Perhaps the most captivating element of the site is the animated flames at the bottom of the navigation device. These serve as a good motif for the space, balancing the inherently synthetic nature of the Internet with its natural physicality.

This is a site where opulence and extravagance are key words. Harvey's agenda is to pour as much creativity and beauty into her website as possible in a bid to overcome the shortfalls of the Internet as it stands and to produce work which goes beyond information and into the realm of art. In her words, 'Art is for all the things you can't say out loud'.

Giles Rollestone

❶

The welcoming screens to the Entropy8 site invite the user to customise the appearance of the browser. You are warned that the site is a 'Hi bandwidth presentation' and that you should hide the control panels of the Web browser and use Entropy8's own customised navigation device to achieve an optimum effect.

A moveable six-panelled navigation device complements the Entropy8 home-page and enables a fluid navigation around the site. If you place your cursor over any one of the six navigation panels, the title of each area appears.

This section offers the visitor background information about the site and its designer.

Hallucinations launches you into the most densely packed area of the site. You are offered three areas to explore: Come in and feel the angst, Portraits and Ephemera, featuring illustration, photography and narrative imagery from sketchbooks.

This screen features various sketchbooks that can be accessed from the Angst section of the site. The images act as an interface to the various collages and stories within. Upon clicking a separate window displays the contents of a chosen sketchbook and offers the possibility of viewing all the pages.

Ephemera is a space for photographic and digital experiments, featuring particularly striking autographic text and imagery — an expressive collage where you can view close-ups of the photography embedded within the background.

The Disease Manifesto contains a series of interlinked pages with handwritten texts and illustrations.

The Family Project page has a scrolling panel with a selection of candid portraits of family members that you can select to view small film sequences, snatches of poetry or simple close-ups of the individuals.

Select the animating flame at the base of the navigation device and you are granted 'Freedom' — a section of the site which allows you to exit and explore a host of other websites that have been selected by the designer.

The Spleen

http://www.mcad.edu/home/faculty/szyhalski/Piotr1

DESIGNER Piotr Szyhalski / YEAR OF DESIGN 1995-96 / PLACE OF DESIGN Minneapolis, USA / COPYRIGHT OWNER Piotr Szyhalski / SCREEN DESIGN, ANIMATION/GRAPHICS, INTERACTION DESIGN, SOUND DESIGN Piotr Szyhalski / PRODUCTION Piotr Szyhalski / EDITOR Piotr Szyhalski / AWARDS New Voices, New Visions Digital Art Competition September 1996, Macromedia User Conference People's Choice Awards September 1996, City Pages Best of The Twin Cities May 1996, Point Survey Top 5% of the Web January 1996, David Siegel's High Five Award September 1995 / SOFTWARE USED Mac: Adobe Photoshop, Adobe Illustrator, Freehand, Sound Edit 16, GIF Converter, GIFBuilder, Macromedia Director, MoviePlayer, Afterburner, Adobe Streamline, Microsoft Word, BBEdit, HTML Editor / DESIGN PLATFORMS Mac: 100%

1

The emblem of the spleen reappears in a variety of forms. Note the slogan borrowed from the US 'Pledge of Allegiance' to the flag: One Art Indivisible.

Piotr Szyhalski's The Spleen is devoted to his own vision of art and propaganda. It opens with an elaborate, animated emblem (a human spleen) and a slogan (Believe!) on a black field. Emblems and slogans play an important part in the design and logic of this site, which uses the bold, theatrical strategies of propaganda art to involve us in its content right from the very first page. The home page offers access to the two main parts of The Spleen: Inward Vessels (Piotr's documents) and Outward Vessels (links).

The interface of Inward Vessels is a single page, in which readers descend vertically through a deep, black space along a couple of veins that branch off into the various 'vessels'. Only when we have been offered entrance to all of the inward vessels do we arrive at the bottom, where descriptive texts about the vessels are to be found.

The vessels are carefully choreographed experiences, many of which retain the feeling of a passageway in which one must choose, step by step, how to advance (which is not to say we always arrive where we expected). This linearity is most emphatically expressed in the design of vessels such as 'Fire Serpents' and 'The Unchangeable': single pages, with one continuous statement in a single line of text, scrolled from left to right, reinforced by background images at critical points. Other vessels are devoted to the development of self-awareness (The Will Power Clinic) or sharing of experience (Chest Piece, about the author's journey back to Poland after a five-year absence). We emerge from the private, dense inner blackness to the body's surface for the 'Preamble' vessel, a medical diagram of the spread and transformation of constitutions in 24 countries, including preambles and even whole texts. Particularly ingenious are the interfaces in 'Wegiel' (Coal), which explore the relation between language, culture and forgetting, allowing readers to alter a 'banner' by exchanging words in a slogan, among other things. The 'Victory' page is the site's most extensive exploration of propaganda art, including pedagogical components and historical information. The visual design here is closest to the emblematic, hierarchical arrangements borrowed from printed media.

In The Spleen we find banners burning in the blackness of a metaphorical space linking the human body (with its profoundly private areas of darkness and silence) with the world beyond its surface. It's a space where the totalitarian dream of the destruction of privacy and extension of control into the individual's innermost depths has been transformed, using its own aesthetics, into an instrument at the service of the individual.

James Boekbinder

The Will Power Clinic

If you are not the man/woman you want to be, if your behavior doesn't measure up to your ideals, probably the trouble is not with your talents, but with your will power. It is true that it is up to you to become more courageous, more enduring, more determined, more disciplined. The task is by no means an easy one, but it is perfectly possible. Here you will find what you need to train your will and to toughen it up.

Take immediate action! By trying out the following psychological experiment on yourself, you will doubtlessly be struck by the fact that you are of drives and motives which contradict each other, that often you are propelled by desires which are equally strong but mutually irreconcilable. That conflict of motives is perhaps the most characteristic phenomenon of human life. This is the core of everything, this is the basis for your self-improvement.

ENTER NOW

This page embodies the iron logic that permeates the site and makes it so coherent: the first choice on our descent is the viewing suggestions. Only at the bottom do we get any information about the vessels.

One of the 'screenplays' in the site: a single line of text, read panoramically in relation to the background. Some of the images can be clicked and examined more closely.

Another screenplay: a perfect example of The Spleen's special visual theatricality.

The Will Power Clinic takes you step by step through a training session, in which you answer 'yes' or 'no' to questions. However, answering 'no' does not mean an easy way out or a retreat.

PLATE VII

① ② ③ ④ ⑤ ⑥ ⑦ ⑧ ⑨ ⑩ ⑪ ⑫

⑬ ⑭ ⑮ ⑯ ⑰ ⑱ ⑲ ⑳ ㉑ ㉒ ㉓ ㉔

Szare Sztandary

(Grey Banners)

Art belongs to the People!

This is a message of good cheer to all the People, to let Them know that They have behind Them an workers who will not flinch or weary of the struggle - hard and protracted though it will be, but that we shall rather draw from the heart of suffering itself the mead of inspiration and survival, and of a victory won not only for ourselves but for all - a victory won not only for our own time, but for the long and better days that are to come.

⑥ ⑦   ⑧ ⑨ ⑩

The interface divides this essay into Hear the Thoughts (a white iconic slide-show on a black screen), Enter the Places, and See the People. It reflects the complexity of this journey home and back.

We re-emerge into a brighter, external setting, reflecting internal processes of will and belief. The constitutions or their preambles of 24 countries appear as eruptions on the surface of a torso.

A simple matrix of one adjective and one noun, in combinations made by the reader, who can move backwards or forwards along the list.

Drawing closely on printed media, this page's Politprop button opens the way to a serious space for learning about and making propaganda art.

The slideshow of black and red fundamental shapes on a white background harks back to early avant-garde art movements of this century, most notably the Constructivists and Suprematists, whose development in the twenties was intimately linked with propaganda art.

Netscape: NIRVANET! A GLOBAL NETWORK FOR LOCAL NOMADS

english 2.0 3.0

français 2.0 3.0

español 2.0 3.0

NIRVANET

①

Nirvanet
http://www.nirvanet.fr

DESIGNER Christian Perrot, Marie-France Perez / YEAR OF DESIGN 1996 / PLACE OF DESIGN Paris, France / COPYRIGHT OWNER Global Theatre Network / SCREEN DESIGN, ANIMATION/GRAPHICS, INTERACTION DESIGN Christian Perrot, Marie-France Perez / PRODUCTION Christian Perrot, Marie-France Perez / EDITORS Christian Perrot / AWARDS Cool site of the day (infinet), Cool music site of the week (CDNOW), latin page of the week (Latin World) / SOFTWARE USED Mac: HTML, WebWeaver 2.5, Adobe Photoshop 3.0, Shockwave, QuickTime, QuickTimeVR, RealAudio / DESIGN PLATFORMS Mac: 100%

The French site Nirvanet. A global Network for Local Nomads aims to 'create a civilisation of the Mind in Cyberspace'; 'we change the Internet to change the world', because 'Culture = Future'. In order to achieve this, the ambitious site builders have set out to catalog the numerous efforts by the (computer) underground to make our world a better place, which is an almost infinite task. Nirvanet gives access to this information in order 'to break the quarantine that has outlawed the terra incognita' of hacking, techno music, fringe science and cyberpunk exploits alike. They have designed an editorial shell at the top of over five hundred linked sites. The visitor can select the Spanish, French or English language. The result so far is a gigantic library of the computer underground.

Upon entering the index page of the site a second browser-window automatically pops up, displaying the abstract shape of a tree as a map for the site. This image captures the various directions the topics branch out in after leaving the roots, which hold the home page, a search engine and tools required to view the audio and video applications of the site. This window remains open and available at all times, an extremely helpful and necessary navigation tool amid the wealth of information offered by the site. Underneath the roots there is also a pop-up menu of the index of the site, which organises the content differently in over thirty subject areas.

The base of the tree is occupied by the magazine. When it is clicked, it becomes an animated contents page holding special features such as a Goa FAQ Travel Guide and pages containing clever methods for linking the user with explicit knowledge. For instance, the feature 'Meet the Best Visions' ranges from topics such as 'Utopia' to 'Extraterrestrials', brought up by activating an AltaVista search for anarchist writer Hakim Bey and alien intelligence respectively. This article was at first accessed through the monthly magazine, yet is part of the much larger area of the Cyberlab.

Nirvanet clicks away like the HTML Book of the Living and Dead, sometimes using the simplest design to organise information, and sometimes choosing Kai Power Tool crazed implosions, esoterically drooling over invisible border frame source design, urging the visitor to conform to the palatine screen font in order to get on with the program. It is through its overall smart design that it manages to synthesise the pleasure of exploration and discovery with the practical need for reference and access. It has transformed the usual presentation of underground fringe media from grey recycled paper packed with 7.0 fonts into a colourful universe of the Web, thereby opening access to previously obscure knowledge.

Adam Eeuwens

❶

The image of a woman's face on Nirvanet's opening page caught in swirls of bright brain waves — her eyes gazing upwards as if in trance, receiving the deeper Meaning of Cyberspace — perfectly prepares the visitor for the experience awaiting...

Cyberpunk

```
Nirvanet radio

INDEX
```

```
* Bruce Sterling "Idea Of A Cyberpunk Library"
* John Perry Barlow "Independence of Cyberspace"
* Bruce Sterling "High-Tech Crime"
* King Fisher "Confessions Of A Cracker"
* Hakim Bey "TAZ, Net Chapter"
* Bruce Sterling "Free As Knowledge"
* Sterling & Gibson "Facing Education"
* John Perry Barlow "The Economy Of Ideas"
* Privacy International "Big Brother Report"
* Hans Moravec "The Age Of Robots"
* Bruce Sterling "Virtual City"
* Bruce Sterling"Computer Freedom Privacy"
* Timothy C. Hay "Crypto Manifesto!"
* Albert Hofman "LSD, My Only Child"
* Nicholas Saunders "E For Ecstasy"
* Nirvanet's Tribute to Timothy Leary
* Timothy Leary : "Chaos and Cyberculture"
* Chaos Computer Club "About Hack Ethics"
* Richard Kern "The right side of his brain"
* Norman Spinrad : "Paradoxes of Technology"
* Dead Addict "In defense of piracy"
* Hakim Bey "Overcoming Tourism"
```

```
Resources          go

REAL AUDIO IS HERE.

COMBAT-ZONE

mitnick
chase

yes

Can you pass the hack test ?

no
```

The index, or map of Nirvanet. At the bottom there is a pop-up menu, which lists all the different features and sections of the enormous labyrinth of information.

Part of the Nirvanet manifesto: 'We live in the culture of clicking, our attention span lasts no longer than a nano-second, surfing the web we let others do all the thinking for us, the click has become more important than the information. So here's a white page for the visitor to think, not click'.

The KISS (Keep It Simple, Stupid) principle in effect. A large image of the ultimate cyberpunk dream of bringing dead icons back to real life in the digital spheres, plus a simple listing of the cyberpunk stories available in this part of the library.

Time to get scared; you are now entering the hacker's zone with a special audio message from convicted hacker Kevin Mitnick to greet you and a quiz to test and prove your credibility.

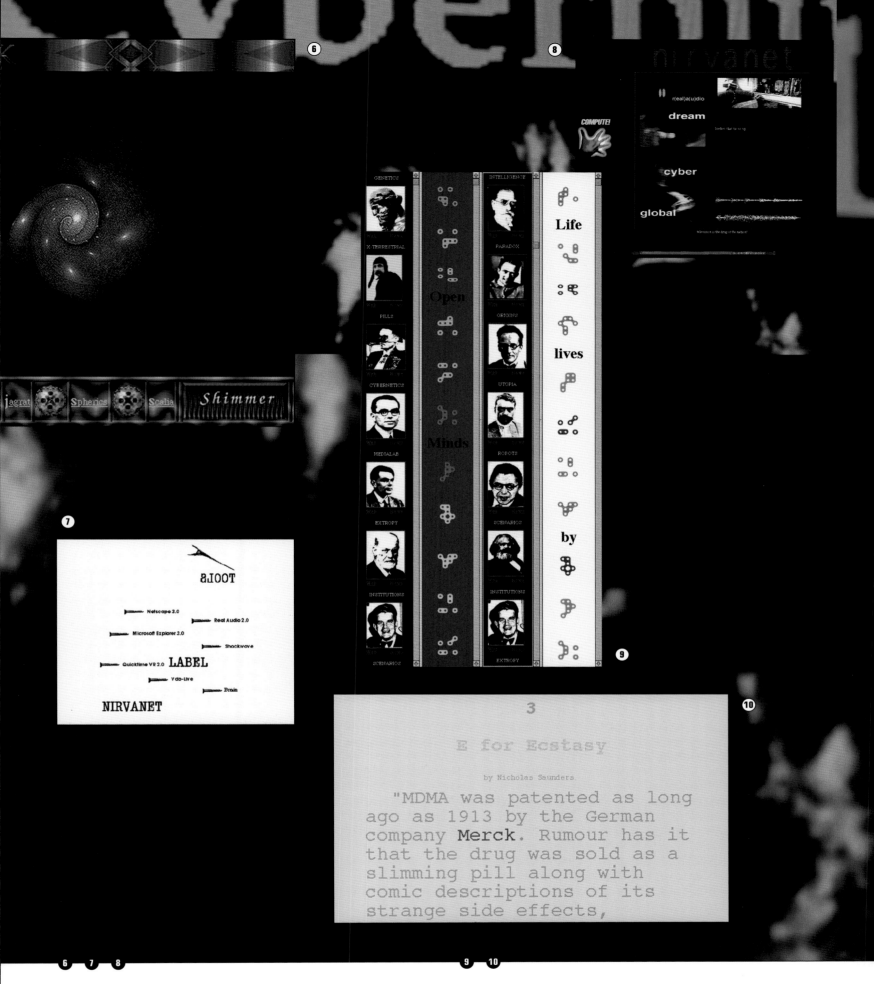

One of the inspirations for Nirvanet, mirrored on their site, is Steve Miller's MkzdK. Here the excesses of Kai Power Tools blossom and frame navigation rules.

The toolbox of Nirvanet is simple and direct, yet playful and pleasant in design.

The contents page after the home page, with a ticker dripping the text in line by line, while some images in the boxes are static and others are animated. Underneath the temperature bar navigation instructions are highlighted.

Four frames making four columns. The left frame holds a list of topics which you have to scroll downwards. The frame in the middle right holds the same list of references, but in reverse sequence. This means that the tedious activity of scrolling down is not necessary.

Favourite bedtime reading for the e-generation, in large type and with fluorescent background.

Corporate communication & product promotion /
Max Bruinsma

Companies these days communicate very differently from the way they did say half a century ago. At that time it was enough to put your products on view and tell folks that they were the best products you could buy. You cannot do that any more. It is not that people don't want to believe you, they want you to make them believe. Advertising is about offering potential buyers arguments with which they can justify their acquisition. And it is increasingly becoming a way of mirroring the people that have already bought your product. They do not have to be convinced anymore, they want confirmation. Nowadays products are about identity more than about functionality or anything else. So corporate communication is not in the first place concerned with spreading factual information on products and prices – that is something which comes later. First of all the company wants to be recognizable as a mirror for its market. The targeted audience has to

recognize itself in the image provided by the company. This is increasingly true for the advertising of products and brands through television, posters and print – although the product remains central in these media. On the Web,where the target is sitting behind a screen, most likely at home, image is everything.

In advertising you cannot elaborate on your glorious past or the genius inventors that are part of your history. You can only hint at the way your product fits in with the lifestyle of your market. Corporate websites try to fill in the gaps left by advertising through other media. On the Web, you can be more specific – or more mysterious. The choice between such extremely diverse ways of addressing your market is motivated by that same market: if you want to bring your car to the attention of dynamic college kids, your site will have to look completely different from a site that confirms the average

suburban person's argument for not driving a Mercedes SEL. In order to attract both categories, Honda made both websites.

On some sites the product is missing completely. All the immersing environment tries to do here, with an extensive use of every feasible multimedia trick, is to attach a brand name to a feeling. The images, the typefaces, the frames with photographs of distant countries or beautiful people, the sounds and moving images all serve to entertain viewers as old acquaintances. The brand presents itself as a good friend, someone to look out for.

1

Netscape: The hands of fate . . .

russian translation

90K read (at 1.3K/sec)

Joe Boxer www Playground

http://www.joeboxer.com

DESIGNER Nick Graham / CLIENT Art & Science W3 Development Ltd. / YEAR OF DESIGN 1995 / COPYRIGHT OWNER Joe Boxer / DESIGN COMPANY Art & Science W3 Development Ltd. / SCREEN DESIGN Joe Boxer, Art & Science W3 Development Ltd. / ANIMATION/GRAPHICS Art & Science W3 Development Ltd. / INTERACTION DESIGN Art & Science W3 Development Ltd. / SOUND DESIGN Joe Boxer / PRODUCTION Jim Connelly, Wayne Bremser, Stefan Fielding-Isaacs / EDITORS Stefan Fielding-Isaacs / CONTRIBUTORS Nick Graham, Kirk Jones, Phil May, Amy Rosenthal / AWARDS Clio (certificate), Angel of Fashion, Cool Site of the Day, High Five, NetGuide Platinum, Japanese Cool Site of the Week / SOFTWARE USED Mac: scanning software, Adobe Photoshop 3.0.5, DeBabelizer Fetch; Linux: BBEdit, native C compiler, Perl Interpreter, Vi / DESIGN PLATFORMS Mac: 90%, Linux: 10%

'Before we start, are you wearing clean underwear?', the visitor is asked on the second page of the Joe Boxer site 6.9. It turns out to be not the marketing squad posing this do-or-die question, but a poodle, smoking and explaining the meaning of life. After hyperclicking a while around the site you will understand where the 'Global Joke Shop' of Joe Boxer is at. The designers of the site take the viewer on a wicked ride past the wacky designs of their warped minds. They are not out to sell underwear, but to 'sell entertainment in such an over the top way that we're certain to knock your shorts off.' Which of course will have you buying new underwear. But first you will enter a Web adventure which has you constantly clicking for more. The sober pages usually feed only one challenging image, sometimes including a bold statement, which leaves you itching to browse on.

The main arena is the Wheel of Fortune of Magic Nick, who is surrounded by icons in a halo shape, representing the further levels and navigation method of the site. Underneath two of them slideshows appear of the people and products of Joe Boxer. Texts are hidden in pop-up menus, so that the design of the pages is not obscured. The background of the pages varies from the fabric of the brand's clothes a fungus culture. This site constantly amuses and amazes: for instance a 'freaks' section is actually an obligatory links page. Instead of simply underlining the linked sites, the sites are presented by funky posters — like the one of the 3-eyed girlfriend, hiding a link to the Peeping Tom site in Sweden, or the one of the World's Largest CEO, which brings you to the fifth column site of Suck.com.

The most spectacular feature of the Joe Boxer site is revealed after clicking on the Statue of Liberty icon. This takes you to The World's First Interactive Electronic Outdoor Billboard, also known as 'The World's Largest E-mail'. It has an option which lets you type a message to be sent to Joe Boxer's billboard, smack on Times Square, where it will be on display to New York for a whole week.

The site offers good-natured, old-fashioned fun, based on a thorough knowledge of the medium. The set-up not only shows what Joe Boxer stands for, but also conveys this experience to the visitor. After having visited this site, nobody will ever forget what this particular brand of underwear stands for.

Adam Eeuwens

❶

On the opening page of the Joe Boxer site hands balance a face whose eyes, by a gentle server push, swirl from one side of the screen to the other. It is a simple, but excellent eye-catcher.

Virtual Underwear Processor™
Be sure you are standing in front of your monitor at all times!
(no need to remove pants.)

V.6.9.

Installing Virtual Underwear Prefs.
Writing: Preference File
[Stop]

②

SOUVENIRS
N.P.R.A.   RANDOM
TALK TALK   FREAKS
TIMES SQUARE   GAMES
US   HELP!
LOOK BEHIND YOU!

③

So glad you could come.
Change your underwear and come with me.

stay a while and I'll tell you my story.
At the end you will find the meaning of life.

④

...forever!

② ③

Before you reach the main arena you involuntarily encounter the fake download of the Virtual Underwear Processor, which uses a make-believe installation window. Frame by frame the meter fills, giving the impression that the application is being downloaded. It is an elegant and very funny use of the server push.

The Wheel of Fortune of Magic Nick. The icons guide you to the homepages of deeper levels of the site. The eight ball brings you back to Magic Nick's haven.

④

The small dot flickers, slowly changing from red to yellow. It is the link to the smoking poodle, which tells of its experiences as a security guard for big logs and also as a fish sniffer until it discovered the smiley 'that changed my life forever'.

How to win a game on a website? In the case of the fortune telling: please, do not put your hand on the screen.

At this precise location in Times Square in New York Joe Boxer has installed a billboard with The World's Largest e-mail. From the site a message can be sent which could be published on the billboard.

This is the core message Joe Boxer wants to get across to the visitor of his site.

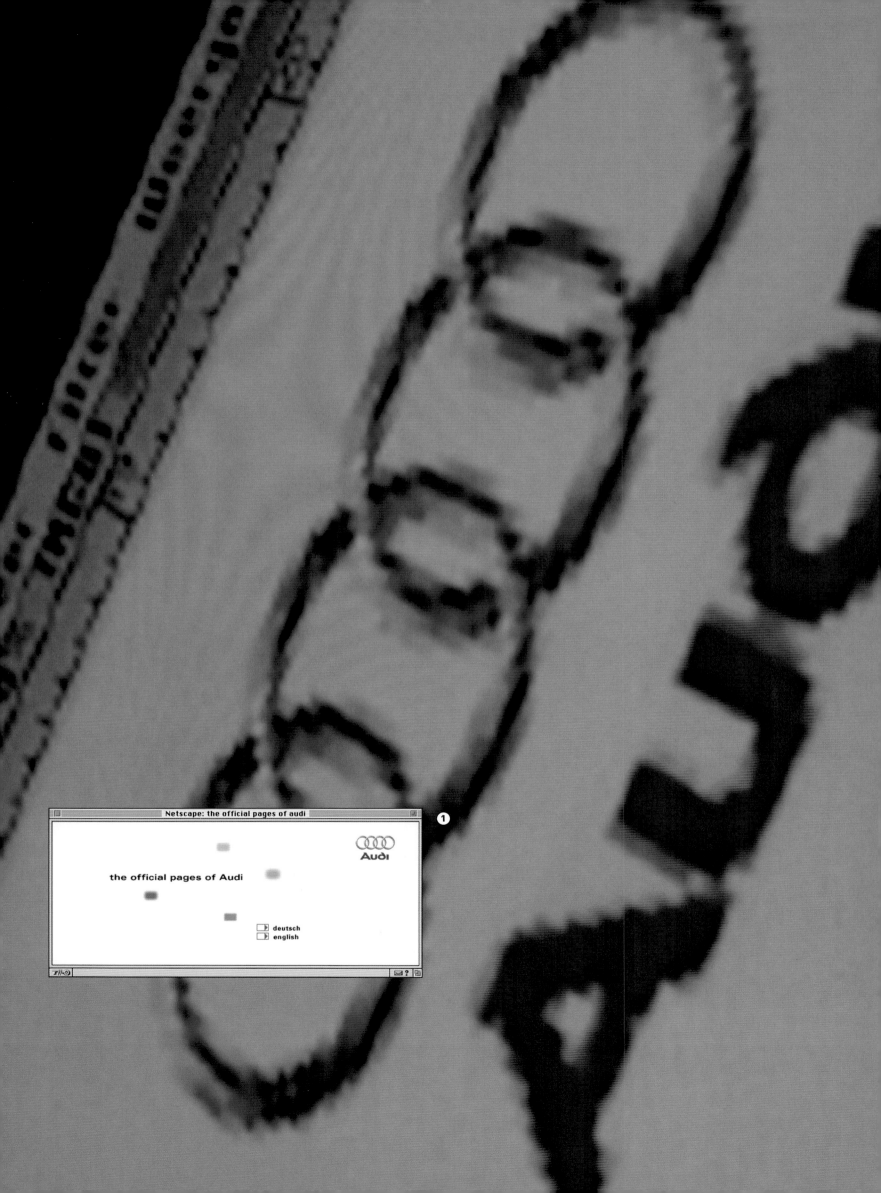

Netscape: the official pages of audi ❶

the official pages of Audi

Audi

▶ deutsch
▶ english

The official pages of Audi

http://www.audi.de/index.html

DESIGNER MetaDesign plus GmbH / CLIENT Audi AG / YEAR OF DESIGN 1996–97 / PLACE OF DESIGN Berlin, Germany / COPYRIGHT OWNER Audi AG / DESIGN COMPANY MetaDesign plus GmbH / SCREEN DESIGN Richard Buhl / INTERACTION DESIGN Charly Frech / PRODUCTION MetaDesign plus GmbH / EDITORS Sonja Studolsky, Roland Metzler / SOFTWARE USED Mac: BBEdit 4.0, Adobe Photoshop / DESIGN PLATFORMS Mac: 100%

As a car manufacturer, Audi is proud of the resounding 'thud' that their well-engineered car doors make as you shut them. In presenting their achievements on-line, they have steered clear of any temptation to use heavy-duty three-dimensional chrome buttons with bevelled edges and have opted for a corporate print brochure aesthetic. The site takes you on a safe, quiet journey through a collection of informative, rigorously constructed pages. With clearly organised content and a comprehensively constructed navigation system, the site provides an abundance of facts and figures about the company's history, current news and product ranges. The site is characterised by moderation of its graphic content and the fact that it delivers a wealth of clear, uncluttered information about Audi.

When you open the official pages of Audi you are welcomed with a splash screen where you can choose to view the site in English or German. At this point you arrive at the main menu or homepage where you quickly get an idea of the Audi site's structure and content.

Audi was founded in 1909 by August Horch. Due to a disagreement with his partner at Horch Works, founded earlier in 1904, his newly established company was not allowed to bear Horch's name. Hence, the name Audi was used. 'Audi' is the Latin translation for Horch, which is the imperative 'Listen!' in German.

This fact, along with a host of others, is brought to you in Report, the on-line magazine within the Audi site.

Apart from Report, the site is divided into the following sections: Models, Service, Facts and News. You also get a 'Navigation' option which, when selected, gives you a pop-up window containing a detailed description of the specific functions of the navigation graphics. Rather than burden each page with text headings describing the different sections, the site designers have chosen a colour key to help the visitor motor swiftly through the site

Grey is the colour used to signify the Models section of the site. It appears in the header for this page, which features the four interlocking circles of the Audi logo. The blue block within the key takes you to the News section. Here, like the Report section, you can browse through the archive of press releases and information, using the vertically scrolling panel on the left of the page.

As a websurfing experience it is hardly Le Mans. However, the Audi site does succeed in serving up clear information in an efficient and unassuming manner.

Giles Rollestone

1

Upon entering the official pages of Audi there is an option to view the site in English or German. The Audi home page has seven main options, from the Report magazine to a help function.

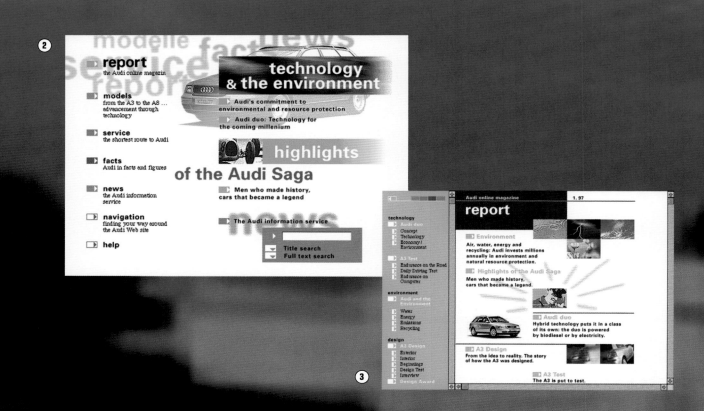

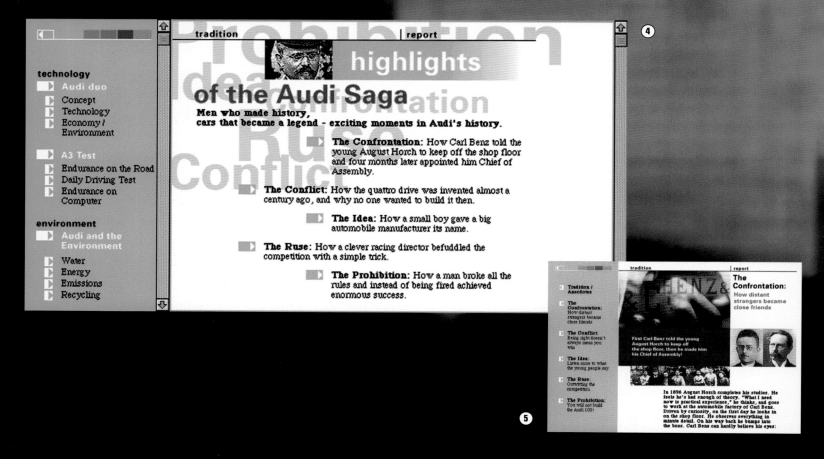

A smaller, separate window accessed from this page provides an explanation of the colour-coded navigation bar and arrows used throughout the site. This key is an essential starting-point, as the featured colors and arrows are used consistently throughout the rest of the site.

The top level of Report features six sections, ranging from Technology through to The Environment, within the main screen area; on the left a frame contains an index of the magazine's contents. This frame uses the yellow from the colour key, which both reiterates the section identity and helps to provide a quick overview of the magazine structure.

Once a topic from the top level of Report is selected, you arrive at a summarising submenu, which in turn takes you to a third tier of information, the articles. From this point you can either browse through the hierarchy of information via the condensed route in the left hand frame or navigate through the illustrated, expanded visual menus provided in the main screen area.

In the Tradition and History section of Report, the anecdotal quality of the text helps to give the potentially faceless corporation some warmth and sets the history of the company into context. The text is accompanied by a tiled collage of sepia-toned illustrations, adding atmosphere to the article.

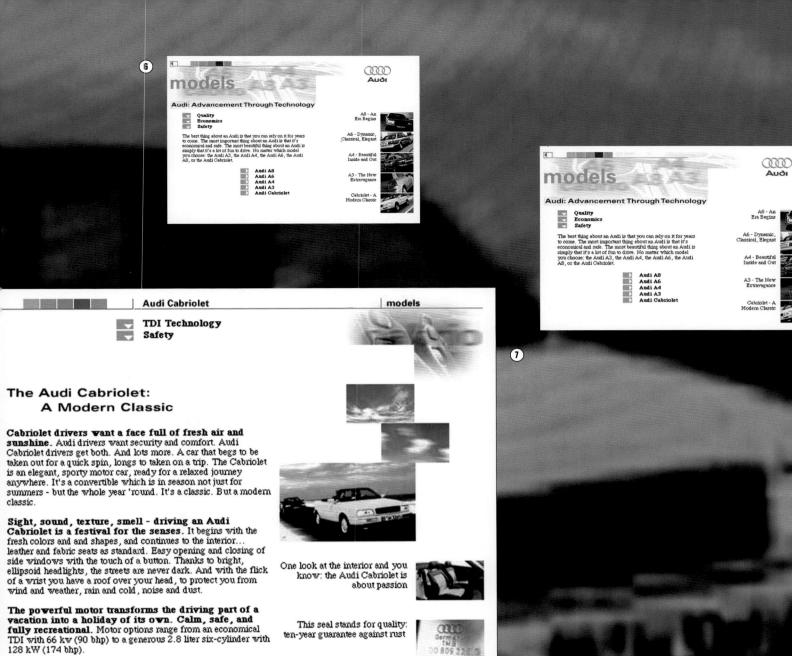

6

models A4 A4 A3 A3
Audi

Audi: Advancement Through Technology

- Quality
- Economics
- Safety

The best thing about an Audi is that you can rely on it for years to come. The most important thing about an Audi is that it's economical and safe. The most beautiful thing about an Audi is simply that it's a lot of fun to drive. No matter which model you choose: the Audi A3, the Audi A4, the Audi A6, the Audi A8, or the Audi Cabriolet.

- Audi A8
- Audi A6
- Audi A4
- Audi A3
- Audi Cabriolet

A8 - An Era Begins

A6 - Dynamic, Classical, Elegant

A4 - Beautiful Inside and Out

A3 - The New Extravagance

Cabriolet - A Modern Classic

7

models A3 A4 A3
Audi

Audi: Advancement Through Technology

- Quality
- Economics
- Safety

The best thing about an Audi is that you can rely on it for years to come. The most important thing about an Audi is that it's economical and safe. The most beautiful thing about an Audi is simply that it's a lot of fun to drive. No matter which model you choose: the Audi A3, the Audi A4, the Audi A6, the Audi A8, or the Audi Cabriolet.

- Audi A8
- Audi A6
- Audi A4
- Audi A3
- Audi Cabriolet

A8 - An Era Begins

A6 - Dynamic, Classical, Elegant

A4 - Beautiful Inside and Out

A3 - The New Extravagance

Cabriolet - A Modern Classic

Audi Cabriolet | **models**

- TDI Technology
- Safety

The Audi Cabriolet:
A Modern Classic

Cabriolet drivers want a face full of fresh air and sunshine. Audi drivers want security and comfort. Audi Cabriolet drivers get both. And lots more. A car that begs to be taken out for a quick spin, longs to taken on a trip. The Cabriolet is an elegant, sporty motor car, ready for a relaxed journey anywhere. It's a convertible which is in season not just for summers - but the whole year 'round. It's a classic. But a modern classic.

Sight, sound, texture, smell - driving an Audi Cabriolet is a festival for the senses. It begins with the fresh colors and and shapes, and continues to the interior... leather and fabric seats as standard. Easy opening and closing of side windows with the touch of a button. Thanks to bright, ellipsoid headlights, the streets are never dark. And with the flick of a wrist you have a roof over your head, to protect you from wind and weather, rain and cold, noise and dust.

The powerful motor transforms the driving part of a vacation into a holiday of its own. Calm, safe, and fully recreational. Motor options range from an economical TDI with 66 kw (90 bhp) to a generous 2.8 liter six-cylinder with 128 kW (174 bhp).

One look at the interior and you know: the Audi Cabriolet is about passion

This seal stands for quality: ten-year guarantee against rust

---

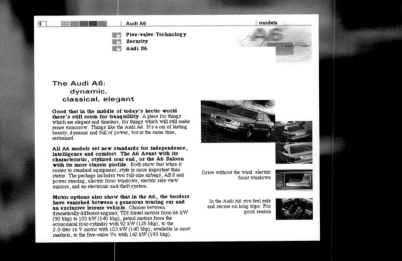

Audi A6 | **models**

- Five-valve Technology
- Security
- Audi S6

The Audi A6:
dynamic, classical, elegant

Good that in the middle of today's hectic world there's still room for tranquillity. A place for things which are elegant and timeless, for things which will still make sense tomorrow. Things like the Audi A6. It's a car of lasting beauty, dynamic and full of power, but at the same time, restrained.

All A6 models set new standards for independence, intelligence and comfort. The A6 Avant with its characteristic, stylized rear end, or the A6 Saloon with its more classic profile. Both show that when it comes to standard equipment, style is more important than status. The package includes two full-size airbags, ABS and power steering, electric front windows, electric side view mirrors, and an electronic anti-theft system.

Motor options also show that in the A6, the borders have vanished between a generous touring car and an exclusive leisure vehicle. Choose between dramatically different engines; TDI diesel motors from 66 kW (90 bhp) to 103 kW (140 bhp), petrol motors from the economical four-cylinder with 92 kW (125 bhp), to the 2.0-liter 16 V motor with 103 kW (140 bhp), available in most markets, to the five-valve V6 with 142 kW (193 bhp).

Drive without the wind: electric front windows

In the Audi A6 you feel safe and secure on long trips. For good reason

---

facts
Audi

Audi in Facts and Figures

- Locations
- Employees
- Production and Delivery
- Annual Report

Only good workers can build good cars. And good workers need good tools. So naturally, our factories are well-equipped. State-of-the-art machinery, high-powered computers, and our commitment to leadership in environmental technology make sure that we produce cars which are success stories. They point the way in areas like safety, comfort, design, performance and environmental awareness.

Locations:
Factories, Cooperations and Joint Ventures

8

---

6 7

8

The Emissions article is part of a rigorously expressed hierarchy. The site as a whole takes its visual and structural cues from corporate graphic design, reflecting a modernist aesthetic whose emphasis on solid structure and form suggests tradition and reliability rather than ephemeral fluidity.

In the pages of the Models section, the corporate brochure style gives way to a more straightforward display of information. The structure and style of delivery focuses the viewer's attention on content rather than form.

The section of facts and figures is another area of the site which successfully communicates Audi's corporate credentials. The unremitting consistency of the page design gives the impression that the company prides itself on its immutability and attention to detail.

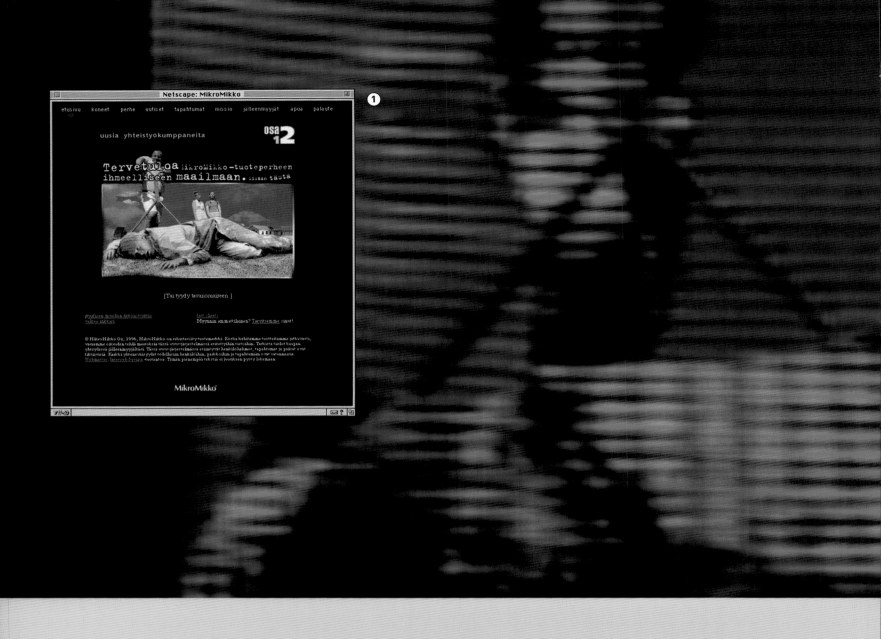

Me tahdomme tietää by MikroMikko

http://www.mikromikko.fi

DESIGNER Interweb Design Oy / CLIENT MikroMikko Oy / YEAR OF DESIGN 1996 / PLACE OF DESIGN Helsinki, Finland / COPYRIGHT OWNER MikroMikko Oy / DESIGN COMPANY Interweb Design Oy / SCREEN DESIGN Juhani Haaparinne, Jarkko Lyyra and Migu Snäll / ANIMATION/GRAPHICS Juhani Haaparinne / INTERACTION DESIGN Juhani Haaparinne, Jarkko Lyyra / PRODUCTION Antti Leino / EDITOR Antti Leino / CONTRIBUTORS Kimmo Koskinen / SOFTWARE USED Mac: Adobe Photoshop, BBEdit, Netscape; sgi: AsWeb, Netscape Navigator / DESIGN PLATFORMS Mac: 80 %; sgi: 20 %

❶

'Welcome to the wonderful world of the MikroMikko product family. Enter here.' The 'family' is introduced here, although it is not yet known that they are the characters in the episodes to follow. The row of words at the top of the page refers to the categories of the site, and is used as a navigation bar throughout the main pages of the site.

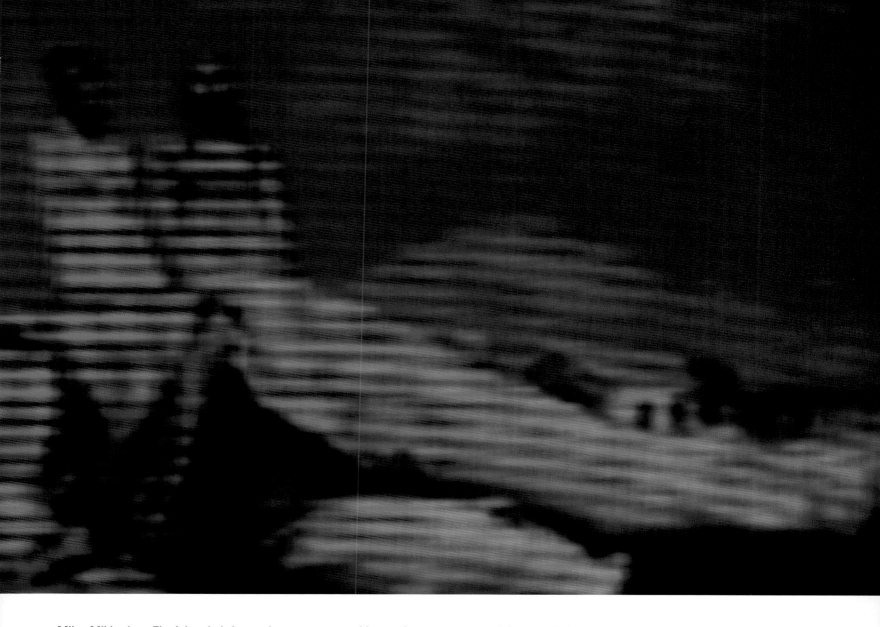

MikroMikko is a Finnish tele-informatics company making and selling their own computers. Their site opens with the question 'Do you listen to Finnish dance music?' and introduces the 'family' of MikroMikko Computers. Then a playful scenario is created with a fictional family and its world, in the form of interactive episodes. The visual language is a rich mixture of theatrical sets with the slick advertising touch of subcultural imagery drawn from computer games and flyers, with text often adding another twisted layer to the story.

Two episodes have been written so far, about the father and the son. They are introduced in their own rooms, where various objects link to their worlds. By moving the mouse across an object the user can read a catchy sentence in the window at the bottom (where the status information of the browser is usually displayed). These lines function as the intermediate narrative for the user, tickling him or her to click. 'Just for you, to know what they talk about.' This is a very elegant interactive feature that appears throughout the site, an example of innovative use of the medium and good screen design, where the problem often is to find the right balance between the visual aspects and the typography, within the technical limitations.

In the first episode, the user navigates through short loops returning to the father's room, or is lured to complete an entertaining psychological test (36 linear pages!). The world of his family portraits and patient reports is coherent, whereas the son's ever expanding world of graffiti, DJs, clothing, sports, and computer games offers less sense of place and continuity. It does, however, offer more surprises: the user may end up reading a list of London clubs, wandering in MUD (multi-user dungeons), or e-mailing his own dreams to MikroMikko. Here one might completely forget that the site is ultimately about MikroMikko's computers (if one ever found out).

Although the main focus is on the growing family narrative, the user is able to read the more factual information about Mikro-Mikko that is presented, parallel to the episodes, as navigational buttons on top of the pages. This navigational system to the site as a whole could do with some restyling. No matter how interested the user is in reading about cockroaches in Bad Mojo, he may want to return to the main interface every now and then and read the corporate information. Coherent navigational tools, such as a row of buttons, could be useful throughout the site. Provided these tools are implemented, the announced 'ride' with the wife and the daughter promises to be even more exciting, giving the needed feminine insight into computers.

Mari Soppela

RASKAILTA

[osa 2. Poika]

[osa 1. Isa]

etusivu   koneet   perhe   uutiset   tapahtumat   missio   jälleenmyyjät   apua   palaute

By pointing to the hot spots of the screen, a line of text is displayed underneath in the browser's window. By 'mousing' over the image and the texts on the screen, the user can read three different lines quickly one after the other: 'The son. Period.' (image), 'To the son's world' (episode 2), and 'The psychiatrist father's thinking corner.' (episode 1)

In Father's room there are 11 links hidden in the image (map): behind the computer screen, the book, all the photos (including the two on the mantel), the newspaper on the table and so on. The Couch of Trust is the least obvious object in the image, and therefore takes you to the most surprising page.

Do you remember how you used to be, before the world corrupted you? Do you remember what you used to think? Send your answers by e-mail.

This page is the main interface of the son's world, and from an interaction viewpoint, it is the most complex page in the site. All the stars and (parts of) the images are interactive. The stars represent and are a link to the chapters in the son's life.

This page is found under the chapter Flyers. It links to the sites of clubs in London, New York and Los Angeles. Other links in this chapter lead to style and clothing sites.

This is the opening page of the chapter Graffiti, where the user can read an in-depth, hyper-linked story about graffiti. Some of the links expand to other sites in the Web. The user can also paint his own piece of graffiti and send it to the on-line Da Helsinki Gallery.

This is the Psych On-Line test with 36 pages of entertaining questions. Similar tests are found in women's magazines.

In the pages under Computers, MikroMikko tell about their computers and strategies. The computers link to more factual pages. All the pages under these buttons are white, in contrast to (most of) the black pages in the episodes.

Netscape: Welcome to Samsung

The opportunity of the 21st Century is the world itself. Its challenges drive us to succeed

Electronics Business Group

Machinery Business Group

Chemical Business Group

Finance Business Group

Other Samsung Companies

Welcome to the World of Samsung

Challenge Samsung!
http://www.samsung.co.kr

Samsung builds the world's largest container ships and crude-oil carriers. It is the largest semi-conductor chip manufacturer. The company also builds excavators, bulldozers and loaders, and was responsible for the fastest 2000 cc Prototype ii racing machine at Japan's 1995 POKKA International 1000k. How was the challenge of designing the website for this megacorporation to be met, without having to invent the world's largest hard disk drive (actually, they have already done that)? The Korean company's Internet presence is not at all a boring bulky catalogue listing too many products. On the contrary, it is a slim, elegant and extraordinarily intelligent site.

The site reads like a confidential annual report to the stockholders, complete with the chairman's obligatory evangelical message proclaiming: 'corporations do not merely offer products – but intellectual assets, philosophy, culture.' The aim of the site is to present Samsung's corporate image and strategy. The entire history of the company is traced, from an image of the house where Samsung started out in 1938 selling fruit and noodles, to its rise as one of the world leaders in the electronics, chemicals, finance and machinery businesses.

Without reserve Samsung spills its beans on how the corporation is run. The income of every division is shown to the last digit, and very detailed specifications are given on how the letterhead corresponds with the corporate identity. This is all done in order to prove that it is deadly serious in its effort to become one of the global top-10 companies by the year 2000. The large amount of information is organised simply and effectively. The core message never exceeds the size of the average computer screen, with navigational arrows at the right leading up and down to the detailed level of a specific section. Another key element in the presentation of Samsung's corporate image is the division into the header sections of Past, Present and Future. Under these are found subsections detailing the roots of the company as well as the present-day and future challenges. In this main section the basic grid of the page rarely changes. It remains sturdy and reliable: the focus is not on a flashy HTML and/or graphic design, but on content.

However, within this self-imposed restriction the design gracefully manages to add value to the content through detailed and manipulated images and by ragging and denting the screen type. The website builders have taken 'Quality First', the most important principle of their chairman Lee, to heart and offer their graphic design colleagues a perfect case study for corporate webdesign assignments.

Adam Eeuwens

1

A modest greeting page with a silent animation of three rotating images. A home page that loads fast, does not intimidate and invites you to continue.

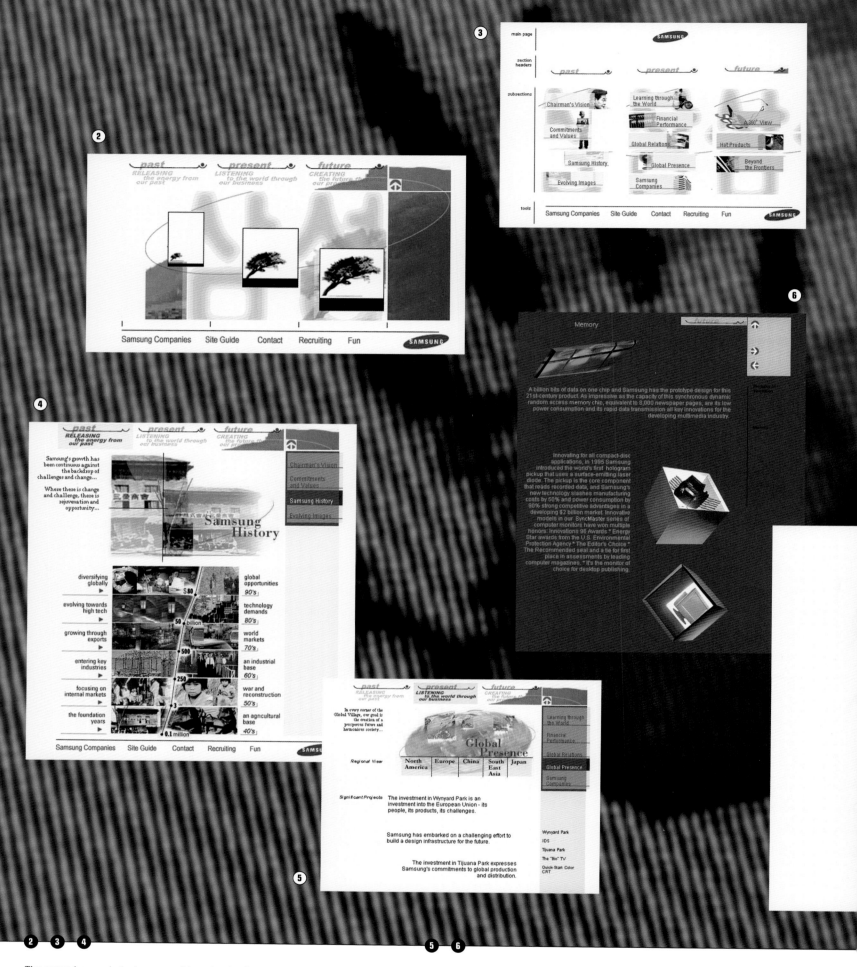

The second page, indexing everything the site has to offer in one clear screen. The line of the ellipse is part of the Samsung logo and plays a role throughout the site.

This map shows the organisation of the site. 'Home' is where the Samsung logo appears. The other elements pictured are the building blocks of the site, which contain many other more specific pages.

The house where Samsung started in 1938. Underneath the clickable info-graphic the complete history of the company is presented.

In the left-hand corner a streamer states Samsung's objective on each topic. The header section 'Past/Present/Future' is always present at the top, while the right side of the screen holds the navigational links, with the very important arrow at the top.

When you go deeper into the detail of a subsection the design grid becomes looser, yet it keeps the navigational tools in the top right corner.

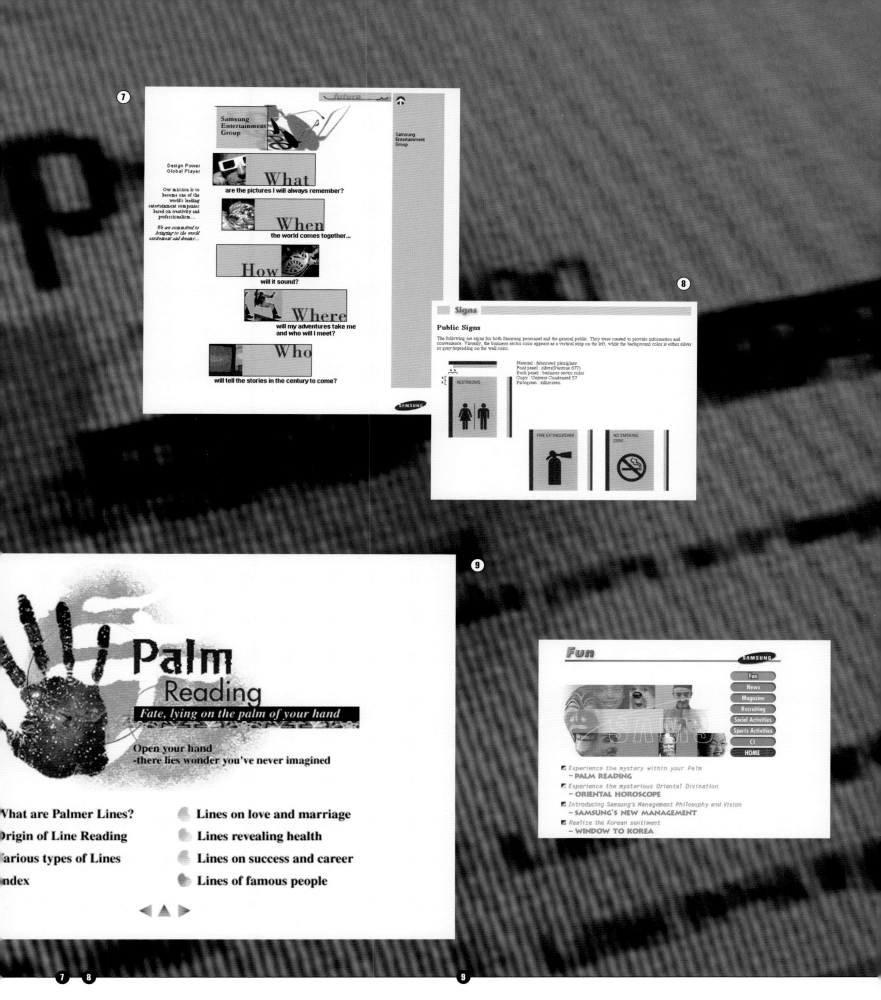

Here the future vision of Samsung is revealed: they want to become a funky entertainment group by the year 2005, realising the current global trend of media development.

All elements of the corporate identity of Samsung are explained.

After all the serious stuff this is the fun page for everybody all over the world and for all ages. Here you can learn how to read your palm, have a Chinese horoscope drawn or read Samsung's magazine.

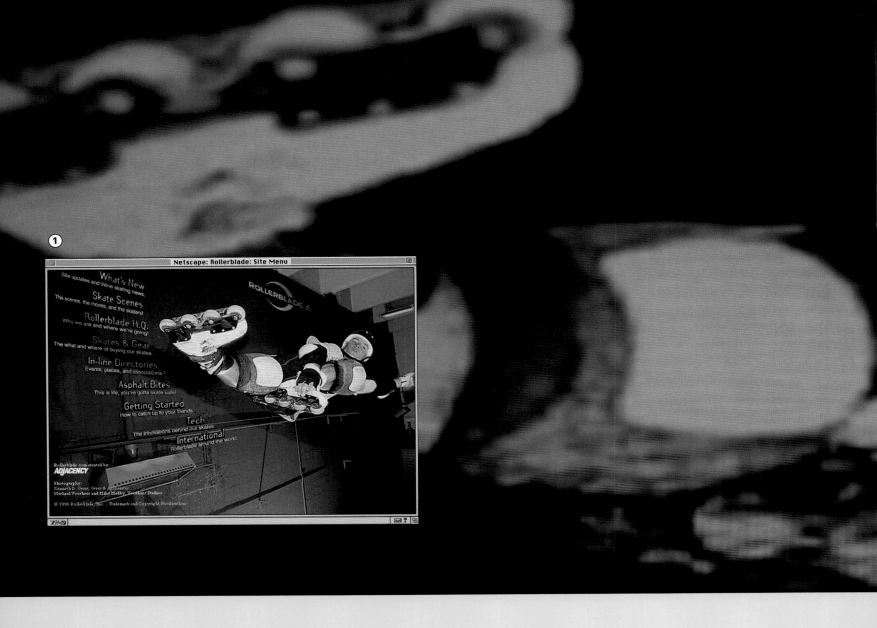

① Netscape: Rollerblade: Site Menu

What's New
Site updates and inline skating news.

Skate Scenes
The scenes, the moves, and the skaters!

Rollerblade H.Q.
Who we are and where we're going!

Skates & Gear
The what and where of buying our skates.

In-line Directories
Events, places, and associations.

Asphalt Bites
This is life, you've gotta skate safe!

Getting Started
How to catch up to your friends.

Tech
The innovations behind our skates

International
Rollerblade around the world.

Rollerblade.com created by:
ADJACENCY

Photography:
Kenneth P. Greer, Greer & Associates
Michael Voorhees and Mike Hedby, Voorhees Studios

© 1996 Rollerblade, Inc. : Trademark and Copyright Notification.

Rollerblade.com
http://www.rollerblade.com

DESIGNER Adjacency / CLIENT Rollerblade Inc. / YEAR OF DESIGN 1996 / PLACE OF DESIGN Madison, USA / COPYRIGHT OWNER Rollerblade Inc. / DESIGN COMPANY Adjacency / SCREEN DESIGN Andrew Sather, Bernie DeChant, Matia Wagabaza, Pascal / ANIMATION/GRAPHICS Bernie DeChant, Matia Wagabaza, Pascal / INTERACTION DESIGN Andrew Sather, Bernie DeChant, Matia Wagabaza / PRODUCTION Pascal, Joe Frost, Jeff Stein, Arturo Pena, Anton Prastowo, Matia Wagabaza, Eric Agnew, Brian Ziegler, Bernie DeChant / EDITORS Rollerblade, Adjacency / CONTRIBUTORS Greer & Associates, Voorhees Studios, Adjacency / AWARDS 1996 Print Interactive Design Annual / SOFTWARE USED Mac: Adobe Illustrator, QuarkXPress, Adobe Photoshop, BBEdit; mpc: Alchemy Mindworks Graphics Workshop, Adobe Photoshop / DESIGN PLATFORMS Mac: 80 %, mpc: 20 %

①

Entering the enhanced site of Rollerblade, this page lists all the goodies to be found. Typography bends and sways across a background image, spitting its message of 'speed, speed, speed!!' at the viewer.

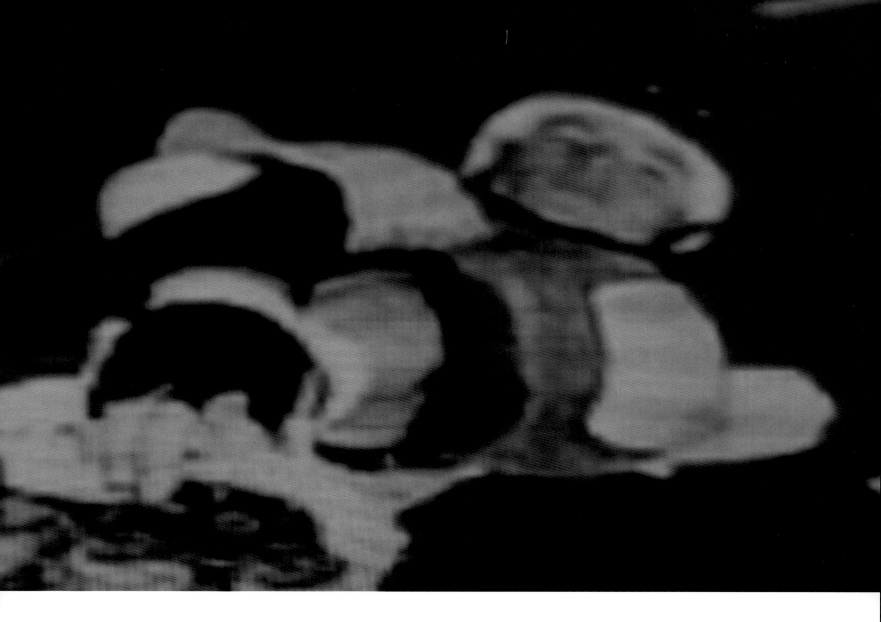

Did you know that in-line skates were invented in the 18th century by a Dutchman who nailed some wooden spools to sticks so he could skate all through the summer? Well, Rollerblade are more than happy to share the credit with this legendary character, although they are quick to add that a lot has changed since then. In-line skating has not only become a sport or leisure activity, it is also a lifestyle – and Rollerblade knows it. Consequently, their website addresses an international audience, ranging from the speedskate fanatic to the casually interested, and aims to establish an on-line skating community. There is information on skating locations, various skating competitions, safety and protective gear, and a host of contact options, from mailing lists to chat-lines. And yes, there is also information about the Rollerblade company and the skates they sell. All of their advanced models are on display, accompanied by technical specs and latest updates.

The visual style of the site reflects the style of the sport – wild, fast and spectacular. The general impact is mainly created by huge background images: action-packed photographs that load amazingly fast. In line with the composition of these images the text flows and sways across the pages. The main links to subsequent sections on the site are captured in images, therefore allowing for a jazzed-up typography and a freedom of layout. Only when the viewer moves deeper into the pages will he/she find default text. Most headings consist of speed-blurred typography, which almost blends with the imagery. These highly-strung pages form a permanent context for the simpler, but frequently updated reports on events, races and celebrities on the international skating-scene. Nothing compares, however, to the pages that show the principal subject of the site, the skates.

The product pages in the Rollerblade site underline the total fetishisation of their skates, from the celebration of the minutest detail of the high-tech design and innovation to the high-gloss product photography. This reaches its apotheosis in the QuickTimeVR enhanced representations of the various models, which allow you to examine the shiny skates from every angle. If the in-line skating virus has not caught you by then, it probably never will, and the helpful pages listing the nearest Rollerblade dealers (world-wide) will be wasted on you.

Geert J. Strengholt

2

The Rollerblade logo in the 'HQ' section is surrounded by links that give background information on the company.

3

In Skate Scenes Rollerblade addresses a wide audience, offering information for the speedfreak in the 'aggressive' section, but also for the leisure skater in Work It. As in many of the pages the main impact is determined by the background images, allowing the designers to play around freely with typography.

Arena provides info about in-line hockey, with tips and tricks to improve your skills. The graphic header reflects the speed and swift turns of this sport. The pop-up menu in Rink Directory allows you to search for the best hockey rinks in the US.

Advertising and selling skates is of course not forgotten: an extensive section showcases the different models. Further navigation to detailed pages is based on image maps.

The Fusion 10K model with the option of checking a 360° view of the actual skates.

A QuickTimeVR movie makes it possible to examine these miracles of high-tech skate-design from every angle.

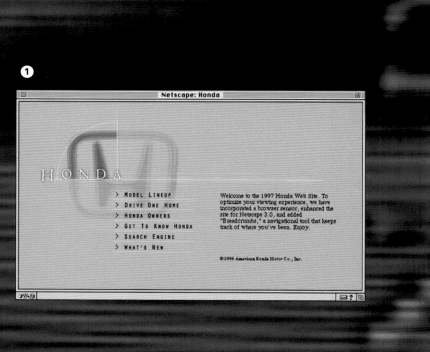

1

Netscape: Honda

HONDA

> MODEL LINEUP
> DRIVE ONE HOME
> HONDA OWNERS
> GET TO KNOW HONDA
> SEARCH ENGINE
> WHAT'S NEW

Welcome to the 1997 Honda Web Site. To optimize your viewing experience, we have incorporated a browser sensor, enhanced the site for Netscape 3.0, and added "Breadcrumbs," a navigational tool that keeps track of where you've been. Enjoy.

©1996 American Honda Motor Co., Inc.

Honda
http://www.honda.com

DESIGNER Rubin Postaer Interactive / CLIENT American Honda Motor Co Inc. / YEAR OF DESIGN 1996 / PLACE OF DESIGN Santa Monica, USA / COPYRIGHT OWNER American Honda Motor Co Inc. / DESIGN COMPANY Rubin Postaer Interactive / SCREEN DESIGN, ANIMATION/GRAPHICS, INTERACTION DESIGN Rubin Postaer Interactive / PRODUCTION Rubin Postaer Interactive / EDITORS Rubin Postaer Interactive / AWARDS International Automotive Advertising Association Gold Award for Internet Design, Pioneer Award, High Five Award / SOFTWARE USED Mac: Adobe Photoshop, Adobe Illustrator, BBEdit, Adobe Premiere, GifBuilder, Progressive Networks; mpc: Macromedia Director / DESIGN PLATFORMS Mac: 90%; mpc: 10%

For a Japanese company, Honda's site is remarkably American-oriented. In fact, about the only explicit mention of the company's homeland is the statement that the first American-built Honda car was exported to Japan in 1988. For the rest it is stars-and-stripes all over. Seen from this perspective, the site is a useful instrument in the PR war between the two economic powers and its Uncle Sam feel is clearly meant as a defence against anticipated anti-Japanese feeling. The pages are built up around a globe-like graph, which becomes a sort of oval scribble deeper into the site, successfully resisting the horror vacui that seems to be the average webdesigner's basic instinct. The design of this site is relatively calm, with an interface that is mainly typographic. You will find no plethora of cool pictorial buttonry at Honda's site. Instead, the designers opted for classic typography around the abstract central image in greys and subdued colours. On various pages an image of a Honda car includes a pull-down menu that accesses model information and in some cases a QuickTimeVR movie allowing you to look around inside the car or view its exterior from all sides. Another visual gadget that is typical of Java-enhanced media is the possibility of changing the colour of a car by 'mousing' over the colour range represented by the dots beside the picture.

With its typographical consistency, the overall design of the site is geared towards an impression of detached, informative communication, and avoids all the clichés of loud advertising and 'we'll-make-you-an-offer-you-can't-refuse' iconography. It's more like a clickable brochure which could also function as a Honda owner's club magazine. There are two breaches in the overall consistency of the graphic design of the site. One occurs on the Made In America page, which is clearly hooked up to an older version of the site's design, based on frames. The other stylistic breach is the link behind the phrase 'Click Here If You Are Under 21' on the What's New page. Actually, this link accesses a new site, the Honda Campus, with a completely different design. This site, which is much 'cooler', with 'handwritten' texts and bright colours, addresses the young college driver who may live for the moment now, but should know that in three years' time — he or she could still be driving the same Honda.

Max Bruinsma

❶

The Honda Welcome page with an index to the site's contents.

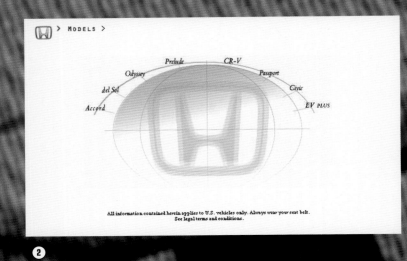

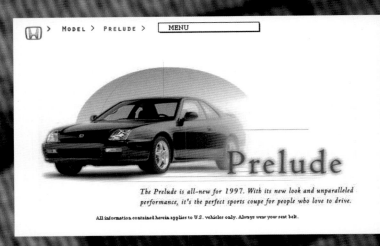

②

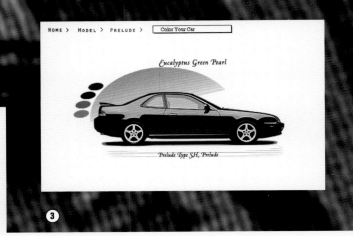

③

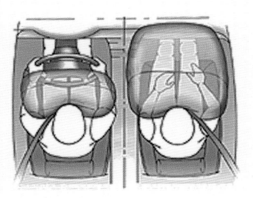

*Dual Airbags, a reinforced body and side-impact be...
put you and your passengers in a cocoon of strength and...*

②

③

The models available in the United States, grouped around a Honda logo.

On the Model Lineup page an image of a Honda model emerges from the digital mist. The image includes a pull-down menu which gives access to pictures and model information, and in some cases to a QuickTimeVR movie that allows you to look around inside the car or view its exterior from all sides. Another visual gadget that is typical for Java-enhanced media is the option to change the colour of a car by 'mousing' over the colour range represented by the dots beside the picture. Notice the standard warning to always wear your seat belt.

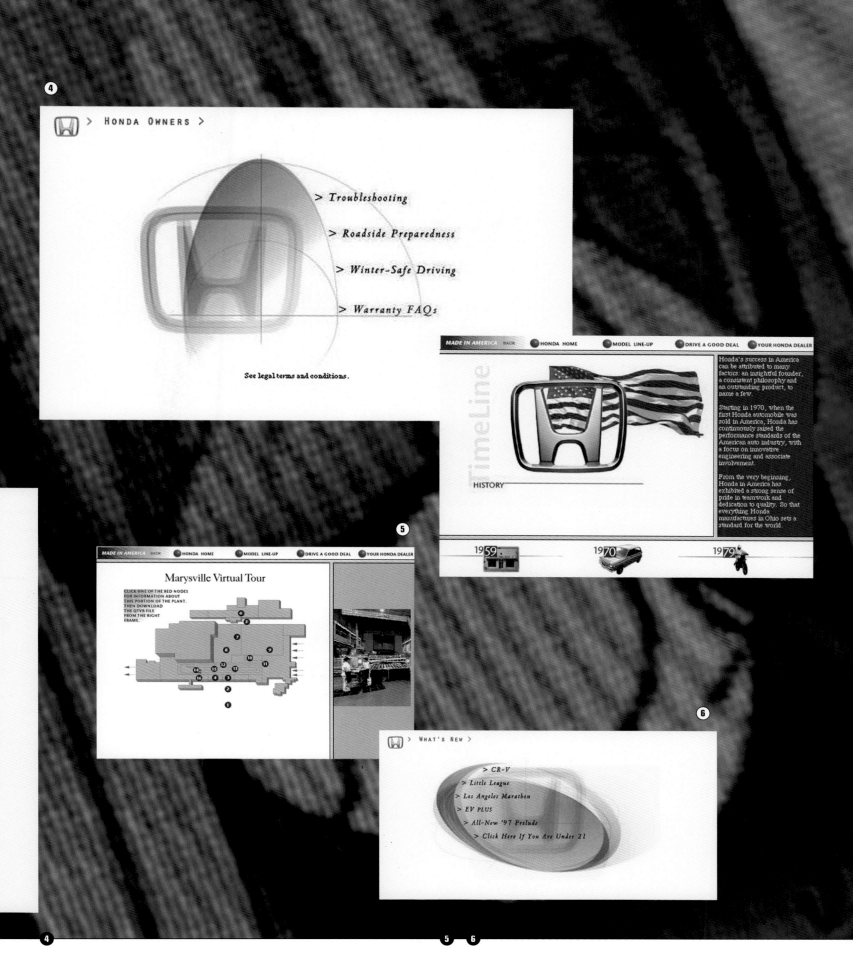

> HONDA OWNERS >

> Troubleshooting

> Roadside Preparedness

> Winter-Safe Driving

> Warranty FAQs

See legal terms and conditions.

MADE IN AMERICA   BACK   HONDA HOME   MODEL LINE-UP   DRIVE A GOOD DEAL   YOUR HONDA DEALER

TimeLine

HISTORY

Honda's success in America can be attributed to many factors: an insightful founder, a consistent philosophy and an outstanding product, to name a few.

Starting in 1970, when the first Honda automobile was sold in America, Honda has continuously raised the performance standards of the American auto industry, with a focus on innovative engineering and associate involvement.

From the very beginning, Honda in America has exhibited a strong sense of pride in teamwork and dedication to quality. So that everything Honda manufactures in Ohio sets a standard for the world.

1959   1970   1979

MADE IN AMERICA   BACK   HONDA HOME   MODEL LINE-UP   DRIVE A GOOD DEAL   YOUR HONDA DEALER

Marysville Virtual Tour

CLICK ONE OF THE RED NODES
FOR INFORMATION ABOUT
THIS PORTION OF THE PLANT.
THEN DOWNLOAD
THE QTVR FILE
FROM THE RIGHT
FRAME.

> WHAT'S NEW >

> CR-V
> Little League
> Los Angeles Marathon
> EV PLUS
> All-New '97 Prelude
> Click Here If You Are Under 21

The Honda Owners chapter gives straightforward information about what to do in the rare event that your Honda does not perform as well as it should. This kind of information is given in default text, accompanied by a heading GIF, which is a combination of the title and the oval scribble that appears in different shapes throughout the site.

On this page we learn that Honda has been active in selling motorcycles in the States from as early as 1959, and are offered a 'cyber-sightseeing' tour through the ultramodern Honda plant in Marysville, Ohio, which produces 380,000 'American' cars yearly, employing thousands of American workers. QuickTimeVR movies allow you to look around in the factory. A time bar offers a brief history of Honda in the US.

Latest updates and a link to the Honda Campus, an altogether different Web site to attract the college-going car driver.

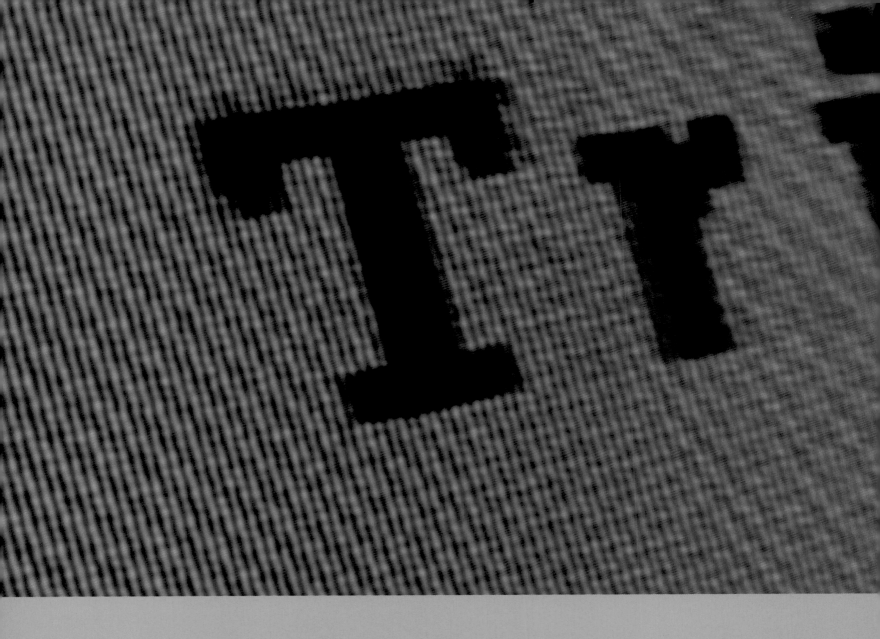

Triple P
House Style Manual
http://www.mediamatic.nl/tpp.html

DESIGNER Mediamatic IP / CLIENT Triple P / YEAR OF DESIGN 1996 / PLACE OF DESIGN Amsterdam, the Netherlands / COPYRIGHT OWNER Mediamatic IP/Triple P / DESIGN COMPANY Mediamatic IP / SCREEN DESIGN, ANIMATION/GRAPHICS, INTERACTION DESIGN Willem Velthoven, Robin Verdegaal / PRODUCTION Willem Velthoven, Robin Verdegaal / EDITORS Willem Velthoven, Robin Verdegaal / CONTRIBUTORS Ric Aqua, Liesbeth den Boer, Mark van Wageningen / SOFTWARE USED Mac: Adobe Photoshop, Pagespinner, Boxtop PhotoGIF, Boxtop ProJPEG

1

The homepage for the House Style Manual features the Triple P logo, consisting of three peas combined with the name in the TheSis-font. The background image of the pea plants unobtrusively underlines the house style concept. The navigation for the site is introduced in the small frame at the bottom, where four icons refer to sections about logo, colours, fonts and grids.

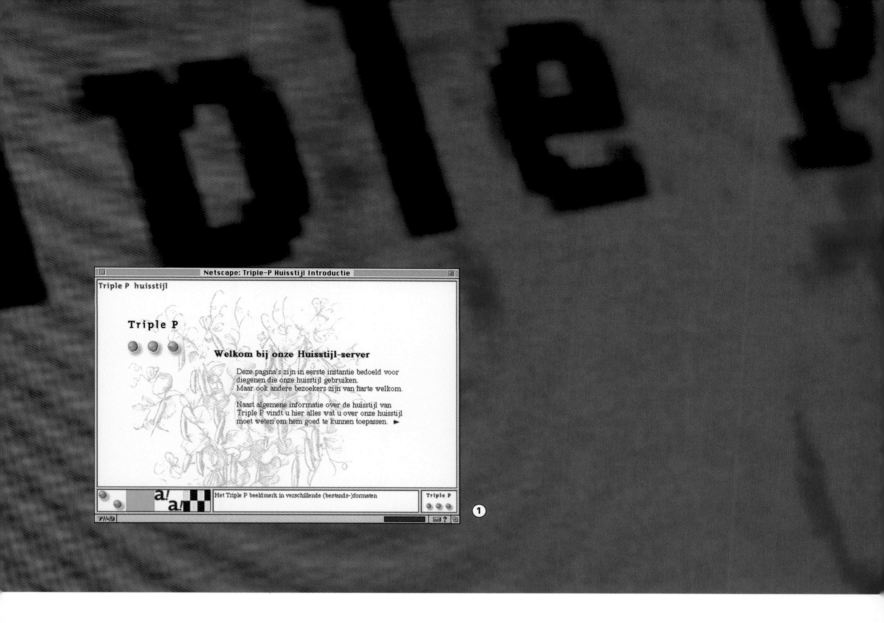

Along with the growth of interest in intranets — corporate websites mainly used for internal communication — designing corporate websites is becoming an important field of Web design. When Triple P completely changed its house style it had to find a way to communicate these changes to the people who needed to know. Usually a printed manual would be published for this purpose. However, in this case Mediamatic developed a website for them, which includes information on the new logo, fonts, colours and grids. Ultimately it will form an integral part of the corporate site of Triple P, where it can be accessed by all internal departments or external branches.

The information on the house style is presented in four main sections. Each section is accessible from the main navigation bar at the bottom of the screen. An index to a particular section is presented when the icons that refer to it are clicked. This index in turn allows random access to several small screens, in which information is kept brief and clear. These screens can also be read in successive order. Crosslinks provide the necessary correspondence between the sections. Therefore the site is in essence non-linear in its structure.

Since people from various departments with various queries have to be able to find answers and material swiftly, the site provides a clear navigational system, but also different ways to end up with the right solutions. In order to prevent too much 'trial and error' searching, the contents of the sections are clearly explained before following a link. Through an intricate interplay of frames and so-called mouse-overs – a Java-script that triggers an event in another frame when 'moused over' – one is able to read a preview of what kind of information is to be expected behind a certain link. This is a powerful tool that enables a swift and smooth scan of the contents of the site. After the initial surprise of the mouse-over activity, it does not take much time to get used to the site. The interface is smooth and clear, and the presentation of the information is very easy to understand. The colours and background images are subtle and subdued, therefore emphasising the text. It is only in the presentation of the TheSis-font that the designers indulge in a GIF-animation extravaganza in order to feature all the font variations. The site is at once an on-line instruction manual and a clear example of how the house style of Triple P should be properly applied in varying circumstances. Last but not least, since the House Style Manual will be accessible to the public at large as part of the website of Triple P, it will also serve a more general PR purpose.

Geert J. Strengholt

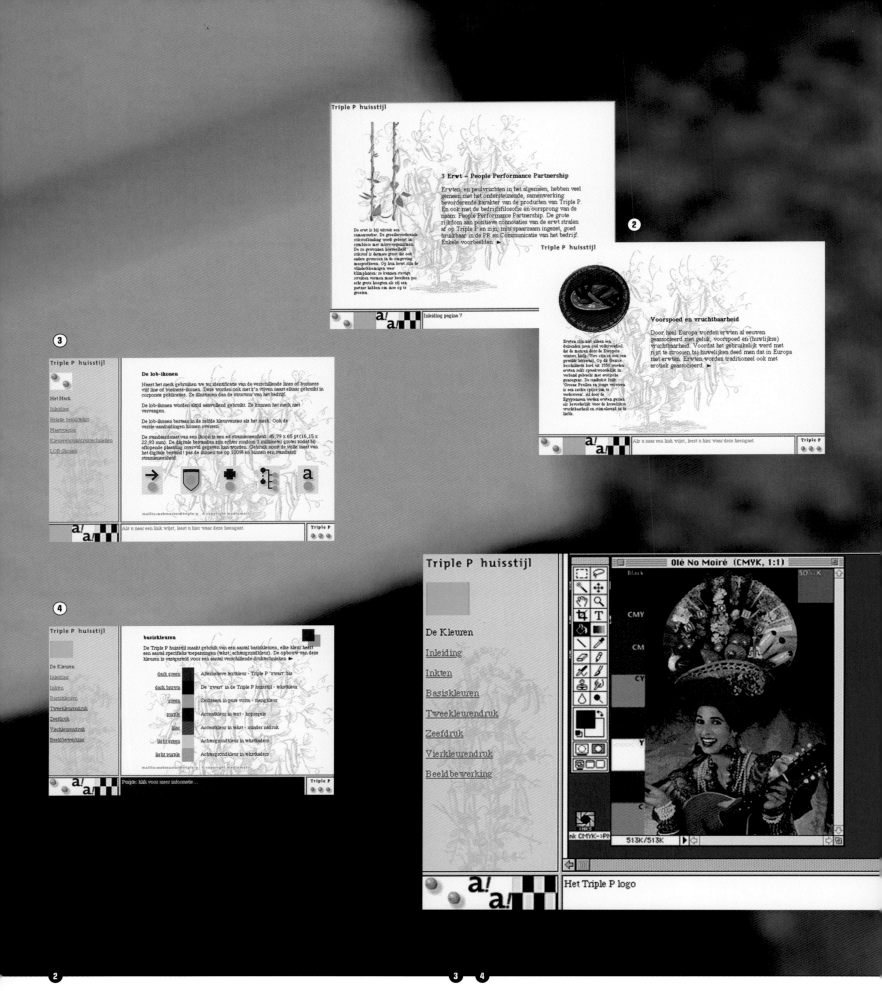

Although rather tongue-in-cheek, the house style is based on a completely researched background of the pea that features in the company logo. As the manual explains, Triple P's corporate philosophy, 'People, Performance, Partnership', has a lot in common with the rich and positive connotations of the pea and its plant. These pages provide a mix of insightful references, ranging from the erotic allusions on a 16th-century plate to biological details, illuminating the concept and imagery of the house style.

Apart from information on the Triple P logo this section also explains the use of five Line-Of-Business icons, representing the structure of the company. Partly derived from the main logo these icons refer to (from left to right) transportation and logistics, financial services, health care, network integration and printing/publishing.

The colour section gives detailed information on the two basic colours from which all house style colours are derived, and when they should be applied. Mouse-overs cause the appropriate colour to be loaded in the lower frame. The frame on the left lists and links to the pages in this section.

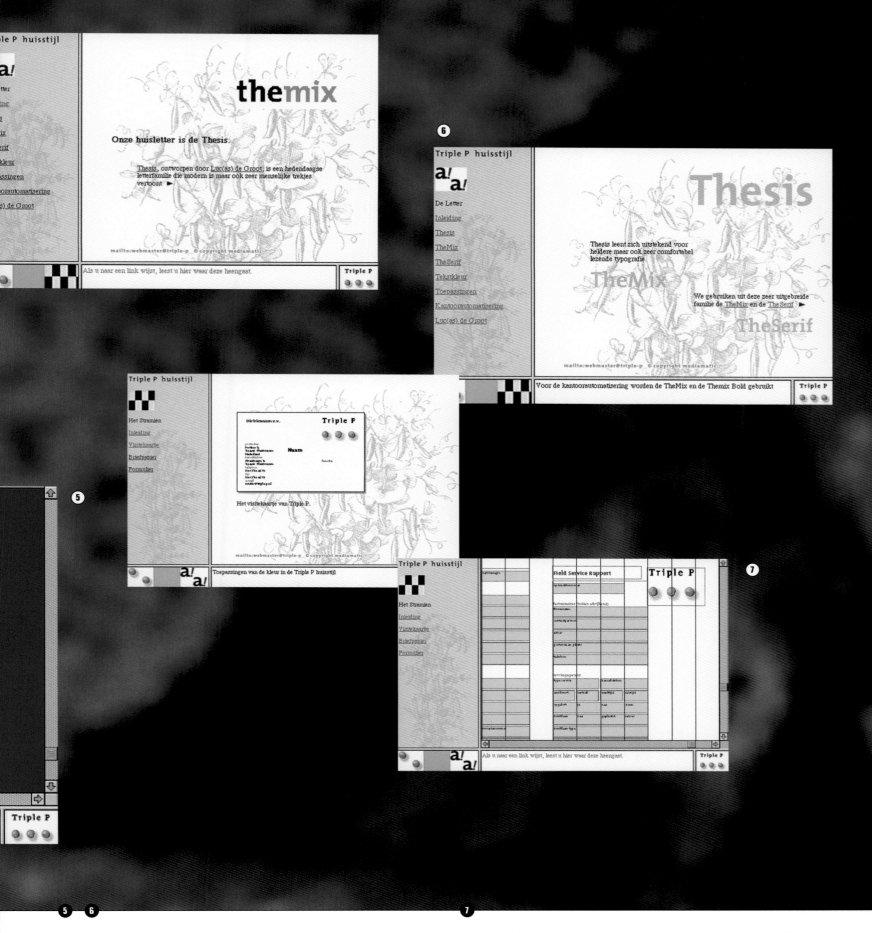

An extensive explanation takes you step by step through the process of adapting imagery to the palette of colours of the house style. Here the final stage is shown.

The first page of the font section introduces the family of TheSis, a font designed by Lucas de Groot, by running a wide range of variations through an animated GIF. Further information about the use of TheSis, or TheMix and TheSerif from the same family, can be browsed through by following the guiding arrows. Of course these pages are also available at random through the links in the left frame.

After a brief introduction The Grid contains a number of examples, like the business card and the field service report. It even contains downloadable templates on a 1:1 scale, to provide printers with all the information and reference material they need.

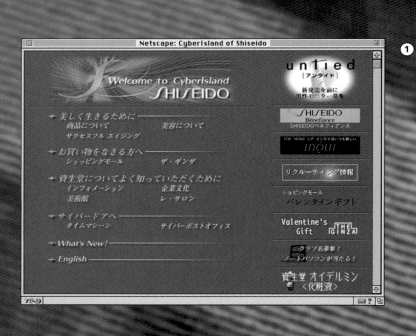

Shiseido Cyber Island

http://www.shiseido.co.jp

DESIGNER Shiseido (Advertising Division) / YEAR OF DESIGN 1995-97 / PLACE OF DESIGN Tokyo, Japan / COPYRIGHT OWNER Shiseido Company Limited / DESIGN COMPANY Shiseido (Advertising Division) / SCREEN DESIGN, ANIMATION/GRAPHICS, INTERACTION DESIGN In-house / PRODUCTION In-house

Shiseido is not so much a corporation as a national institution. Founded in 1873 by Yushin Fukuhara, the corporation started as a pharmacy and over the past century has expanded internationally. Its business now includes the retail of cosmetics, clothing, pharmaceuticals and health and food products. In 1995 the Shiseido Cyber Island website was launched. The site is not an on-line shopping opportunity – it is a comprehensive guide to Shiseido's history, current activities and product ranges.

What is impressive about the site is the sheer volume of information that it delivers. The home page presents you with no less than twelve different sections to explore – and this is just the English version. Selecting one of the icons on the home page takes you to the top end of the section represented. The same twelve options then appear consistently at the bottom of each page, condensed into a text-only version in a block of horizontal lines. While you browse a section you will notice that its heading is highlighted at the bottom of the page, ensuring that you always know where you are. Discipline and consistency in design are key elements: vital when there is so much information to manage.

Each department of the site is characterised by different visual qualities. Using simple white backgrounds and neatly cropped photography, the Shiseido Story is communicated with a highly corporate gloss.

Information in this section is presented without any predominant metaphors or superfluous decoration. The most interesting part in this section is perhaps the chronological archive, which covers almost a century of Shiseido's advertising graphics, and in particular the influence of Serge Lutens in the 1980's. His use of slick black marble and red lacquer is evident in Le Maquillage.

The Les Salons pages, with decorative purple borders, are imbued with a sense of history and a nostalgia which are somewhat difficult to represent in digital space. In contrast, the strong visual and structural metaphor of the Time Machine rescues the situation with humour. The machine's control panel, with its textured, bevelled surfaces, takes you on a tour of Shiseido's history, from its formative years up to the present. The digital patina of the pages is similar to the scratch tiles used on the original exterior of the Shiseido store of 1928. This, together with the accompanying sepia images and animations, effectively evoke a sense of the era.

In the Science and Technology pages you learn about the corporation's approach to product development, Science wrapped in Art, which is a fitting summary of the Shiseido philosophy.

Sophie Greenfield

❶

The 'S' of Shiseido is the center of focus at the top of both the Japanese and the English home pages. The style of the 'S' is redolent of the corporation's past, when products and advertising were distinctive for their 'arabesque' graphics.

English home page features twelve finely rendered icons that
ckground colour with graduated tints from blue to vermilion.
he Japanese home page presents a series of links to new
ne for Untied, a new men's line shown here.

The colours used for the headers at the top of the pages are reminiscent of
makeup colour swatches and give the pages a distinct identity. In these
examples the glossy pack shot of the cosmetics works well with the overall
colour scheme used on the page.

Each of the sections of the site have an array of topics, all of which have
meticulously constructed pages containing a careful blend of text and illustration. The copy-writing is succinct and successfully balanced with the
graphics. In the Science and Technology pages you will discover that Shiseido
takes its scientific research as seriously as its creative design.

In Les Salons du Palais Royal the lingering Art Nouveau influence harkens back to when the Shiseido design department was set up in 1916. Its abiding interest in exotic luxury with a western style is demonstrated in these pages, which showcase Parisian haute couture fashion. The current section of the site is highlighted at the bottom of the page within the summarising navigational menu. This graphic device appears at the bottom of each page throughout the site, making navigation effortless.

The Time Machine acts as a navigational metaphor for the history section. Your first stop is a hand-rendered map of the old Ginza or commercial district. Water colour strokes loosely delineate the streets between the key buildings in which Shiseido began back in the 1920's. Select a building in a pale grey halo and explore its interior in greater detail.

The evocative, sepia toned photography and short cinematic sequences are complemented by the old fashioned control buttons. You can select a different feature of the architecture, like selecting a different floor of a department store from an antiquated elevator.

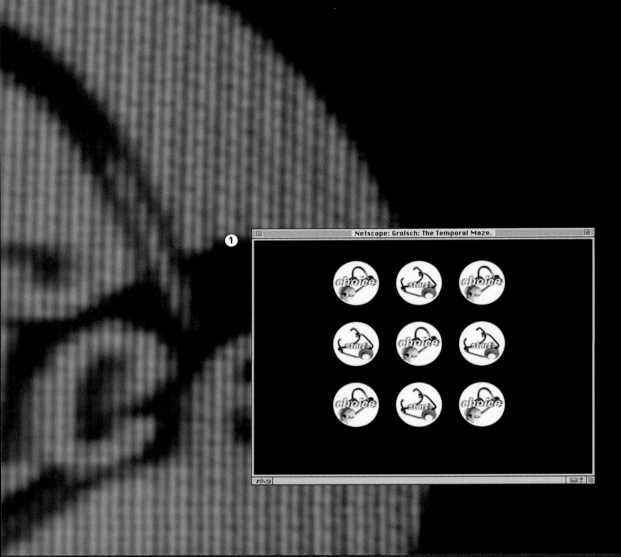

1

Grolsch:
The Temporal Maze
http://www.grolsch.nl

1

The home page: just a short hello from Grolsch, and a play with a highly typical feature of their beer bottles: the 'swingtop'

It is an age-old trick to make a place seem irresistibly attractive and warn the visitor not to enter unprepared. When you access the Grolsch site you are warned to beware of their 'heavily Shockwaved' environment, and brace yourself for an overwhelming experience of moving images and sound, before clicking on the 'travel at ease' link. And yes, there is music and the screen shows an animated introduction, before freezing again into the welcome image of the Temporal Maze of Grolsch where the 'Time Traveller' is told that this is a place 'where the physical restrictions of our linear existence do not apply'. Another short animation ('it's time... the unknown...') glides over the screen. Here the shockwave stops and you have to surf on all by yourself.

The site map on the navigation bar gives an overview of 15 pages, with titles that suggest the kind of bold exploration of the unknown that we know from TV-series like Star Trek. However, the voyages do not go very far, and usually end after one or two clicks on an 'interactive page', where visitors are invited to give their comment or opinion. Links between brackets in the top right corner mostly access other sites related to films, sports or weird Web things such as the 'giant button', which you can click but does nothing in return. Apart from offering information on the range of beers from Grolsch, cinema is the most conspicuous topic on the site — Grolsch sponsors the International Film Festival in Rotterdam.

From the vantage point of graphic design the site is clearly formulated; the elaborate introduction and subsequent pages all look fresh and stylistically up to date. Typography and image have been welded together into attractive screens, without demanding too much time to download. The design combines visual effectiveness with an economy of means. A flaw of the interface is that in most cases the site map can only be accessed via the browser's 'back' button or through a detour back through the shockwaved introduction.

On the whole the graphic design of the Grolsch site is much better than its content. The hyped-up texts that accompany every page invariably suggest or promise a lot more than there is to be found behind links such as Ancient Memories. After all this breathless searching for scraps of knowledge you want to see the real thing to quench your thirst, which is to be found on the product line-up page.

Max Bruinsma

(IT'S TIME)

Grolsch

here is the
lost and found
department
of the soul

?nfo

Memories...
turned into stone

Watch o

improve

stop

It's probably an optical illusion, but a sandy plain stretches in all directions. The only object that catches your eye is an uncut block of solid marble and a chisel lying on the ground beside it. It's up to you; create something, a site, a thought, a memory... anything. Or leave your comments. Hopefully you enjoyed the show. So long, traveller!

e-mail

name

reaction

send

2 3

An introductory image in the form of a fingerprint tells the visitor about the things to come. Clicking on the center of the image triggers another short animation.

Within shockwaved images that suggest a solar eclipse or an unidentified blue space, mysterious little sentences appear: 'it's time... the unknown...'. Clicking the dot in the navigation bar brings you to the site map.

4 5

The Grolsch Temporal Maze consists of fifteen pages that are accessible from the site map. Behind each page is another page which invites you to comment on a question or make a statement, or to link to another site.

This page is typical of the kind of interaction pursued on the Grolsch site: a short mystifying introduction basically asks you to do it yourself, and then says 'so long, traveller'.

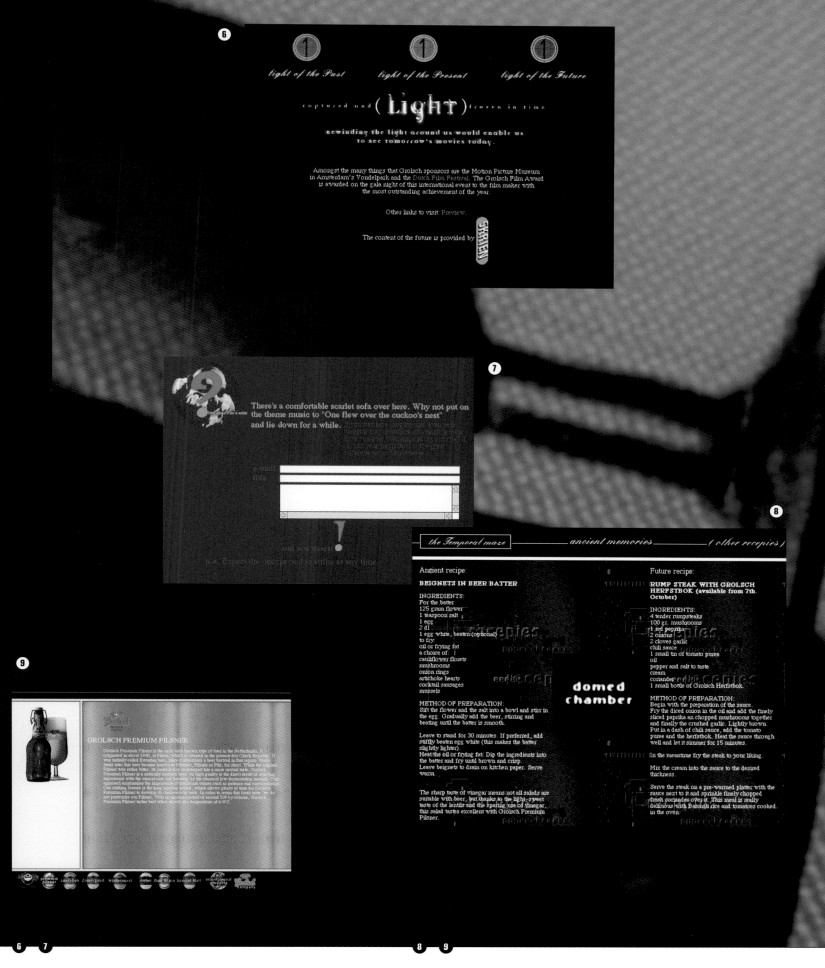

Grolsch is very much involved in film culture, as a sponsor of the International Film Festival in Rotterdam; the festival website is accessible via this page. There are other links, for example to a film encyclopaedia on the Web. The clickable dots at the top of the page count up and down from past to future.

Another cryptic invitation to share your thoughts with Grolsch. These are an idealistic attempt to break down the walls between the producers of the page and their audience. Clicking the button in the bottom right hand corner produces a response page.

The animated text in the center of this page reads: 'You're standing in an domed chamber. High above you light filters through a crack, illuminating the ancient writing on the wall around you.' A slightly off-beat way to introduce two recipes in which beer is used. The default text is on an elaborately designed background.

Clicking the 'pit stop' image in the site map takes you to the product line-up of Grolsch beers. The range in the bottom image bar is clickable and offers information on the different brands, displayed in the double screen above.

Designers / Max Bruinsma

When graphic designers start their career, their first natural assignment is to create their own personal house style. For many designers this is a nightmare. I have known seasoned graphic designers who would rather go to the card-printing machine at the supermarket than design their own address card...

For graphic designers, making a presentation for themselves is a trial. Every formal detail, every content-oriented association will immediately trigger a response, like 'ah, that's what they are about...' But they have so much more to offer! This may be one of the reasons graphic designers love the Web. Here they can show all their different faces at the same time. Not only can they present their port- folio of work, but they can also pontificate about what design is all about ('We are in the midst of profound changes in consumer attitudes...'), and how they can help you out. The true attraction of the World Wide Web as a medium to promote the activities and skills of designers is its broad scope. Professionals have the possibility of designing and presenting their work on experimental pages, where they can show a more personal side and present their work as an artist.

Such experimental environments, where one is warned not to enter without a bag full of plug-ins, are regular features of designers' sites. Rather interesting things can be seen on them. That is, if you have enough time to download ingeniously moving alphabets, images and texts that morph into each other, colours and sounds, and 3D spaces which give a glimpse of what communication spaces may become.

And there is always room for input from the outside world. An interesting way to interact with colleagues and clients is the Surrealists' technique of 'cadavre exquis': a drawing or text or image by one artist is commented on by another and another ad infinitum. The added value of the site is that a few days or weeks later visitors may be tempted to return, curious as to what changes have taken place since their last visit. Other designers make their site a place for discussion or an opportunity to share their cultural interests with you, sometimes transforming part of their website into an e-zine on music or the visual arts. After all, designers' work is not only about what they make for clients. It also embraces research and development, and cultural responsibility. There is a world of software out there that yearns for creative and sensitive application, and an enormous territory of not yet fully explored communication tools and possibilities. Designers who take their role as cultural agents seriously are enhancing their self-portraits on the Web by showing everybody what they are creating for themselves.

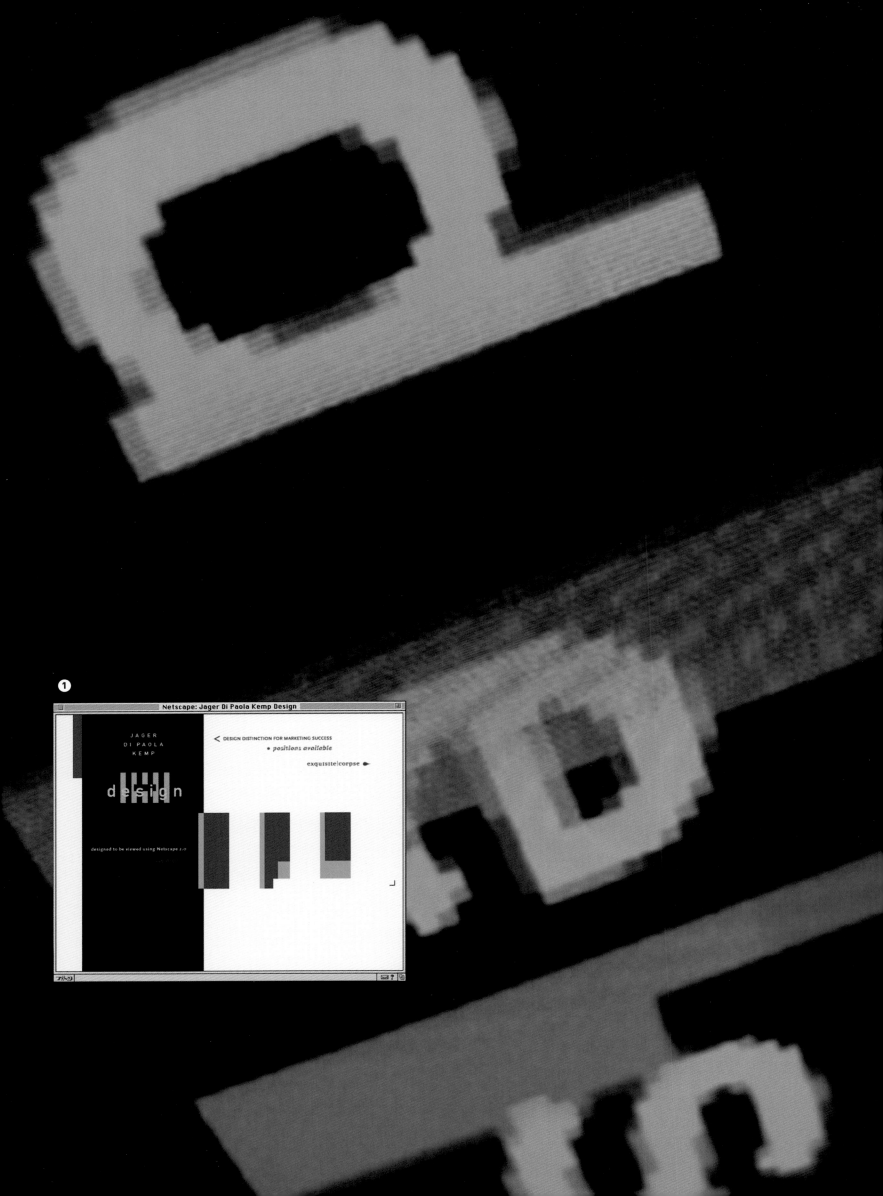

❶

Netscape: Jager Di Paola Kemp Design

JAGER
DI PAOLA
KEMP

design

designed to be viewed using Netscape 2.0

< DESIGN DISTINCTION FOR MARKETING SUCCESS

• positions available

exquisite|corpse ►

Jager Di Paola Kemp Design

97

http://www.jdk.com

DESIGNER Jager Di Paola Kemp Design, Mark Sylvester, Chris Bradley / YEAR OF DESIGN 1996 / PLACE OF DESIGN Burlington, USA / COPYRIGHT OWNER Jager Di Paola Kemp Design / DESIGN COMPANY Jager Di Paola Kemp Design / SCREEN DESIGN Michael Jager, Mark Sylvester, Chris Bradley / ANIMATION/GRAPHICS Michael Jager, Mark Sylvester, Chris Bradley, Anne Barrett / INTERACTION DESIGN Chris Thompson, Kevin Murkami, Dave Winsler / PRODUCTION Chris Thompson, Kevin Murkami, Dave Winsler / EDITORS Jager Di Paola Kemp Design / CONTRIBUTORS Michael Jager, Mark Sylvester, Chris Bradley / SOFTWARE USED Mac: Adobe Illustrator, Adobe Photoshop, Perl / DESIGN PLATFORMS Mac: 100%

A website is a window to the outside world. It is a way to present who you are and what you stand for. The company Jager Di Paola Kemp Design (JDK) use theirs to present a portfolio of their own design work. They have done this in such a way that it is difficult to pinpoint who they actually are, which makes them all the more interesting. These guys are clearly aware of the new 5 Ps of marketing (Paradigm, Paradox, Persuasion, Perspective and Passion). Their homepage, for instance, has a distinctly corporate, modernist, 'annual-report' feel to it. When you click on the weighty title 'design distinction for marketing success' the page Consciousness of Chaos comes up. An animated loop of a skinless head appears whose veins pump up the bare brain, making an eyeball pop out, which gets dropkicked back again by a very long tongue. It is in complete contrast to the previous page.

Next up is JDK's contemporary philosophy on marketing design, a two-fold manifesto for 'marketers to boldly embrace the new reality without fear' (passion), and three theories on how a strategic tool in brand characterisation should be designed (perspective). The continuing click is nicely located in the word 'work', in which the 'o' blinks to create a perfect button feel. Twenty-seven pages of commissioned JDK work are showcased, including a short description of the briefing, how the assignment was tackled by JDK and the final image produced (persuasion). An added feature here is the indication of the design categories to which these commissions related. There are eleven categories, ranging from identity design, packaging and advertising. For every project one or more of these categories is highlighted to indicate what kind of effect the design was meant to have. It is a very informative kiss-and-tell journey through work for quite impressive clients, such as TDK, Benetton and Burton.

The other part of the JDK site is found under the only other link on the homepage, sporting the rather esoteric title 'exquisite corpse'. It is a place for 'a global dialogue of ideas and images', based on a concept borrowed from the French surrealists. A very long list of designers have volunteered to respond to the invitation to write something and/or place an image, in order to see if the total has a deeper meaning than the sum of its parts.... Maybe the opening image, with its Rorschach resemblance, already indicates that this section can be interpreted in a manifold way.

The JDK site is a good example for other design consultancies contemplating how to present themselves on the Web. JDK have decided to show their portfolio and reveal their design philosophy, simple and straightforward. They do not fall for the so-called paradigm shift of design transferring from paper to screen, yet use design as a paradigm which can itself be applied to any medium.

Adam Eeuwens

❶

The Jager Di Paola Kemp Design homepage is designed in a very structured and simple manner, showing a high level of professionalism and sophistication. The colours are the height of contemporary chic and the typeface Din is the coolest around.

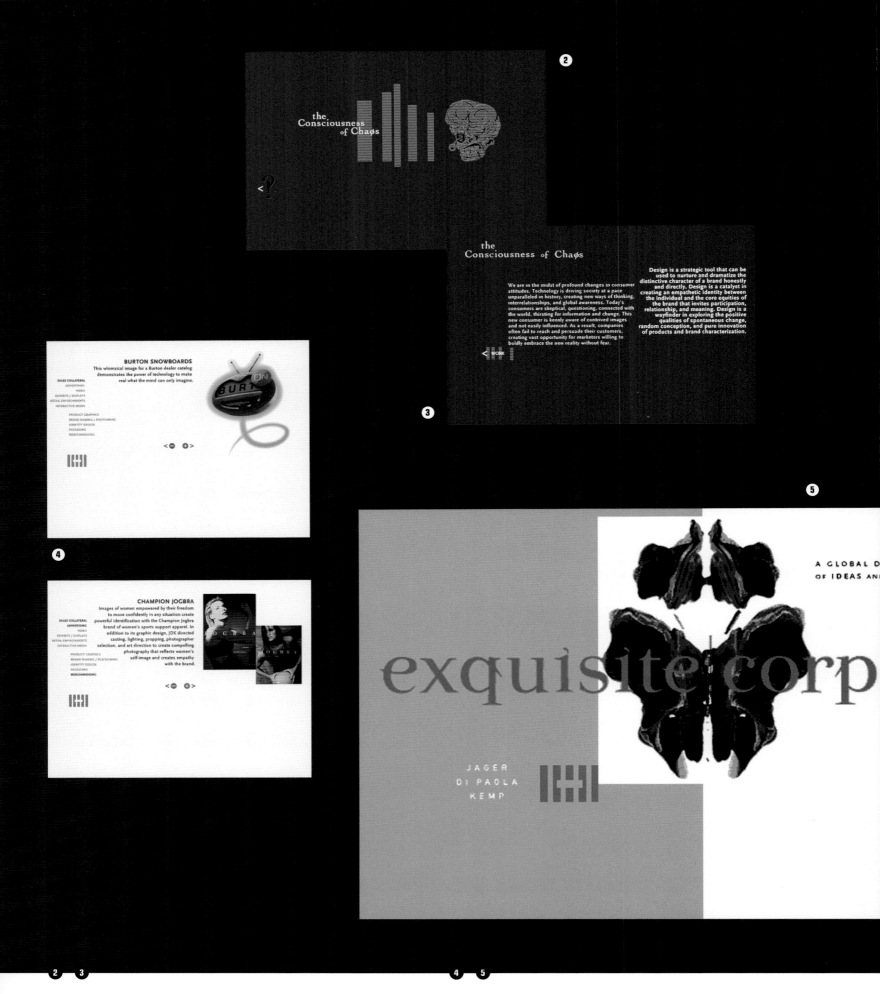

The Consciousness of Chaos page. Every heartbeat makes the eyeball pop out and the tongue kick it back in. The exclamation/question mark hides the only link.

The next page consists of two columns of neatly designed text plus an animated header in which the letters of the word 'chaos' constantly shift around.

Several pages of JDK's portfolio. The size of the layout never exceeds the size of an average computer screen. On the left-hand side categories are high-lighted to indicate the nature of a particular design assignment, so presenting the range of creative and problem-solving capabilities of JDK.

Clicking your way into the most obscure page of the JDK site, you will find the entrance to a collage of statements and images.

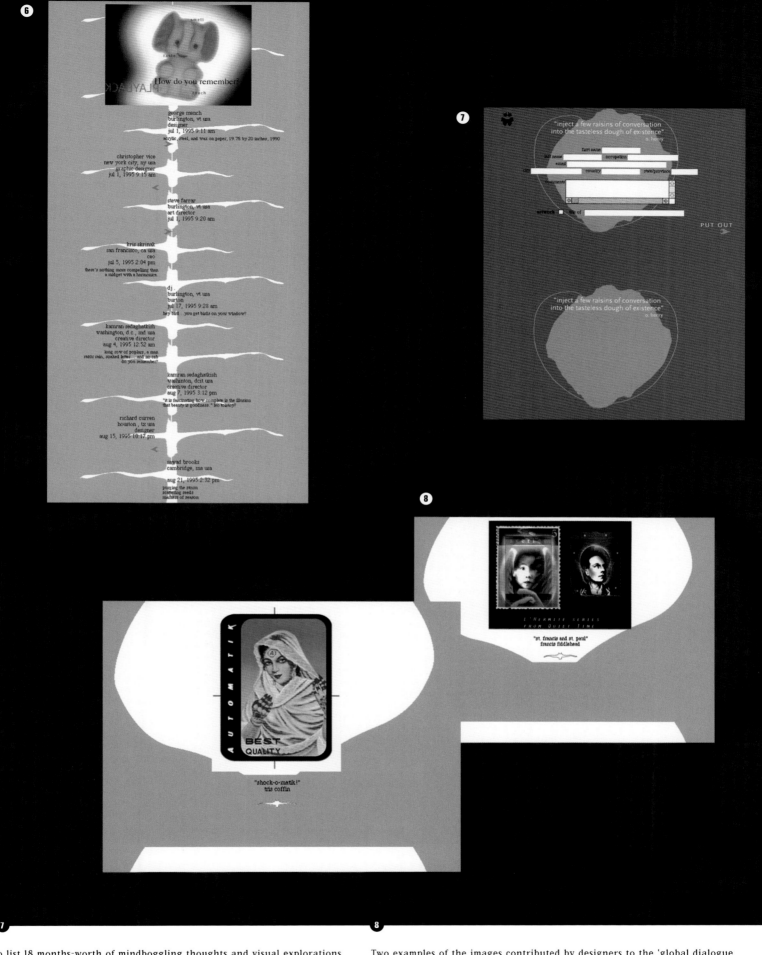

6 7

How to list 18 months-worth of mindboggling thoughts and visual explorations submitted by designers and design aficionados? The compilation of responses follows a 'stem' that grows as the dialogue extends. 'Buds' are links that lead to visual submissions or extended texts.

The exquisite corpse section provides a framework that is variable and immediate. Artists can respond either in written or visual form. This is the 'vocalisation' entry form.

8

Two examples of the images contributed by designers to the 'global dialogue on ideas and images'.

Netscape: i|o 360 Digital Design

① 1

i/o360.com

http://www.io360.com

DESIGNER i/o 360° Inc. / YEAR OF DESIGN 1996 / PLACE OF DESIGN New York, USA / COPYRIGHT OWNER i/o 360° Inc. / DESIGN COMPANY i/o 360° Inc. / SCREEN DESIGN, ANIMATION/GRAPHICS, INTERACTION DESIGN i/o 360° Inc. / PRODUCTION i/o 360° Inc. / SOFTWARE USED Mac: Adobe Photoshop, Macromedia Director, QuarkXPress, VRML, Adobe Illustrator, Live Pictures, Future Splash; mpc: Adobe Photoshop, Adobe Illustrator / DESIGN PLATFORMS Mac: 60%; mpc: 35%; unix: 5%

● 1

i/o 360 °'s conventional but elegant homepage allows you to access 'Oy' for a painless, low bandwidth experience, featuring a range of commercial projects much like an on-line company brochure. 'Yo!' is for a more experimental, introspective look at i/o 360 °'s achievements and 'What's New' is accessed via randomized screen shots offering short-cuts to i/o 360 °'s extensive portfolio.

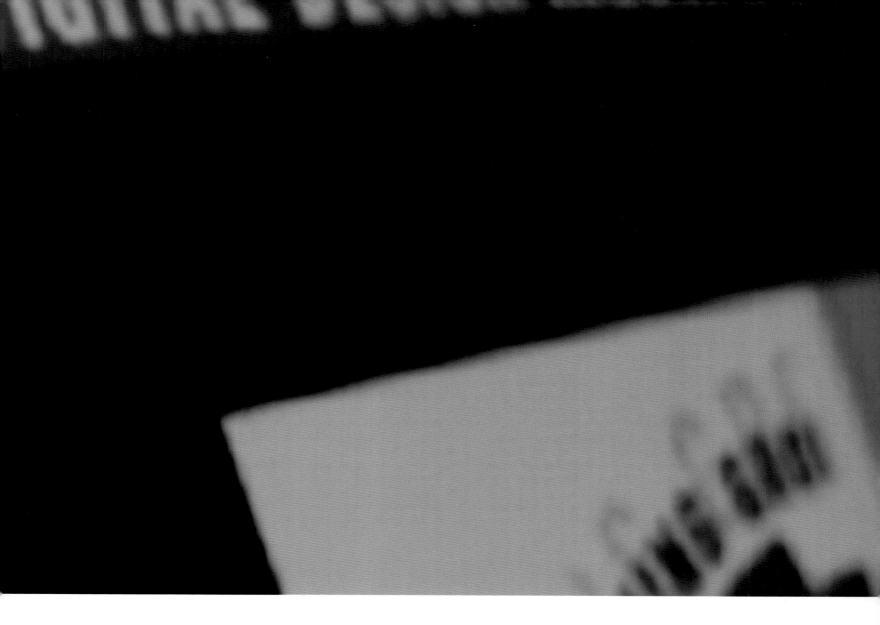

'We always seek to operate at the nexus where evolving technology and innovative design converge.'

i/o 360° is a digital design company in New York. Its name describes the nature of the company, whose input and output all-rounders work around the clock. It was founded in 1994 by a group of young individuals, from various backgrounds including architecture and graphic design. Their website contains a summary of their company, staff and clients, along with examples from their portfolio and their coverage in the media.

The homepage displays both Japanese and English text. This is because i/o 360° aspires to a successful Internet presence in both market places. By selecting the Japanese headline at the top of the page, you can browse through the Japanese version of the site. The spare, lean style of the site perhaps is reminiscent of a certain strand of Japanese minimalism. The quiet, black pages are intersected by one pixel-wide grey lines which form a grid through the entire site. This minimalist, almost austere design works well. The subtle visuality of the site delivers the content seamlessly, allowing it to stand out, while its container runs invisibly beneath.

The main body of content within the site is divided loosely into two main sections. From the homepage you can start your journey with either 'Yo!' or 'Oy'. When you enter the outward looking 'Oy' section, i/o 360° assure you that there will be 'nothing painful, we promise'. The pain is the interminable wait often inflicted on users wanting to view pages with added memory- consuming features. But this promise of painlessness has a punch-line. The next thing you get is a green-screen, text interface nightmare which you thought did not exist any more. Looking around, after the initial burning of the retina caused by the lurid green, you realise that they were only joking. The sleek headers are still in their rightful place within the grid and you quickly move on to explore their voluminous projects portfolio. The 'Yo!' section is a loosely structured, modular environment where i/o 360° promote screen-based experimental projects. This section requires a range of specific software, which adds animation and sound to complement the graphics. The experimental work in 'Yo!' and the website as a whole stand as a testimony to the innovative digital creativity of the producers.

Giles Rollestone

Green screen text, the witty punch-line to a promise of painless surfing through the Web. The navigation grid at the top echoes the site hierarchy and helps to guide the visitor through i/o 360˚'s portfolio. The other sections: 'profiles', 'public realm', 'experiments', 'alliances' and 'links' act as secondary contextual levels of information and provide access to experimental work.

From this portion of the site you are offered a gamut of portfolio features including: Web-based prototypes, Intranet, Off-line, Video and Print. A distinction is made between recent projects and Web makeover projects, reflecting that much maligned area of webdesign — window dressing!

The individual project spaces are all rooted in the same modernist template. Its static grid is a framework for the sample images and explanatory text and also reflects the site's hierarchical structure. This graphic minimalism lets the information stand out, without being weighed down by superfluous detail.

Like many other successful interactive media companies, i/o 360˚ has often been featured in print. The 'public realm' section contains excerpts from recent articles. The circular icons on this page work like portholes or windows to other spaces within the site. They help to entice the visitor to journey on to the next level of information.

Journeying through one of the portholes in the Public Realm press screen, you arrive at one of five articles featuring i/o 360˚. Here you learn that the company has worked on a range of multimedia design and programming projects, ranging from websites and CD Roms to installations.

All the vertical lines within the background grid change from grey to red. Selecting any of the semi-transparent blocks of red and black typography layered over the fine array of lines takes you to one of the experimental i/o 360˚ projects.

The 'Variations on Cryptography' installation involved the projection of digital media live from two webservers, creating an ever mutating digital performance experience in a gallery space, which lasted for four weeks.

'Yo!' is composed of modules which attempt to address and explore the particular creative possibilities offered by the Web.

One of the highly recommended activities of the site: downloading i/o 360˚'s acclaimed off-line experiments, their 1994 and 1995 demos. Like the site, these are eloquent examples of integrated graphics and interactive design.

103

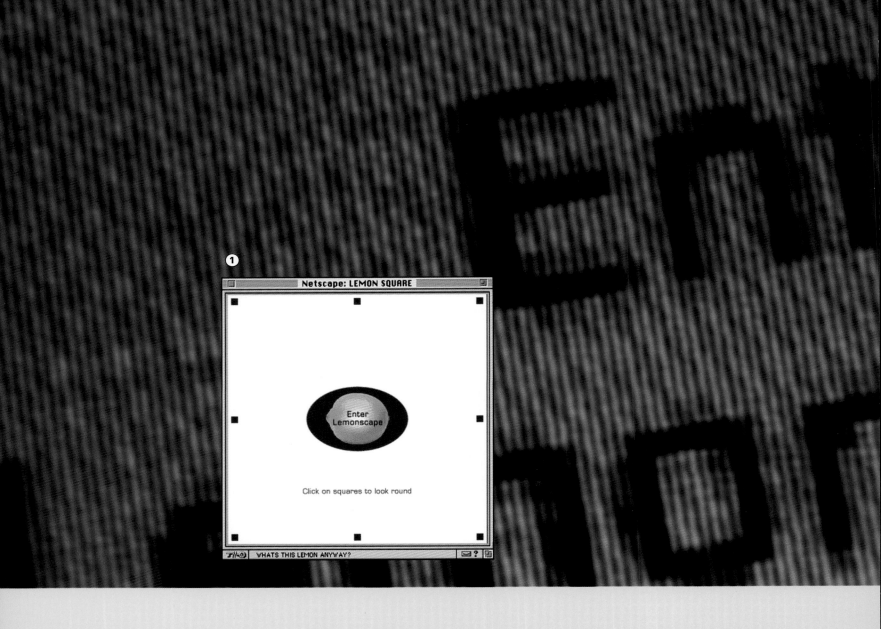

The World of Lemon

http://www.lemon.com.hk

DESIGNER Lemon (HK) Ltd. / YEAR OF DESIGN 1996 / PLACE OF DESIGN Hong Kong, / COPYRIGHT OWNER Lemon (HK) Ltd. / DESIGN COMPANY Lemon (HK) Ltd. / SCREEN DESIGN David Mok, Christopher Potter, Everett Rodriguez / ANIMATION/GRAPHICS Christopher Potter, Everett Rodriguez / INTERACTION DESIGN David Mok, Christopher Potter, Everett Rodriguez / SOUND DESIGN Andrew Ingkavet / PRODUCTION LEMON / EDITORS David Mok, Victor Mehra / SOFTWARE USED Mac: Adobe Photoshop 4.0, Adobe Premiere 4.21, Adobe After Effects 3.0, BBEdit 4.0, Fetch 3.01, Netscape 3.01, Macromedia Director 5, Adobe Illustrator 6.0, Macromedia Freehand 7, FormZ Renderzone 2.82, Electric Image Animation System 2.7, Avid Media Suite Pro, GifBuilder, Equilibrium DeBabelizer, Apple QTVR Toolkit; mpc: Netscape 3.0 / DESIGN PLATFORMS Mac: 99%; mpc: 1%

1

A Java-based panel, appropriately called Lemonsquare, features some demos of state-of-the-art web-tech. Mouse-overs in the edges and corners of this square compass display preview images of the demos in the center.

'You're only as good as your latest website'. This line from Lemon Design's corporate statement sums it up all right. 'Fresh' is the key word here. Lemon is an interactive multimedia agency on the move, specialising in designing websites and delivering cutting-edge technology. As such the aim of their own site is obviously to get their company message across by displaying their technical capabilities and presenting a portfolio of work done so far. Most webdesign companies show their portfolio as images on the pages of their own site, or simply refer to them. At the risk of laying too much claim to fame Lemon have taken a different approach.

Upon entering the Lemon site you are dazzled by a nine-part demo of technical wizardry, featuring VRML Hell, a shockwaved version of Robbie the Robot, Virtual Spam (QuickTimeVR) and various forms of animation. All of these goodies are available through Lemonsquare, a Java-based navigation device that allows you to travel any way the wind blows. Through the central panel, which reads 'Enter Lemonscape' over the Lemon icon, a new browser window opens and the company presentation begins. Suddenly you realise that your trusted tool and location bar have disappeared and that you are at the mercy of Lemon-scape. A toolbar mimicking Netscape's buttons, with a shiny 'L' where the 'N' used to be, provides your navigational interface within the Lemon site.

'The Internet – the ultimate manifestation of our collective consciousness'. In a series of bright, colourful screens Lemon blast off a couple of their so-called 'Mind Grenades'. Set against the backdrop of Armstrong's first footstep on the moon they give their views on the Internet, new technologies and communication. No lengthy default texts, but short catchy phrases in images set the tone here. Cut up into words or short phrases, messages are strewn across the pages in a playful typographic setting. Positioning these compact statements over background imagery allows Lemon to design the average page to fit within a minimum screen size.

But what about the clients? Lodged amidst these energetic pages, a rather basic page presents Lemon's Web achievements to date in a pop-up menu. However, by simply linking to websites designed for Cathay Pacific, Hong Kong Telecom and many others from within their frame-set, they cleverly assimilate these sites within the Lemonscape browser. All of a sudden, through this very basic trick, complete websites have become part of an on-line portfolio. Although these sites obviously show a wide range of design possibilities, the message they convey in this setting leaves no doubt: 'Lemon(scape) rules'.

Geert J. Strengholt

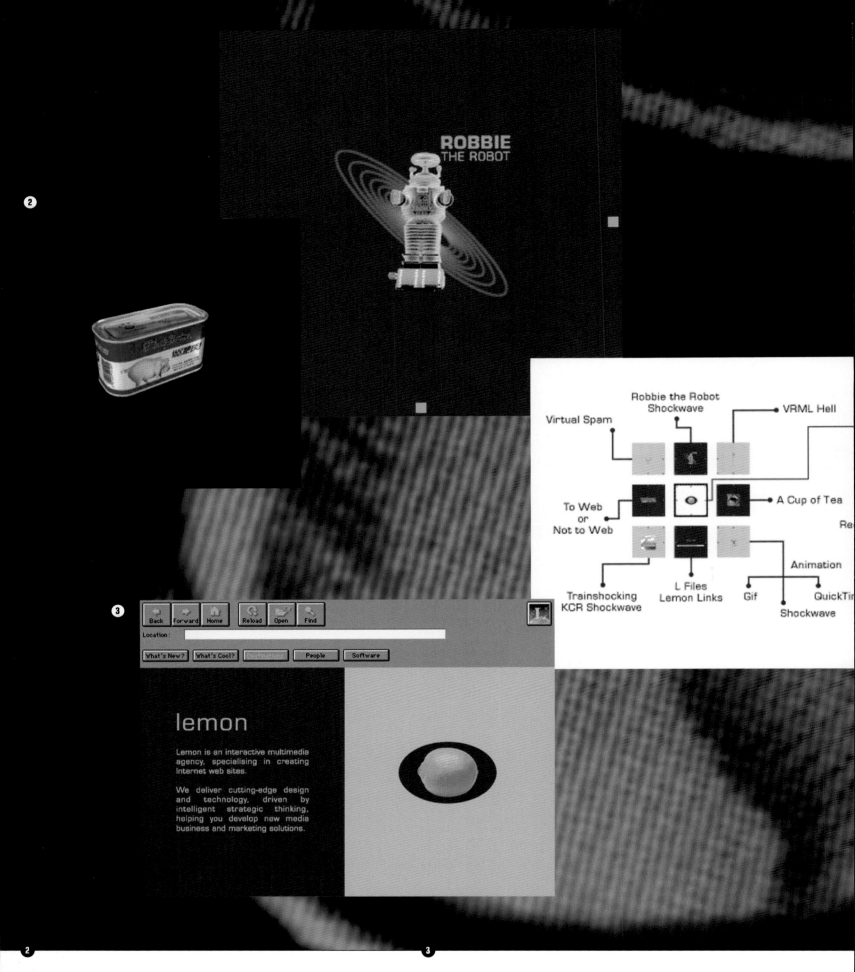

ROBBIE
THE ROBOT

Virtual Spam

Robbie the Robot
Shockwave

VRML Hell

To Web
or
Not to Web

A Cup of Tea

Re

Animation

Trainshocking
KCR Shockwave

L Files
Lemon Links

Gif

QuickTi

Shockwave

Back   Forward   Home   Reload   Open   Find

Location:

What's New?   What's Cool?   [Destinations]   People   Software

lemon

Lemon is an interactive multimedia
agency, specialising in creating
Internet web sites.

We deliver cutting-edge design
and technology, driven by
intelligent strategic thinking,
helping you develop new media
business and marketing solutions.

2

Robbie the Robot (found if you head towards north) demonstrates a number of
Shockwave experiments and in Virtual Spam, QuickTime VR allows you to toy
around with a virtual can. The images are taken from old TV-series (Lost in
Space in Robbie's case) or commercials. The 'Enter Lemonscape' panel
introduces the main body of the site.

3

Upon entering Lemonscape a mock-up of the familiar Netscape buttons
provides a navigation through this company section of the site. Mouse-overs
show clarifying instructions, so you cannot go wrong here. Most subsequent
company pages are loaded in the lower frame. The page design has been
adapted accordingly, so that the pages neatly fit in an average size screen.

These two pages of company 'Mind Grenades' are constructed from a number of transparent images, interlocking and positioned over the yellow background colour. In this way each single image can function as a link to a next page.

This site map not only lists all pages and elements in the site, but also works as a flow chart indicating the navigational possibilities from page to page. On the left the Lemonsquare is graphically dissected into detailed components. All pages displayed here are immediately accessible through this map.

The pop-up menu links to recent sites created for corporate clients. Cleverly assimilated within the Lemonscape frame, the pages of the sites developed for Cathay Pacific and Bank of Asia have become showcases in Lemon's portfolio.

Juliet Martin

http://www2.sva.edu/threads/juliet/Resume/Resume.html

DESIGNER Juliet Martin / YEAR OF DESIGN 1996 / PLACE OF DESIGN New York, USA / COPYRIGHT OWNER Juliet Martin / DESIGN COMPANY Juliet Martin / SCREEN DESIGN, ANIMATION/GRAPHICS, INTERACTION DESIGN Juliet Martin / PRODUCTION Juliet Martin / EDITORS Juliet Martin / AWARDS For the site titled: oooxxxooo, 1996 DNP International Achievement Award, 1996 Macxibition: Honorable Mention, 1996 David Siegel's High Five Award / SOFTWARE USED Mac: Adobe Photoshop, Adobe Illustrator, Macromedia Director, GifBuilder / DESIGN PLATFORMS Mac: 70%; sgi: 30%

Seldom do you find such a synthesis of creative endeavour within a single website. This site is about language and self-expression and is a convincing example of the potential of the Internet as a powerful and vivid medium. Juliet Anne Martin is currently a Master of Fine Arts student of Computer Art in New York. In this website she harnesses her skills as an artist, writer and programmer to produce a creative, personal space.

As you enter the site, there are links which take you to three examples of commissioned projects. These include webdesigns for other artists and writers, such as Supergirl by Laura Perry. Two of the links are hosted by Razorfish, a design consultancy in New York. In these commercial projects certain elements of Martin's graphic style become apparent, like the playfulness of its coloration and layout of text.

On Martin's own homepage her aims are clarified by her statement that as a writer she is weaving text into a literary environment for the reader to navigate. Indeed, the emphasis of the site is on text rather than on elaborate illustrations. The most interesting thing about the site is that it shows just how creative a designer can be when using a limited palette of options. It is testimony to the strength of the ideas that the pages can be so simply constructed and at the same time inventive and expressive. The use of colours is restricted to its barest minimum, while the text is displayed in a basic 'default' format. Where most designers would opt for smoothly blended typography, Juliet Martin uses the most basic building blocks to create content. With a combination of simple commands written in HTML, the type is cleverly arranged into a collection of 'carmina figurata' or pattern poems. In some cases these shaped blocks of type are subtly shaded with monotone tints, while elsewhere they form typographical structures which guide you from page to page.

In essence Juliet Martin's personal website is as much about graphic design as about the expressive nature of language. It is a collection of writing and imagery laced with reverie and catharsis. One of the most interesting elements of the site is a page with an oval block of fractured prose where the user is invited to submit a statement. When you enter this area you can read the wide range of responses her work provokes. Some feel at home on her site, while others are baffled. However, everybody is intrigued.

Sophie Greenfield

❶

This page is the gateway to Juliet Martin's site. You can either click on the graphic arrows or on the text headings to reach your destination. Selecting Resume takes you through the artist's CV and to the main body of the site. Selecting Artist Statement takes you to the top of this page, to a summary outlining the aims of the site.

The Web Samples page is in the Resume section of the site. From here, a panel of six buttons allows you to navigate to the education, skills and experience of the artist. If you select any one of the black and white icons, you can link directly to specific sections of previously designed websites.

This navigation totem-pole serves as the main menu for Juliet Martin's experimental site. Without text labels, these enigmatic symbols soon become meaningful once you visit their linking pages. The icons are a set of visual mnemonics, symbolic motifs representing the content of each section of the site.

This simple graphic construction presents you with negative and positive options. The big composition allows ample use of the scroll bar. Clicking on either 'yes' or 'no' along the length of this typographic ribbon takes you on a poetic text-oriented journey through the pages of the site.

Much of the descriptive prose contained within the site is carefully composed and laid out, so that the text forms illustrative structures. An example of one of these pattern poems is this typographic incarnation of 'the silicon serpent'. Many of the compositions sprawl tall and wide, making full use of the scroll-bars as navigational tools.

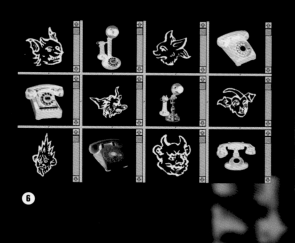

6

7

8

ou salavate as you taste salt on your tounge. Your eyes fixate on the fish[girl]fish and boy. He takes a blade
m his pocket as you stare. He lifts his arm in an arc that reminds you of swimming. You rush forward trying
top the knife, but you stop yourself instead. You look and lick up the lust that gushes from her gut. My heart,
you whisper, as you watch her spleen, liver, and heart fall to his feet. You can feel

9

SUBMIT

submission

Wild rat
lies in my
computer dump
"But the mind of rat
could not understand
trigonometry," quipped
James. It was that branch of
mathematics that dealt with the
relationships between the sides
and the angles of triangles and
the calculations based on them.
My computer knew it was the branch
that made me sweat and pulse and

touched my thumb to my thumb and my
index to my index and placed the
triangle over my vagina. I looked
inside the three angles and was
beyond the reach of the conceptual
rats. But without the rat
the pulsing was gone so I
climbed out and lay with my
belly pressed to the
ground and let my
little rat lick
my clitoris.

RESIST

10

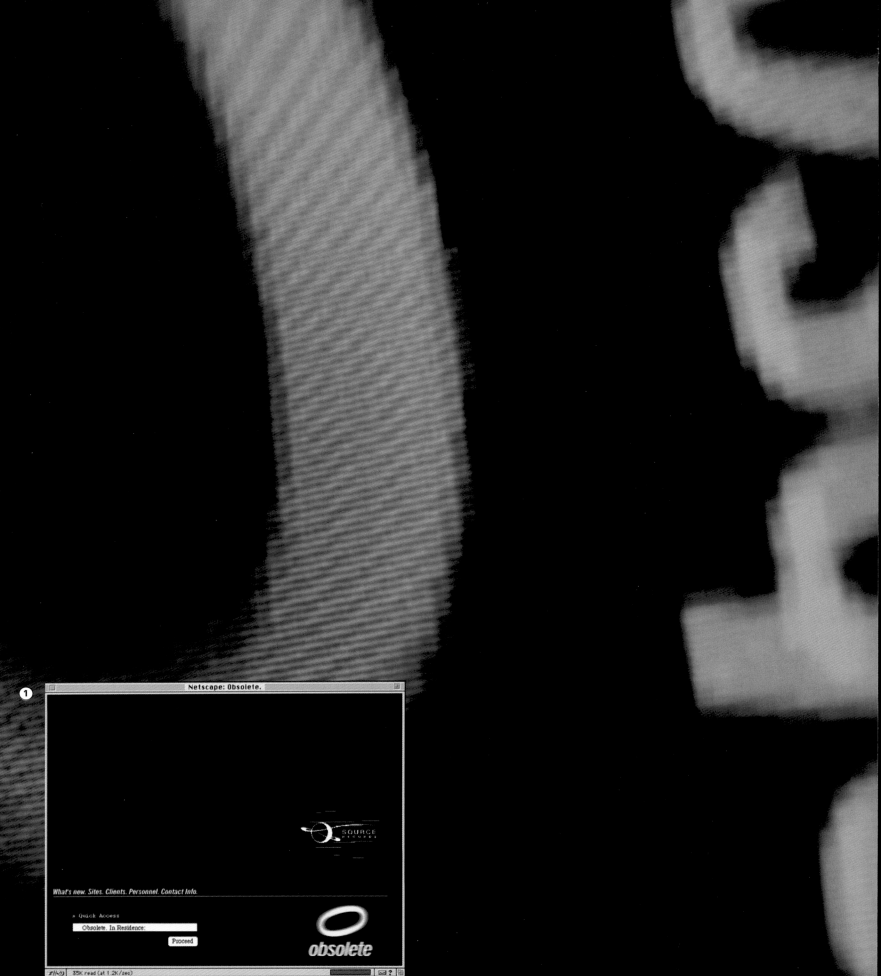

Obsolete

http://www.obsolete.com

DESIGNER Obsolete / YEAR OF DESIGN 1996-97 / PLACE OF DESIGN London, UK / COPYRIGHT OWNER Obsolete / DESIGN COMPANY Obsolete, China Records, Metalheadz, Warp Records / SCREEN DESIGN Chris McGrail, Dorian Moore / ANIMATION/GRAPHICS Chris McGrail, Dorian Moore / INTERACTION DESIGN Chris McGrail, Dorian Moore / PRODUCTION Jon Baines / CONTRIBUTORS James Bigson, Kim Bull, Simon Grab, Damian Reeves, Adam Twiss, Sam Jones, Jamie Cansdale

'Obsolete is a young and persuasive group committed to the invigoration, subversion and demystification of Web culture.' As an Internet design and facilities house, Obsolete started out dealing mainly with underground record labels, musicians and artists. Clearly their background is the London music scene, where jungle, techno and ambient rule. This has been the testing ground for their Web design practice. Consequently the Obsolete site is more than a portfolio of the company's achievements; it provides a digital platform for the communication of a range of artists' work and functions as a gateway to an entire creative on-line community. By now their website represents a creative smorgasbord, ranging from e-zine cyber ephemera and music promotion to the corporate cool of Levis.

The Obsolete site interface design addresses issues such as the impatience of users and hardware inadequacies. The homepage allows you quick access through five main options appearing in a simple sentence format: 'What's New', 'Sites', 'Clients', 'Personnel', 'Contact' and 'Info'. Selecting 'Sites' from the home-page takes you to 'Obsolete in Residence', which features a range of categories from 'Record Labels' to 'Merchandising'. This list provides links both with self-contained sites and pages served by Obsolete. The record labels featured within Obsolete's site, such as China Records, offer extracts from audio tracks and are characterised by their fresh simplicity and often quirky graphic style.

Obsolete also collaborated in the production of large-scale on-line communication sites like that of the Levis corporation, or budding record labels like Metalheadz, whose energetic pages feature rippling navigation buttons and a live video link which directly funnels sights and sounds from the sessions of a night-club DJ. In bringing you this collection of pages and sites, Obsolete have applied a range of software innovations. Quickdraw 3D is combined with Shockwave to deliver a three-dimensional version of their main interface. They also tie in sound and on-line shopping capacities to their music-based pages, such as Hydrogen Dukebox.

What is inspiring about the site is that Obsolete clearly operate as creative catalysts and facilitators rather than just directive designers. The site successfully provides a digital forum for a range of geographically diverse companies, creating a sense of community that would otherwise be difficult to achieve.

Giles Rollestone

1

The succinct homepage of Obsolete has a flickering, low-resolution animation, which features snatches of imagery extracted from the main body of the site. From the industrial yellow and black pages, there are five ways you can start your journey. As an alternative, you can simply use the button and menu combination to connect directly to the large range of websites 'residing' in Obsolete's collection.

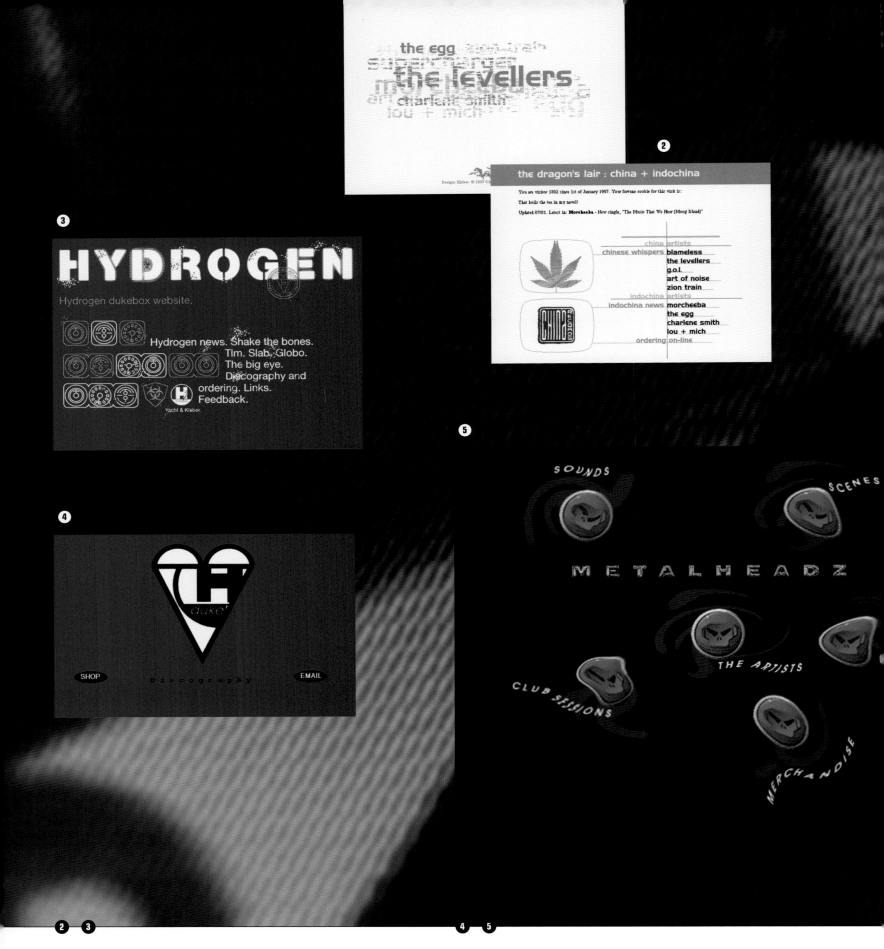

HYDROGEN

Hydrogen dukebox website.

Hydrogen news. Shake the bones.
Tlm. Slab. Globo.
The big eye.
Discography and
ordering. Links.
Feedback.

Yacht & Kleber.

the egg
the levellers
charlene smith
lou + mich

Design: Kleber. © 1997 Ch

the dragon's lair : china + indochina

You are visitor 1302 since 1st of January 1997. Your fortune cookie for this visit is:

That boils the tea in my navel!

Updated 07/01. Latest in: Morcheeba - New single, "The Music That We Hear (Moog Island)"

	china artists
chinese whispers	blameless
	the levellers
	g.o.l.
	art of noise
	zion train
indochina artists	
indochina news	morcheeba
	the egg
	charlene smith
	lou + mich
ordering	on-line

duke!

SHOP   Discography   EMAIL

SOUNDS   SCENES

METALHEADZ

CLUB SESSIONS   THE ARTISTS

MERCHANDISE

② ③   ④ ⑤

These pages evoke the spirit and unique style of Beyond Records, a small label representing musicians such as the Levellers and Zion Train. This part of the site features music with a small niche market and shows how Obsolete offer a platform to such underground labels for contacting an audience within the digital domain.

Armed and dangerous graphics grab your attention at the Hydrogen Dukebox homepage with its enormous spray-stencilled header. The curved squares containing altimeter-style icons flash white and orange in a random pattern, drawing attention to the loosely arranged section headings of the site.

In the Hydrogen Dukebox discography, the label presents its music products in a bold, uncluttered style. This site was developed from scratch by Obsolete. Obsolete's work reflects the diversity of its clients, large and small, with an emphasis on capturing the energy of the moment.

The creative energy of this jungle label is effectively communicated through the use of both interactive and graphic design. The Metalheadz icons, linking to artists, merchandise and even live video-links, seem captured in mid jostle.

6

7

8

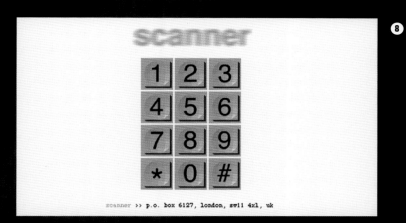

9

6 7   **8 9**

At the Warp Records site you are guided effortlessly through the sleek, low-colour pages of the 'complex and beautiful Warpnet experience' by the responsive control bar at the bottom of the screen. As you roll your cursor over its slim-line cells, the section headings appear instantly on the right hand side of the bar, accompanied by a confirming 'beep!'

In the Gallery you can use the scrollers to select a specific album cover. Clicking on the smaller icon of the album opens an enlarged version of the artwork in a separate pop-up window. The image quality is sufficiently high to keep you browsing; it is like searching the shelves in a real music shop.

Scanner's key motif, the ubiquitous touch-tone dialling pad, becomes the central visual menu and metaphor for these pages. Known for his use of the much maligned scanner technology, this renegade music maker browses the air waves sampling and collecting random snatches of conversations, signals and other ephemera that permeate the digital ether.

'Please replace the handset' is the sound bite emanating from the pop-up window; this page represents a playful juxtaposition of sound and imagery. It is one in a series of nine sections exploring the synthesis of aural and visual communication and cogently expressing the artist's work.

115

John J. Hill's on-line portfolio is a sophisticated and successful example of graphic design on the Internet. This carefully orchestrated site leaves you in no doubt as to the character and quality of the designer and his work. The strong identity and style of his graphics are clearly communicated and the information about his work and inspirations is concisely written and easy to navigate. This is not a site showered with buttons or menus. The navigation options are very clear and despite the use of raw, untamed typography and layered imagery, the organisation and logic of the pages within the site are consistent and controlled. Right from the start you are presented with striking page headers and image maps where information is carefully woven into textured, illustrative collages. The means of navigation is creatively integrated into the overall design of the site, one effortlessly complementing the other.

The homepage presents the user with the option of setting the correct screen width to suit the page layouts. Then you can either enter the Haus of Jinn, which is the main portfolio section, or enter the domain of 52mm, a design company started by Hill with a couple of partners. The Haus of Jinn main menu adds a sense of counterpoint to the site. The black backgrounds of the 52mm pages are balanced by the bright translucence of the portfolio pages. Throughout the two parts of the site, the designer uses this contrast, balancing positive and negative space to great effect.

The main menu of Haus of Jinn is a collage composed on a white background which features the same Easter Island statue found on the homepage, but here in a positive rather than negative incarnation. From this page you can browse through the four main areas of Hill's solo site: 'Gallery', 'Information', 'Soapbox' and 'Fun Joints'.

The Gallery includes a cross-section of digital illustrations and sketches. One particularly inviting touch is to be found in the Miscellaneous section, where you are encouraged to 'dial up' an image. This section is not an after-thought, but a cleverly conceived content-driven device which adds character to the site. Hints of this same Miscellaneous dial are to be found in the header for the Gallery, creating a sense of connection and continuity between the pages of the site.

The Information page gives you more details on the designer and his background. The Soapbox functions much like the letter of the site editor and the menu of Fun Joints with its particularly eye-catching header provides links to Web pages which reflect Hill's eclectic interests and influences.

Sophie Greenfield

❶

The dark and dramatic front door of the site consists of one image map with layered autographic typography. The graphic style and structure of the page sets the tone for the site and also acts as a top-level visual menu, giving you access either to the Haus of Jinn, the designer John Hill's personal portfolio, or to 52mm, the promotional site featuring Hill's design company.

The 52mm logo, couched in textured, organic forms, functions as a visual sub-menu and has enigmatic sounding options such as Lobotomy and Memoir arranged around the central motif.

'...autechre . bluencreame . hong kong . ramen . underground . rust . gorilla . mignola . outworld . digital . styles ...' A simply constructed yet expressive page delivers Hill's profile. It consists of his portrait and a column of evocative key words. The portrait is framed by the rough texture of a torn spiral bound page and the plain, default text presents a condensed summary of Hill's inspirations and preoccupations.

The image map centers around the Easter Island statue motif also used in the doorway to the site. Woven into the visual menu are layered and fractured words representing the different sections of the designer's portfolio.

The Information page within the portfolio uses a striking green and black duotone header. When scrolling downward, simple, flowed text provides information about Hill's background. The lavish header does not present any clickable options, but works as a showcase example of the designer's expressive graphic style.

[— **Hootie and the Blowfish Enhanced CD** (Old Man and Me single) —]
[— Design and Interface, produced for Engine.RDA —]

[— **Newangel**. Another sketch —]

The Gallery main menu uses earthy, tertiary colors and harnesses the white space of the page in a constructive way, lending form and structure to the graphic header. From this point within the portfolio, you can browse through the collection of digital illustrations or read about other sites designed by Hill.

The Miscellaneous page uses an inventive, graphic device which allows you to select and view a collection of random images by clicking on the various numbers encircling the CD. In this way you can dial up the digital illustrations that don't fit within any of the other categories in the site.

The Digital Illustrations menu uses a brain motif divided into thirty square cells containing thumbnail-sized portions of the digital imagery featured within the section. Traces of graphic elements from other areas of the site, for example the dial from the Miscellaneous page, are collaged into the image map.

New Angel is just one example of the many digital illustrations accessed from the Gallery section. Each illustration has a carefully composed frame: a collage of graphic elements from the main Gallery menu interwoven with simple navigational references.

119

Institutions / Max Bruinsma

In general an institution is a framework set up by a group of people who share a certain interest or activity. The activities facilitated by an institution can be manifold. Parliament is an institution, as is the local art center. They all share the task of informing a broad interested public of what they are doing. This is why they were set up in the first place; their raison-d'-être is their public base. This high priority of informing their audience reflects on the communication policy of institutions: they use any means necessary. So it is not surprising that institutions, especially educational and cultural institutions, were among the first extensive users of the World Wide Web. There are few universities, museums or government institutions who by now do not have their own website. The possibilities of on-line media for communicating the activities of institutions are great, considering the types and categories of information that an institution can provide to the public: policy statements, calendars of events, archives, databases or search services... the list is endless. A well-developed institutional site provides all these informational entrances. This means that the graphic design of the interfaces for these sites is very important. The visitor has to be guided step by step through a complex maze of interconnected data. And most important of all, the data have to be organised in a way that makes them accessible from many different angles.

Therefore structure is of paramount importance in the design for institutional websites. These sites are probably the most frame-intensive around, and more often than not they have much default text and few images – information comes before entertainment. The most conspicuous elements in these designs are the pictograms and buttons structuring the navigation. Sometimes these are simply hot words, grouped in frames or on differently coloured backgrounds, sometimes they are elaborate images that visually organise the complex structure behind them. Often there will be a clickable plan of the institution's building, with the endless corridors that characterise bureaucratic organisations. But in most cases there is a choice of interfaces and navigational tools, text-based or image-based, to make the institution a truly open space. Ultimately, a well-designed institution is an invaluable tool in the hands of the public.

Ars Electronica

http://www.aec.at

DESIGNER Ars Electronica Center, NL-Design / YEAR OF DESIGN 1996 / PLACE OF DESIGN Linz, Austria / COPYRIGHT OWNER Ars Electronica GmbH / DESIGN COMPANY Ars Electronica Center / SCREEN DESIGN, ANIMATION/GRAPHICS, INTERACTION DESIGN Manuel Schilcher, Mieke Gerritzen & Marjolijn Ruyg / PRODUCTION Ars Electronica GmbH / EDITORS Christa Schneebauer / CONTRIBUTORS Matt Smith, Lisi Schedlberger, Sylvia Mueller, NL-Design: Mieke Gerritzen & Marjolijn Ruyg / SOFTWARE USED Mac: Adobe Photoshop, Netscape Navigator, Texteditor; mpc: Adobe Photoshop, Netscape, Texteditor / DESIGN PLATFORMS Mac: 80 %; mpc: 20%

1

The home page introduces the five main sections of the website. At the same time it presents the general design of the interface; these icons will be used as 'landmarks' in the rest of the site.

Ever since its foundation in 1979 the Ars Electronica festival has been at the forefront of electronic Media Art, always focusing on a fusion of arts, technology and science. Recently the Ars Electronica Center opened its doors as a permanent exhibition and research space, and completed the first phase of its website. Its aim, of course, is to represent the AEC on the Web, but also to make the extensive festival archive accessible and to create an on-line space for discussion and research. This means that the site has a substantial content, but at the same time has to remain flexible to accommodate additions for future festivals and projects. This is achieved by using a plain but elegant overall design, which can be varied.

The site is divided into five main sections: the Center, ACCU (an open zone for projects), Festival, Prix and Service. An interface derived from the logo provides navigation buttons which return throughout the site in various forms. The clarity of navigation successfully prevents you getting lost in the tremendous amount of information.

Among the best pages on the site is the presentation of the Center itself. A cross-section of the physical building shows the location of the departments and gives access to them. This creates a clever interplay between the physical and virtual functions of the Center, as the user switches from the real-life location to the various on-line functions and services.

The festival archive – obviously one of the most extensive parts of the site – has been designed very clearly. The image map of this festival database gives easy access to all successive festivals without becoming a straightforward listing. At the same time it suggests the interrelations and connections between the festival topics. When you click through a single festival edition, the page design becomes more basic. The lowest level consists of simple arrangements of image and monospaced text, but here of course the information is what counts.

Apart from the clarity of its overall design, one of the more interesting phenomena on the AEC-site is the fact that previous festival websites and projects will remain part of the archive, while new ones will be added each year. When comparing for instance the 1995 festival site to that of 1996, the evolution of the Web and webdesign becomes apparent. Since each new festival or project will demand its own visual design and structure, there will be a rapid growth in form as well as content on the AEC-site, making it well worth your bookmark.

Geert J. Strengholt

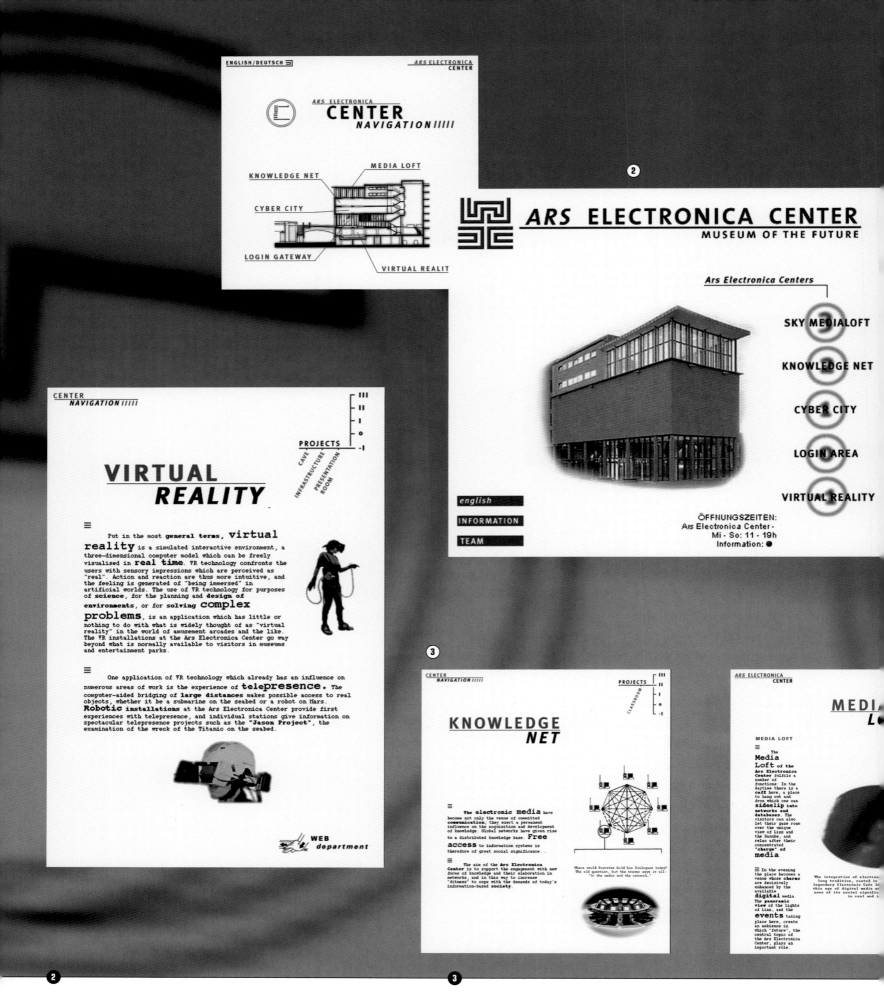

Pages presenting the Ars Electronica Center as the Museum of the Future. A cross-section of the actual AEC-building provides virtual access to the various departments in the AEC. Each link leads to different levels offering information or user interaction.

The basement is dedicated to Virtual Reality and Tele-presence. On the second floor visitors have access to the latest network technologies. The Media Loft functions as an Internet cafe and meeting place, both virtual and in real life. In the top right corner of the screen a simple but effective representation of the building gives access to other floors or departments on the same level.

124

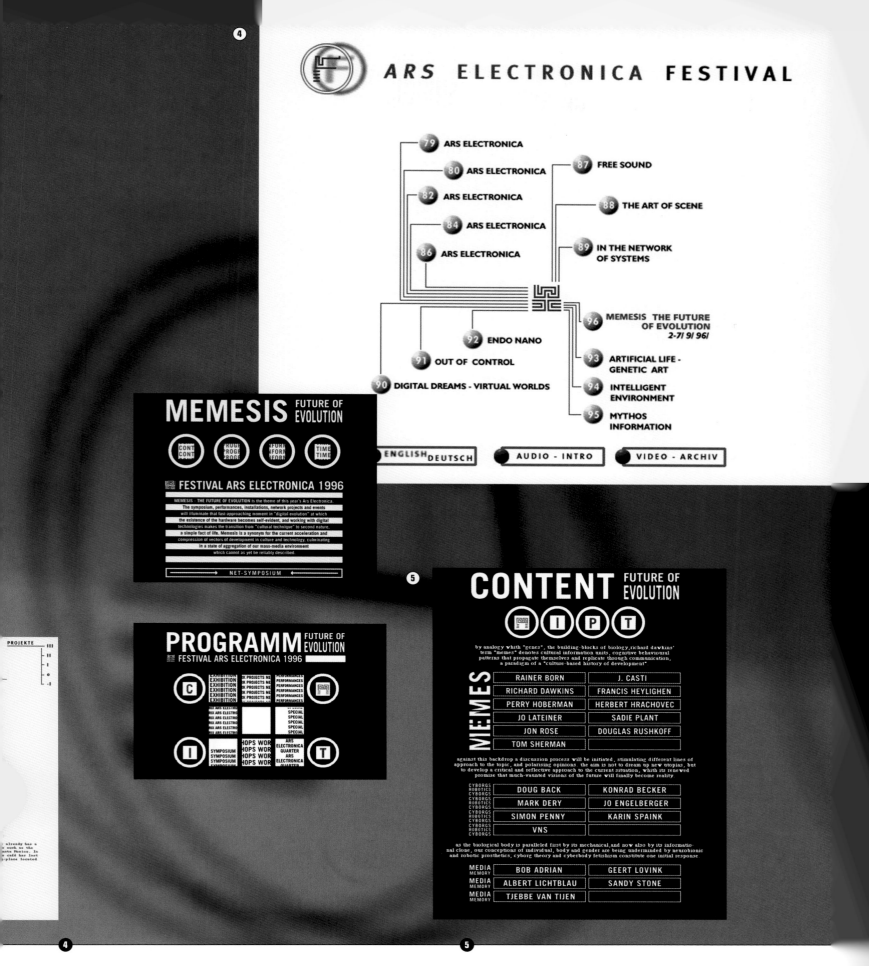

④ This image map, derived from the AEC-logo visible in the center, is the interface to the extensive festival archive. There are also options to switch from English to German, load an audio introduction or visit the recently opened video archive.

⑤ The festival section also accommodates new additions for future festivals. The 1996 festival, Memesis, was designed by NL-design and demonstrates the occasional departure from the unifying design of the AEC-site. In a way the '96 site seems the inverse of the design of the rest of the site. The circular icons are repeated as main elements of navigation.

① Netscape: Introducing Norway: Homepage

http://odin.dep.no/ud/publ/96/norway

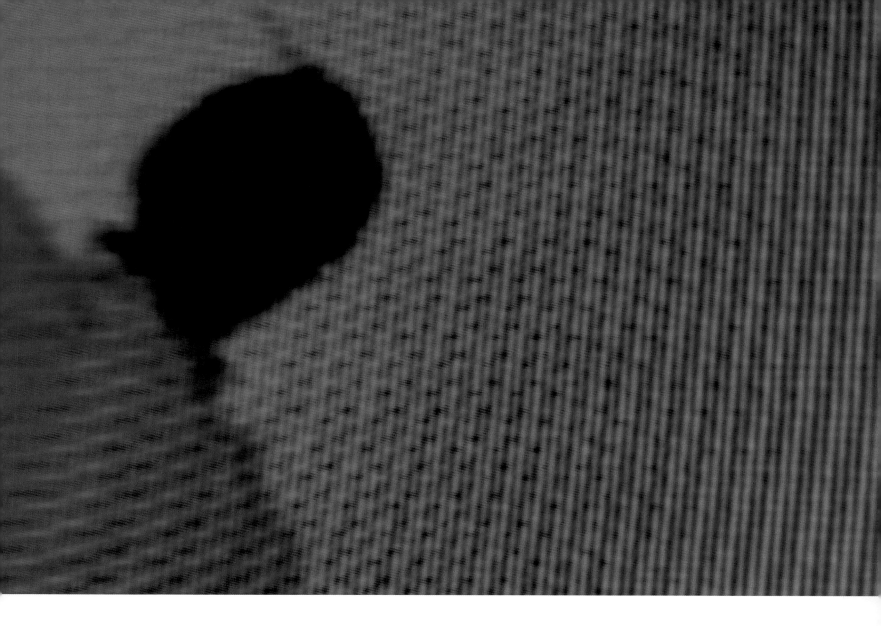

Tucked away in ODIN, the official Web server for the Norwegian Government, Introducing Norway was created by the Ministry of Foreign Affairs as an educational tool to teach foreign kids some facts about their country. Two children, Kari and Øyvind, are our personal guides through a well-balanced dose of Norway's geography, culture, society and much more. Reading through this on-line geography book, we are introduced to the ways and whims of the Norwegians, their country, their cultural heroes and national inventions such as the paperclip and the cheese slicer.

The designers focused on the clarity of the navigation and on making the various topics available. Each page basically has the same navigation banner and the same typography. The main variation in the design of the site is created by simply using different colours for banners and backgrounds in every section. Occasional animated GIFs, such as the morph between the portraits of Kari and Øyvind, are used to enliven the pages. In general a functional separation is made between the textual information and the illustrating images. The text pages with small images load quickly, but provide the option to view the illustrations much bigger on a second page.

The navigation banner displays a clear overview of the topics of the sites, and also includes a subject header for the current page. Two simple arrows indicate that there are more pages in a section, and a 'continue' link at the bottom of the screen will load the next page. By linking back to other parts of the government site, the basic information on cultural celebrities such as Grieg or Munch can be fleshed out – the only drawback being that the pleasant design is lost once you enter other regions of the ODIN site.

Some of the best pages on the site are to be found in the geography section, where an image map provides links to a collection of pictures of cities and countryside in Norway. Another particularly successful page is about the peculiarities of the Norwegian alphabet, introducing the Æ, Ø and Å by way of a GIF animation. Although general interaction is limited to reading by clicking or searching for keywords, the site makes pleasant browsing – and not only for kids.

Geert J. Strengholt

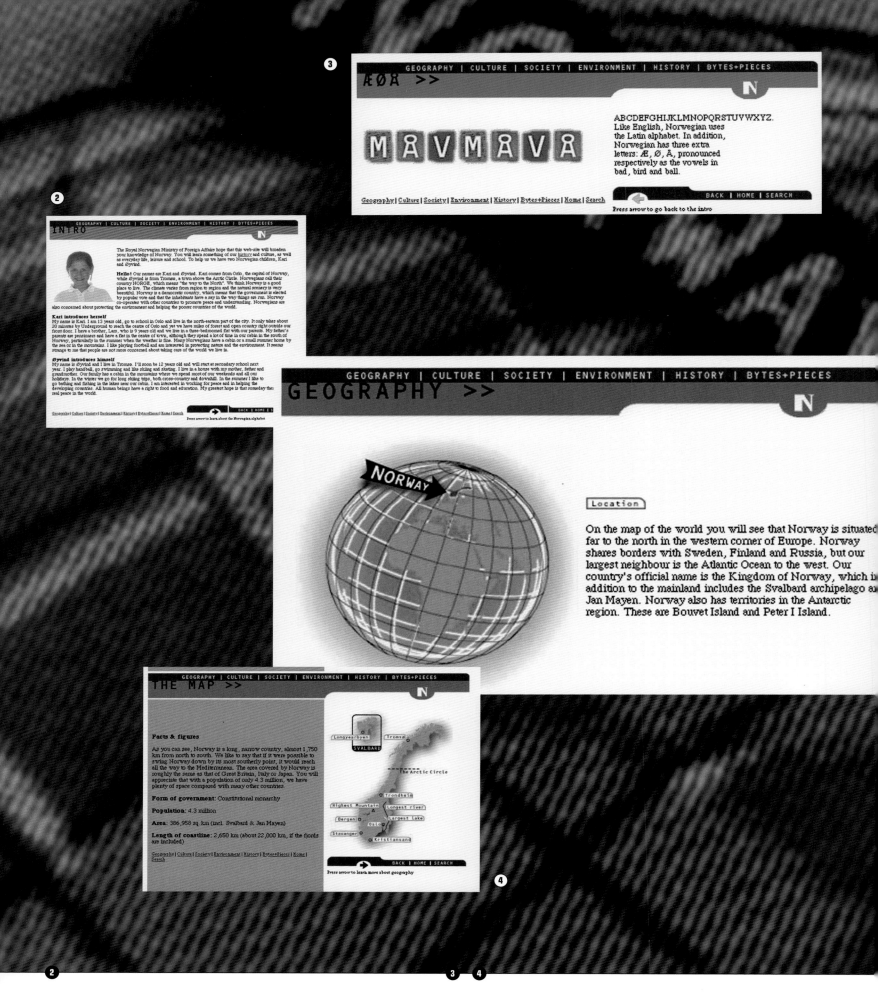

ÆØÅ >>

ABCDEFGHIJKLMNOPQRSTUVWXYZ.
Like English, Norwegian uses
the Latin alphabet. In addition,
Norwegian has three extra
letters: Æ, Ø, Å, pronounced
respectively as the vowels in
bad, bird and ball.

Geography | Culture | Society | Environment | History | Bytes+Pieces | Home | Search

BACK | HOME | SEARCH

Press arrow to go back to the intro

INTRO

The Royal Norwegian Ministry of Foreign Affairs hope that this web-site will broaden your knowledge of Norway. You will learn something of our history and culture, as well as everyday life, leisure and school. To help us we have two Norwegian children, Kari and Øyvind.

Hello! Our names are Kari and Øyvind. Kari comes from Oslo, the capital of Norway, while Øyvind is from Tromsø, a town above the Arctic Circle. Norwegians call their country NORGE, which means "the way to the North". We think Norway is a good place to live. The climate varies from region to region and the natural scenery is very beautiful. Norway is a democratic country, which means that the government is elected by popular vote and that the inhabitants have a say in the way things are run. Norway co-operates with other countries to promote peace and understanding. Norwegians are also concerned about protecting the environment and helping the poorer countries of the world.

Kari introduces herself
My name is Kari. I am 13 years old, go to school in Oslo and live in the north-eastern part of the city. It only takes about 20 minutes by Underground to reach the centre of Oslo and yet we have miles of forest and open country right outside our front door. I have a brother, Lars, who is 9 years old and we live in a three-bedroomed flat with our parents. My father's parents are pensioners and have a flat in the centre of town, although they spend a lot of time in our cabin in the south of Norway, particularly in the summer when the weather is fine. Many Norwegians have a cabin or a small summer home by the sea or in the mountains. I like playing football and am interested in protecting nature and the environment. It seems strange to me that people are not more concerned about taking care of the world we live in.

Øyvind introduces himself
My name is Øyvind and I live in Tromsø. I'll soon be 12 years old and will start at secondary school next year. I play handball, go swimming and like skiing and skating. I live in a house with my mother, father and grandmother. Our family has a cabin in the mountains where we spend most of our weekends and all our holidays. In the winter we go for long skiing trips, both cross-country and downhill. In the summer I like to go bathing and fishing in the lakes near our cabin. I am interested in working for peace and in helping the developing countries. All human beings have a right to food and education. My greatest hope is that someday there real peace in the world.

Geography | Culture | Society | Environment | History | Bytes+Pieces | Home | Search

BACK | HOME | S

Press arrow to learn about the Norwegian alphabet

GEOGRAPHY >>

Location

On the map of the world you will see that Norway is situated far to the north in the western corner of Europe. Norway shares borders with Sweden, Finland and Russia, but our largest neighbour is the Atlantic Ocean to the west. Our country's official name is the Kingdom of Norway, which in addition to the mainland includes the Svalbard archipelago and Jan Mayen. Norway also has territories in the Antarctic region. These are Bouvet Island and Peter I Island.

THE MAP >>

Facts & figures

As you can see, Norway is a long, narrow country, almost 1,750 km from north to south. We like to say that if it were possible to swing Norway down by its most southerly point, it would reach all the way to the Mediterranean. The area covered by Norway is roughly the same as that of Great Britain, Italy or Japan. You will appreciate that with a population of only 4.3 million, we have plenty of space compared with many other countries.

Form of government: Constitutional monarchy

Population: 4.3 million

Area: 386,958 sq. km (incl. Svalbard & Jan Mayen)

Length of coastline: 2,650 km (about 22,000 km, if the fjords are included)

Geography | Culture | Society | Environment | History | Bytes+Pieces | Home | Search

BACK | HOME | SEARCH

Press arrow to learn more about geography

Since the target audience is kids, the intro-page presents two young companions who join the visitor on this do-it-yourself tour of Norway. Their portraits are morphed in a GIF animation, so that one face gradually changes into the other.

A series of 7 GIF animations shows the Æ, Ø and Å in the Norwegian alphabet, while a brief practical text explains the peculiarities of the Norwegian language and its pronunciation. The double arrow in the navigation banner indicates that this section contains further pages to explore.

Facts and figures about Norway's geography are combined with a map of the country; the map is clickable, marked places linking to pictures of towns and landscapes. Text and images, as is the case in the rest of the site, are clearly arranged by means of invisible tables.

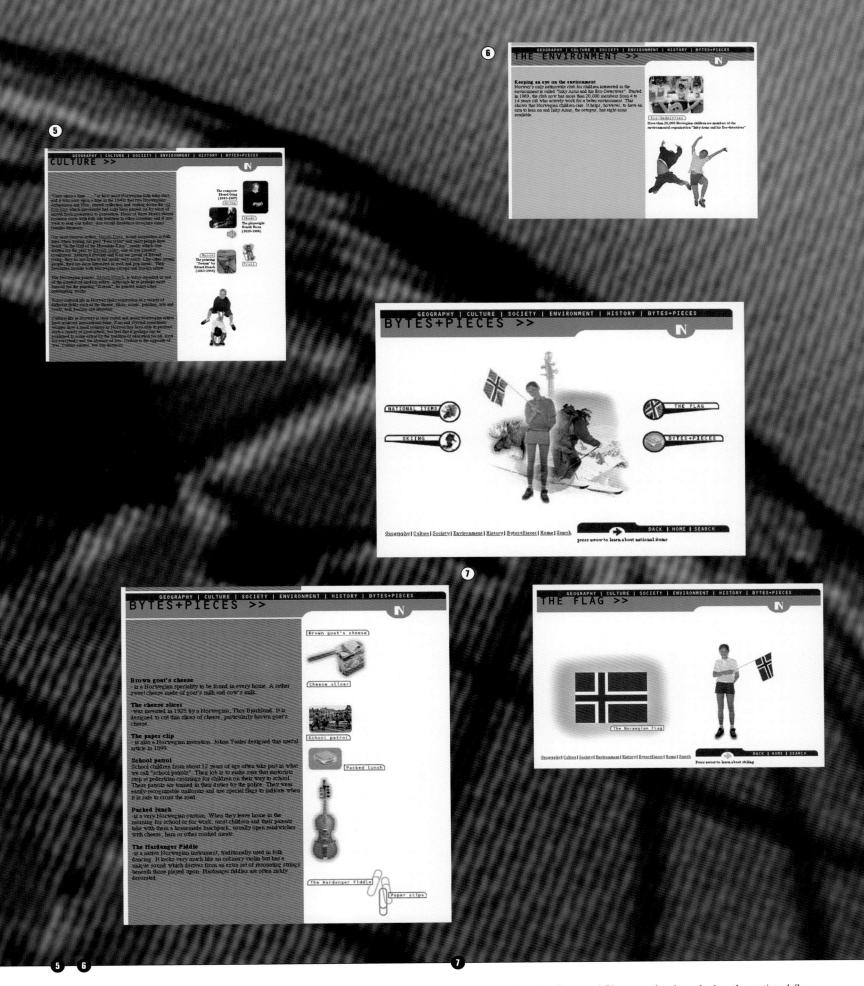

This page introduces some of Norway's cultural heroes such as Ibsen, Grieg and Munch, enhanced by links to more detailed information stored in other parts of the ODIN server. In the animated GIF below, the guides demonstrate one of their favourite games.

In this section the national concern with environmental issues is evident: eco-detectives are presented. 'Inky Arms and his Eco-detectives', as the full name goes, is one of the largest environmental organizations for children.

Three pages from the Bytes and Pieces section introducing the national flag, activities like skiing and national inventions like the paperclip and cheese slicer. Some links are provided to more detailed pages such as one about the flag. Once more an animated GIF shows the guide waving the Norwegian flag.

KABD

Kunst- und Ausstellungshalle der Bundesrepublik Deutschland

http://www.kah-bonn.de

DESIGNER KABD, Christoph Schubert (KAH), Norbert Kanter (KAH), Sebastian Weiss (Dimedis), Neville Brody, Arthur Schmidt (Digital World) / YEAR OF DESIGN 1996 / PLACE OF DESIGN Hamburg, Germany / COPYRIGHT OWNER Kunst- und Ausstellungshalle der Bundesrepublik Deutschland / SCREEN DESIGN Norbert Kanter, Christoph Schubert, Arthur Schmidt, Sebastian Weiss / ANIMATION/GRAPHICS Norbert Kanter, Christoph Schubert, Neville Brody / INTERACTION DESIGN Norbert Kanter, Christoph Schubert, Arthur Schmidt, Sebastian Weiss / PRODUCTION Norbert Kanter, Christoph Schubert, Arthur Schmidt, Sebastian Weiss / EDITOR Norbert Kanter / CONTRIBUTORS Kunst- und Ausstellungshalle der Bundesrepublik Deutschland / SOFTWARE USED Mac: WebWeaver, Adobe Photoshop; mpc: Premiere, HotMetal, Adobe Photoshop / DESIGN PLATFORMS Mac: 90%; mpc: 10%

Although it is inevitable that the design of websites for existing institutions will be largely determined by the physical image and tradition of the material body they represent, this is all too often a restriction. After all the Web, which is medium and context in itself, imposes special visual and communicative demands. Therefore, when designers and editors create such a non-web-specific site, it is their challenge to create a site that clearly distinguishes itself in its form, function and content from the other media through which these organisations are expressed.

In every way the site of the Kunst- und Ausstellungshalle der Bundesrepublik Deutschland in Bonn serves the promotional and public aims of the museum, but it also convincingly uses the visual opportunities of the Web. It is above all a service-providing, interactive version of the real museum, in which it is easy to navigate. The pages are surprisingly diverse, through variation in text rather than images. The tight typography, in combination with a carefully considered screen layout, delivers information about the content and structure of the KABD in a clear and simple way – for example about exhibitions, conferences, theatre and music shows, and film presentations.

The monochrome homepage immediately shows the three main sections of the site: 'exhibitions', 'information' and 'calendar'. A submenu gives access to a range of extra facilities, such as e-mail, a guest book and photo archive. An alphabetical index makes all information readily available, and by clicking on 'press' you can download the press releases.

Many on-line museums are still struggling with the new, dynamic and immaterial context of the Web, and how to bring to this context both the historical and cultural tradition of their physical presence, and their symbolic, ideological aims. This means that very often their digital presence is merely a refined semi-interactive flyer, or a weak, electronic imitation of the physical building. The KABD did not attempt to imitate its architecture. Instead it provides an insight into its internal structure. The possibilities of the Web have been utilised to create an archive of real practical use. The accessible way in which the tremendous amount of information has been organised keeps you from being swamped. As a result the site leaves a lasting impression, which is more than can be said of most websites.

Jorinde Seijdel

❶

The German homepage indicating the three main sections; at the top left is the logo of the KABD, reflecting the institute's distinctive architecture. When the page loads for the first time, the letters appear in an apparently random order. By means of the orange bars — white, black, grey, orange and red are the most important colours of the site — you can switch to English.

The Kunst- und Ausstellungshalle's program is based on a broad definition of culture that includes science and technology as well as art and cultural history. The museum's task is to present intellectual and cultural developments of national and international importance and to promote dialogue between leading figures from the world of art, culture and scholarship as well as from the realm of politics. Exhibitions, congresses, theater and musical events, film presentations and lectures take place here. Comprising an exhibition area of 5,600m2, the Kunst- und Ausstellungshalle can present five alternating exhibitions of various sizes simultaneously. All other events take place in the Forum, a multi-purpose room with seating for up to 550 persons.

EXHIBITIO NSI

OVERVIEW   CHRONOLOGICAL   SYTEMATIC   PUBLICATIONS

5 JULY 1996 - 12 JANUARY 1997: THE GREAT COLLECTIONS IV /
MODERNA MUSEET STOCKHOLM

5 JUNI 1996 - SPRING 1998: F U T U R E
G A R D E N   PART 1 - THE ENDANGERED MEADOWS OF EUROPE

6 DECEMBER 1996 - 2 MARCH 1997 - THE GREAT COLLECTIONS V
NAPOLI ... MATEGNA, RAFFAEL, TIZIAN, EL GRECO ...
IL MUSEO NAZIONALE DI CAPODIMONTE, NAPLES

KUNST- UND AUSSTELLUNGSHALLE DER BUNDESREPUBLIK DE...

EXHIBIT SI

6 DECEMBER 1996 - 2 MARCH 1997 - THE GREAT
NAPOLI ... MATEGNA, RAFFAEL, TIZIAN
IL MUSEO NAZIONALE DI CAPODIMON

6 December 1996 to

NAPOLI!

... Mantegna, Ra...

The Museo Nazionale ...
important museum ...
Attention: 160kB JP...
in Bonn for the fir...
comprehensive sele...

The collection's h...
century. It has 'li...
and culturally impo...
Italian princely fa...
the Borgia or even...
Paul III (1534-159...
example, is compar...
collections. Examp...
Renaissance, Manner...
of sculptures and ...
comprising all the ...
are represented in...
from, among others,...
Greco, Pontormo, C...

EL GRECO ...

By clicking on the logo you can view a scale model of the building and get an impression of the distinctive architecture by Gustave Peichl. The KABD, directed by the Swede Pontus Hulten, opened its doors in 1992, so the site is not burdened a long history. The cubical building, with an enormous roof garden used for sculpture exhibitions, is pierced by 3 protruding light cones, which appear in the logo and represent the main focus of the museum: architecture, painting and sculpture.

The main menu of the section 'Exhibitions', with an option to bring up a list of all exhibitions, arranged chronologically or thematically. In particular the latter option is interesting, because it shows how the museum categorises its own content. You can also view information about accompanying publications. The list of exhibitions consists of colourful frames, designed as posters, with titles and dates.

By clicking on an exhibition announcement, detailed information is accessed about the event in question, including photos which can also be displayed at full-screen size.

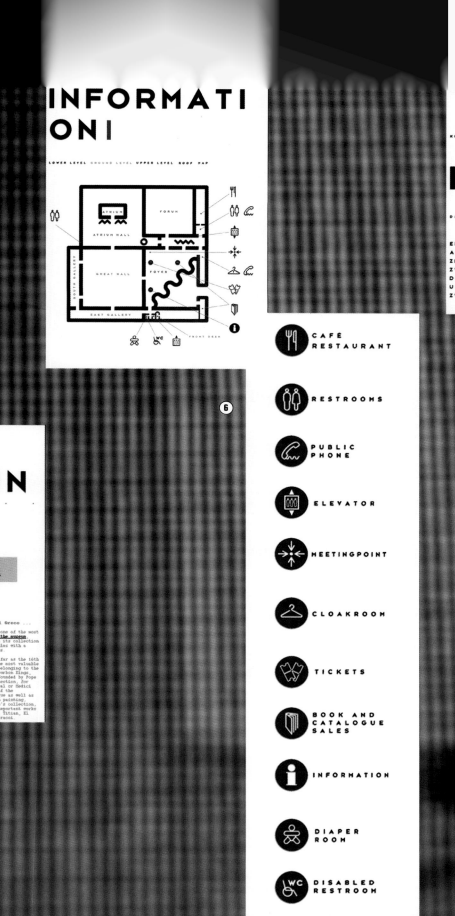

INFORMATI
ONI

LOWER LEVEL GROUND LEVEL **UPPER LEVEL** ROOF MAP

ON

El Greco ...

is one of the most
of the museum
ent its collection
Naples with a
ces

as far as the 16th
the most valuable
belonging to the
Bourbon Kings,
. Founded by Pope
ollection, for
t of the
roque as well as
ish painting,
em's collection,
y important works
l, Titian, El
Carracci.

CAFÉ
RESTAURANT

RESTROOMS

PUBLIC
PHONE

ELEVATOR

MEETINGPOINT

CLOAKROOM

TICKETS

BOOK AND
CATALOGUE
SALES

INFORMATION

DIAPER
ROOM

WC DISABLED
RESTROOM

KUNST- UND AUSSTELLUNGSHALLE DER BUNDESREPUBLIK DEUTSCHLAND

KALENDERI

DEZEMBER

EINS ZWEI DREI VIER FÜNF SECHS SIEBEN
ACHT NEUN ZEHN ELF ZWÖLF DREIZEHN VIERZEHN FÜNF
ZEHN SECHZEHN SIEBZEHN ACHTZEHN NEUNZEHN
ZWANZIG EINUNDZWANZIG ZWEIUNDZWANZIG
DREIUNDZWANZIG VIERUNDZWANZIG FÜNFUNDZWANZIG SECHS
UNDZWANZIG SIEBENUNDZWANZIG ACHTUNDZWANZIG NEUNUND
ZWANZIG DREISSIG EINUNDDREISSIG

KUNST- UND AUSSTELLUNGSHALLE DER BUNDESREPUBLIK DEUTSCHLAND

INSIGHT

LIVE-IMAGE
from the Kunst- und Ausstellungshalle der Bundesrepublik Deutschland

Event:
Exhibition <u>The Great Collections IV: Moderna Museet Stockholm)</u>

Since:
1 November 1996, 11:30 am (<u>location of the camera</u>)

From 'Information' you can call up impressive plans of all floors of the building, which, like the icons that show the visitor the way in the physical building, were created by the English designer Neville Brody.

A list of all icons, some of which provide more information about certain functions and services of the KABD.

When the 'Calendar' page is loaded, the letters appear in a random order on the screen, which is fascinating to see. By clicking on a date, you discover what was/is/will be shown in the KABD on that particular day.

A live picture is available 24 hours a day of a room in the KABD (although nothing can be seen after closing time because the lights are out then). Every 60 seconds the image is renewed.

Dutch Parliament

http://www.parlement.nl

DESIGNER DC3 Interaction Design / CLIENT Tweede Kamer / YEAR OF DESIGN 1996 / PLACE OF DESIGN Amsterdam, The Netherlands / COPYRIGHT OWNER DC3 Interaction Design / DESIGN COMPANY DC3 Interaction Design Elma Wolschrijn, Hayo Wagenaar, Rik Koster, Joost Holthuis, Marc Bokeloh / ANIMATION/GRAPHICS Sander Hassing, Hayo Wagenaar / INTERACTION DESIGN Elma Wolschrijn, Rik Koster / PRODUCTION Marcus Bremer / EDITOR Mirjam Boone / CONTRIBUTORS Bert Mulder / SOFTWARE USED Mac: BBEdit, Adobe Photoshop, DeBabelizer, Freehand, Adobe Illustrator, Claris Homepage, Macromedia Director, Shockwave / DESIGN PLATFORMS Mac: 100%

1

The homepage is composed of frames, with the 'Tweede Kamer' (Lower House of Parliament) showing images of empty chairs in the meeting hall, a part of the Parliament building.

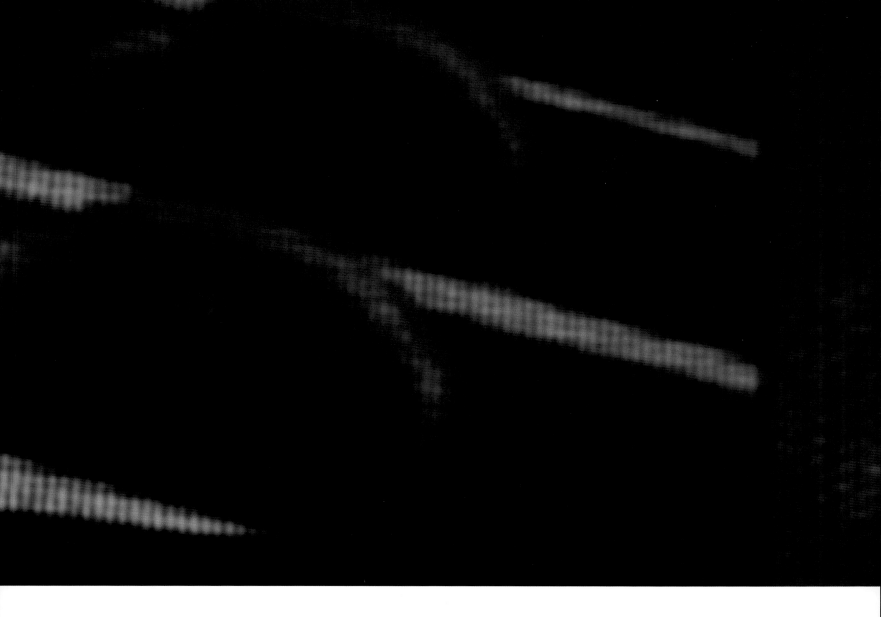

Like most others, the Dutch parliament consists of two houses: an Upper and a Lower House, which together are called the 'States General'. This bicameral system was introduced in 1815. In 1996, the Dutch government introduced the Parliament website, in a modern attempt to take the flow of information to Dutch citizens into its own hands.

Although the homepage offers access to the Upper as well as Lower House, only the latter option functions as yet. Clicking on it takes you to the central menu, in which a cream-coloured main frame is flanked by other, predominantly grey and blue-purple frames. At the top left a banner with a start button and a menu bar with 5 icons represent the table of contents of the site. The homepage also has search and help functions, and direct access to information about the daily agenda or to the international section of the site.

From this well-organised structure, which in comparison with many other rather dull government sites has a remarkably progressive design, it is possible to explore the Lower House of Parliament and gain an understanding of how Dutch politics function. The layout of the pages always remains relatively simple, varied only by the use of a number of standard colours and by shifting typography and colour surfaces across the screen. The design of the site has been geared to its educational and promotional function. It is structured so that less experienced websurfers can use it with relative ease. The information, which is brief and clear, discusses the history and organisation of the Lower House of Parliament as well as the legal opportunities for the Dutch citizen to participate. In addition there are more important official documents and data, like dates of meetings or political programs. The website functions as a vehicle for government information. It is the public relations site of Parliament. The image it evokes is that Dutch politics are clean, open and dynamic – like the design of the site. However, it lacks the informal anecdotes and vicious discussions of 'real' political life in the Netherlands.

Nevertheless, it is quite remarkable that the government has decided to make its internal structure more transparent and accessible. As well as a means of orientation for MPs themselves it is also a very suitable means for other people — for example children, students or immigrants — to become familiar with the workings of the Dutch government. Now the vigilant Dutch citizen can press a button at home at any moment, view the political agenda of his government and scrutinise its activities.

Jorinde Seijdel

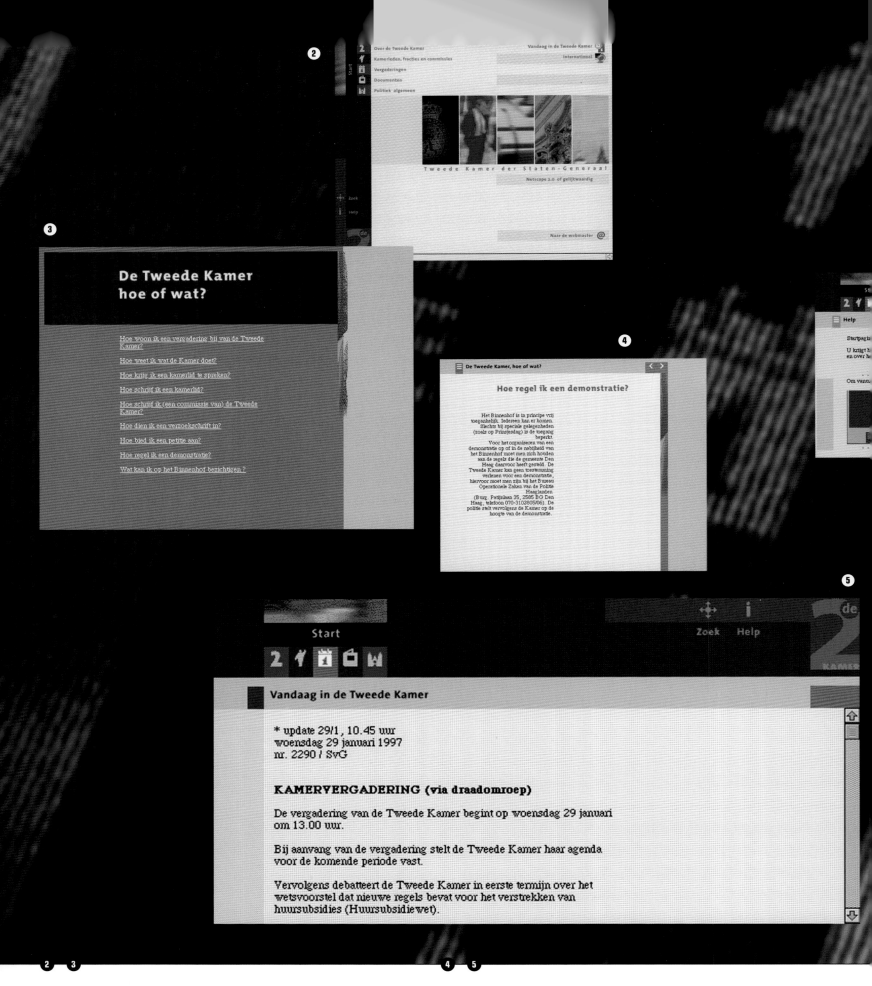

The page with the main menu: by clicking on one of the icons at the top left you open a specific subject. Architectural fragments and glimpses of interiors are also displayed, creating an impression of vitality.

The guide to the Lower House of Parliament. A number of concise questions have been formulated, which examine the opportunities of the citizen to participate ('How do I submit a petition?' for example or 'How can I sit in on a session of the Lower House of Parliament?')

'How do I organise a demonstration?' Click on the arrows at the top right to browse through this section backwards or forwards.

The agenda of a parliamentary meeting, reached from in the main menu through the button 'Vandaag in de Tweede Kamer' (Today in Parliament). The menu bar with 5 icons has changed position here.

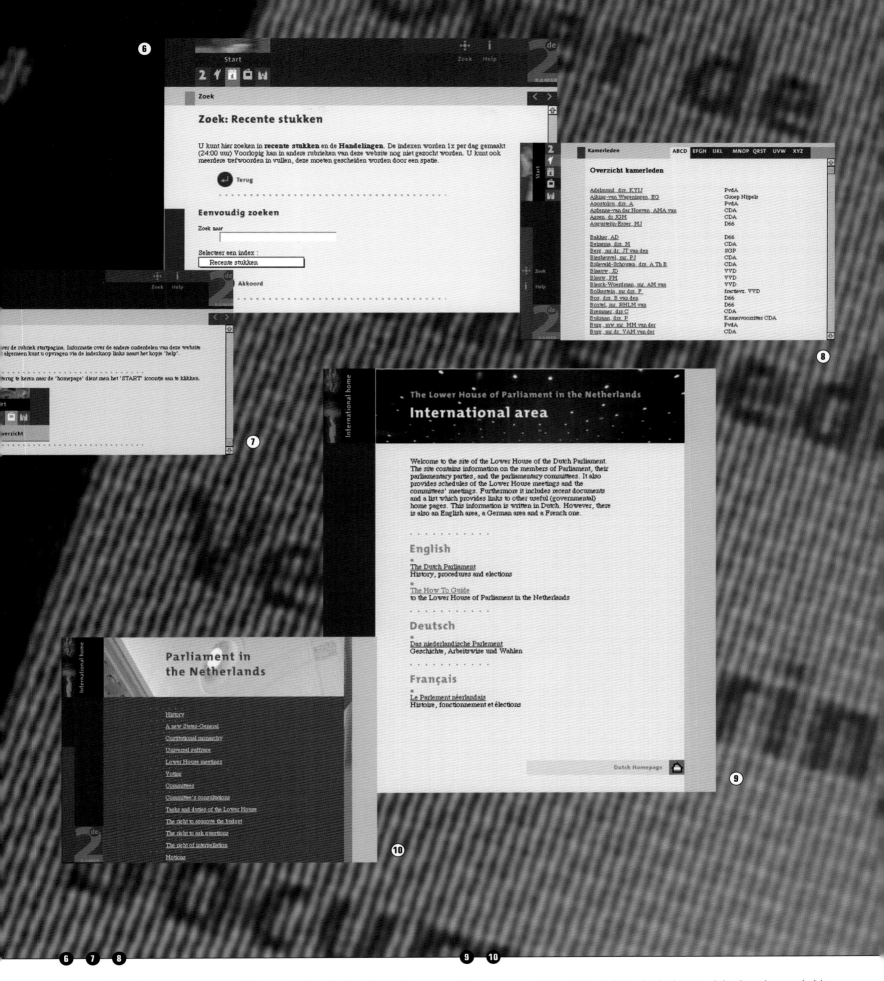

The search function, again in grey and blue-purple. For the time being it is only possible to search for 'Recent documents' and 'Official Reports', though these are a mine of information for anyone interested.

The very accessible help function explains, as it should do, the way the buttons work, the contents and layout of the site.

A list of the names of all MPs. By making use of the alphabet bar you can speed up the search for a particular person.

The homepage of International Area. At the bottom right there is a symbol in the 3 colours in the Dutch flag, which takes you back to the Dutch version.

The table of contents of the English section. The architectural detail in the top frame is used a number of times throughout the site.

Netscape: Art Center College of Design

ART CENTER COLLEGE OF DESIGN
@

http://www.artcenter.edu

It is a considerable challenge to design a coherent and dynamic website for an educational institution, even more so when it is for Art Center in Pasadena, California, which is one of the premier art and design schools in the world. Not only do they have an excellent reputation to uphold in their venture on-line, but one also expects a vision, an unveiling of what the future holds when the students of Art Center leave school and join the forces currently designing the digital revolution.

Art Center is a private school, so one of the primary functions of the site must be to attract and inform the potential new student. It approaches this goal in a very clear way; first of all by soberly listing all the hard information one needs to know to enroll, and secondly by adding a very strong visual identity that provides the visitor with a sense of the character and signature of the place. This begins on the homepage where the first element loaded is an orange '@' sign on a black background, an effective translation of the school's logo. Then the name of the school appears in several layers of overlapping type. The '@' is the active element which is clicked to continue. A subtle change takes place, with an index and an atmospheric background merging with the first two elements of the homepage. The type

used for this section is a simple Courier, but the way the words are spaced and placed is evidence of a long tradition of well-considered design. The same applies to the section containing the thirteen departments of the school. The first page of each department is black, with text presented in an erratic combination of centered and uncentered columns of type, with a blur of bold running through. Then, loading slowly, the title of the department appears in customized type — fusing a sans-serif with a serif letter — blended with a large diffused background photo.

The design of the Art Center website is beautiful, slightly mysterious, somewhat dysfunctional, yet very organic. An open structure has been created that will grow and prosper with time, once the presently void space for the students and the alumni becomes filled. A promising sign in this direction is the Art Center Palace site, an interactive virtual chat space built by students and displayed under Events. It will be interesting to visit this in the future and see if it has become just as lively a place as the campus itself is.

Adam Eeuwens

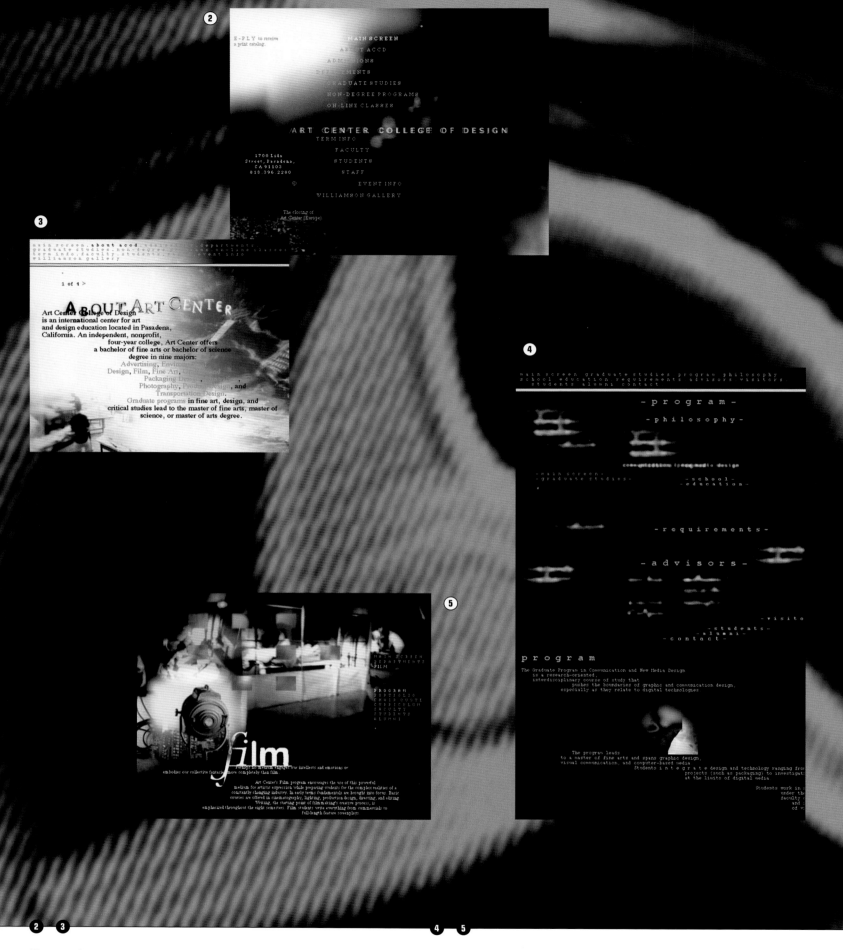

The second page is the index, which plainly states what the visitor can find in the site with only the odd added feature.

A typical page of the Art Center site, using customized typography, along with a column of type and images blended in the overall layout.

The New Media Design page takes a long time to load, since the designers have put all the information about the departments on one single page, like an on-line poster. It is worth the wait though, because when you click on the words, you are transported rapidly to the subject in question.

The main page of the Film department, using images of the film classroom as a background. The text column bears the Art Center signature of organic, lively text design.

A few examples of portfolio pages, in which the work of the students is beautifully represented in the on-line environment. Images or colour form the background, strengthening the impact of the main work.

Each departmental section has a neatly designed quote from the department's head. The dot underneath the index bar on the right, the logo of Art Center, is also the navigation tool taking you to the map of the site.

A map does not need to be fancy, but it has to be easy to use. This accessible site map lists all the contents within a small screen, providing a useful overview.

When you click back to the main page in the site structure, you will find surprising quotes advertising the philosophies and/or virtues of the design profession.

Magazines / Max Bruinsma

The World Wide Web could be conceived as a very large magazine which is updated every split second. It is too large to actually fit into a table of contents; nobody knows exactly what the magazine is about and what is to be found on its pages. The Web is a magazine without filters. It is entirely up to the readers to find articles of interest to them in this vast billion-page publication.

However, using this metaphor for the Web, one quickly realises why it actually is not a magazine: there is no editorial point-of-view. That is where the electronic magazine comes into play. It has been said before: the main problem of information technology is not the content but the context. Formulated more precisely: it is the way you filter content through context. Lost in an ocean of info, the browser looks for anchors. One of the most precious things a Web magazine can do is provide a well-structured set of links to a well-defined subject.

That is what will make the viewer come back. It goes without saying that a Web-based magazine also provides its own content. In a sense it works as the World Wide Web at large. It offers a variety of material, which is connected in more than one way. The interfaces of e-zines mirror this in that it is rather common for Web magazines to provide multiple ways of navigation. The content itself may change in a way which is not feasible for paper magazines: a Web magazine can be updated at any time. Therefore the difference between 'issues' is not that clear – they tend to grow gradually and organically. And, more than in printed magazines, the design of e-zines is the design of links between pages, sites, images and texts — the consistency is in the linking itself. At all times you can choose between exploring the information on a deeper level or continuing to link 'on' or 'out'.

The difference from printed media is not only non-linearity — printed magazines themselves are largely non-linear media — but also multimedia. From the pages of an e-zine you can play RealAudio-music while reading and browsing. Short animations will pop up around the text and sometimes the text will flip its own pages, or change into an illustration, which in its turn will change into another illustration.

Most e-zines try to appeal to a specific audience. The graphic design of a magazine mirrors the lifestyle of the targeted group of readers. They have to be able to identify with the magazine and its editors. This is maybe even more important for Web-based magazines than for their printed counterparts which can check the loyalty of their readers through subscriptions. The reader of an e-zine has to bookmark it. The more they can identify with the form and content, the more frequently they will return to their anchor in the Web.

Node 246

http://www.softmachine.co.jp/node246.003

DESIGNER Soft Machine Inc. / YEAR OF DESIGN 1995 / PLACE OF DESIGN Tokyo, Japan / COPYRIGHT OWNER Takeru Esaka / DESIGN COMPANY Soft Machine Inc. / SCREEN DESIGN, ANIMATION/GRAPHICS, INTERACTION DESIGN Hikaru Mochizuki, Madoka Iwabuchi / PRODUCTION Takeru Esaka / EDITORS Takeru Esaka, Masaaki Hara, Kazuya Kawasaki, Kouji Yoshida / SOFTWARE USED Mac: Adobe Photoshop, Adobe Illustrator, Macromedia Director 4.0.4, GifBuilder / DESIGN PLATFORMS Mac: 95%; sgi: 5%

A node is a porthole which takes you into a network. Node 246 is an e-zine that gives access to contemporary 'japanese alt.culture', specifically the 'tokyo backbone'. It jacks you into the brain of the creators of Japanimation (issue one), techno music (issue two) and, in the latest issue, fashion. The content is a representation of what these people stand for, and especially their view of their work versus the rest of the world. This is achieved in a very graceful manner, keeping the typical 'Japlish' at a very low level and offering an original inside look into Japanese pop culture.

The excellent Photoshop and Illustrator design of images combined with meticulous screen-typography — often fearlessly taking on the gruesome hassle of denting and ragging every single textline with crafty HTML-code — show that the makers of Node 246 are totally dedicated to perfection. Like modern day monks, they make each page into a little work of art, fabricated in the same way that a glossy magazine presents its content. The metaphor of old-style paper publishing is apparent everywhere in Node 246's presentation. Its covers and headlines and opening images are like those of a conventional newspaper with a story to break. Yet here the images can be animated: a completely new dimension in story presentation.

Node 246 unveils a wealth of new design possibilities, while new options are invented with each issue. The most significant gain is the control of timing — it is as if the designer were able to take the visitor on a short enforced walk through a slide show before delivering the page which contains the story. Some ideas they have come up with are not successful. For example, text sometimes becomes illegible. However, other solutions certainly work. All these different results can be viewed on the adventurous Node 246 website.

Node 246 shows that the Web can be a perfect medium for recreating and further enriching the lifestyle magazine. The content, look and feel of Node 246 closely resemble the image and role of the English magazines The Face and I-D. Every feature has its own customised approach, jamming in hip dynamics along with groovy style experiments. By sticking to the conventions of producing a magazine, and sensibly applying the bag of tricks provided by on-line technology, Node 246 definitely has made a statement of its own webdesign style. It forges a subtle blend of an old and a new medium, and offers an inspiring experience.

Adam Eeuwens

1

The opening pages of Node 246 work like covers of a magazine.

While in the first two issues the homepage displayed the contents, the third relies more on a conventional magazine design, trusting that the index on the second page will suffice to guide the visitor.

The equivalent of a magazine opening layout is demonstrated in these three successive pages of a feature story in the first issue of Node 246 in 1995. The first page shows the headline and title. On the second page stills from a video clip are shown when you click on the pistol (just like the opening images of an article), and then page 3 is automatically loaded. On this page the body of text starts.

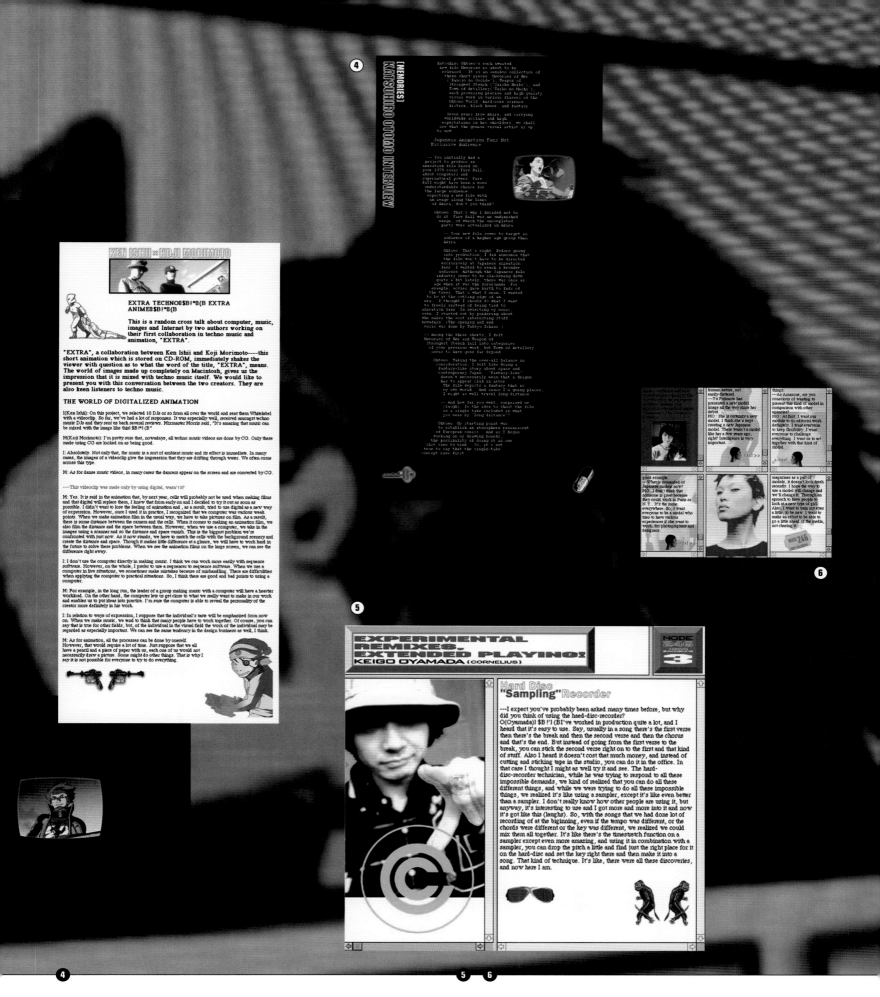

A beautiful example of indented text and ragged lines — a successful experiment in pleasant on-screen reading.

February 1996, the 'free bomb inside' second issue of Node 246, now with frames. Above are the title and 'home button'; below the navigation index. One window frame shows the animated interviewee, the other frame holds the scrollable body of text.

The stories never have an endless screen scroll as the designers have been very inventive. For instance, in these six frames it only takes a little scrolling until a clickable 'next' arrow appears, continuing the story on the next screen.

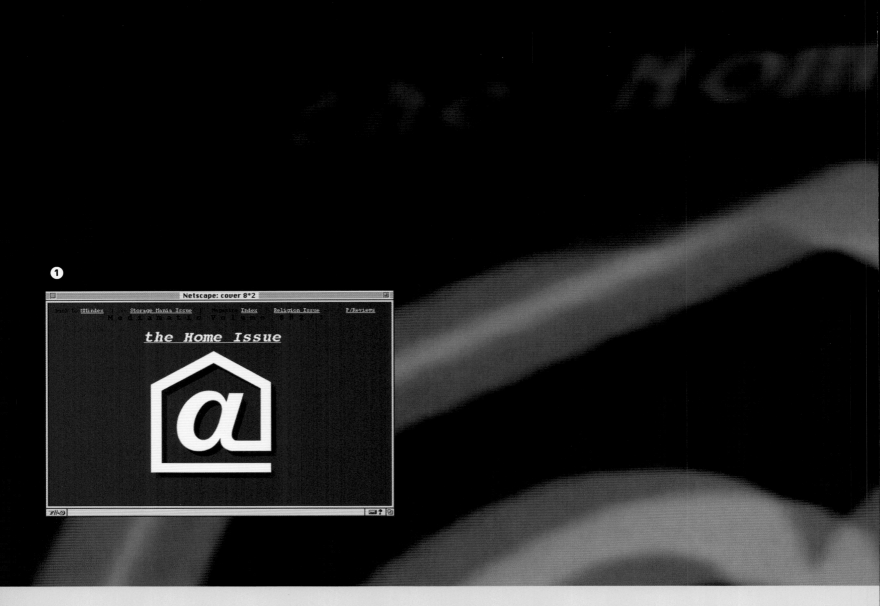

❶

Mediamatic Magazine

http://www.mediamatic.nl/

DESIGNER Mediamatic / YEAR OF DESIGN 1994-97 / PLACE OF DESIGN Amsterdam, The Netherlands / COPYRIGHT OWNER The Mediamatic Foundation / DESIGN COMPANY Mediamatic / SCREEN DESIGN Zsa Zsa Linnemann, Peter v/d Hoogen, Chris Remie, Willem Velthoven / ANIMATION/GRAPHICS Zsa Zsa Linnemann, Peter v/d Hoogen, Chris Remie, Willem Velthoven / INTERACTION DESIGN Zsa Zsa Linnemann, Peter v/d Hoogen, Chris Remie, Willem Velthoven / PRODUCTION Jans Possel, Geert J. Strengholt / EDITORS Arie Altena, Paul Groot, Jans Possel, Jorinde Seijdel, Geert J. Strengholt, Dirk van Weelden, Willem Velthoven / CONTRIBUTORS James Boekbinder, Erkki Huhtamo / AWARDS European Design Prize 1997 / SOFTWARE USED Mac: Adobe Photoshop, Pagespinner, Adobe Pagemill, PhotoGIF / DESIGN PLATFORMS Mac: 100%

❶

On the cover page of the 'Home' issue the modified '@' reflects the theme of this issue. The unobtrusive navigation links allow hyperjumps to the table of contents in the present issue, to future or previous issues or to the review section. Although it is varied through the site, this is the basic set-up for navigation.

Browsing through on-line magazines on the Web one cannot help but notice their struggle to shake off the traditions of printed media in their search for new ways of publishing, new content and new design. As a printed magazine about the cultural implications of new media, Mediamatic has always had a keen interest in the (design) challenges of new interactive media. Now its on-line counterpart is actively assessing the possibilities and limitations of electronic publishing. Until now four issues of Mediamatic Magazine have been published on the Web. These issues not only show the evolution of webdesign over recent years, but also represent a clear shift in the specific challenges, both in content and design, being addressed by Mediamatic's editors and designers.

Mediamatic is a text-heavy magazine, so at the outset of its on-line existence it showed a close resemblance to the academic world of the Web. In time the attention has clearly shifted from transposing printed content to the Web in such a way that people would be willing to read it on the computer screen to developing new content in the context of the digital realm. Moreover, Mediamatic has changed its focus from writing about the Web to writing and designing within the Web environment. This is basically a shift towards an aestheticism of the digital zap, the link or connection between multiple (con)texts. One of the more interesting examples of this is the editorial to the 'Religion' issue, which focuses on the role of religious material on the Web and uses search engine technology to generate new associations and links. The new content is not found in a new text, but in the unexpected results of linking and shifting from one context to the next. In a piece called 'Meta-morfussed' three versions of Finnegan's Wake and an accompanying essay are simultaneously presented, allowing the reader to jump back and forth between texts. Frames and Java-script are used here to create an intuitive interplay of texts, context and references, exposing secret textual alliances.

Visually, most pages in Mediamatic Magazine show a restrained combination of text and images, while the clear, plain text navigation bar determines the logic of the site as a whole. Whereas previous issues were mostly set in black and white, each recent issue and separate sections have been based on a limited palette of colours that work well on the Web. Generally the design of the site is well-balanced, presenting its challenging content in a clear, readable format, while it continuously explores new directions. But then again, what else may one expect from a 'new media' magazine that features a graphic designer as its editor-in-chief?

Geert J. Strengholt

Like a traditional table of contents this page lists the articles available in this issue. Apart from links to the articles themselves there are also links to pages containing biographies of the writers. The image of the 'Halo' reflects the theme of this issue, 'Religion'.

The editorial to the 'Religion' issue explores the occurrence of a number of words on the Net related to religious matters. Accompanied by a previous word count, the words in the top frame of the second page are linked to a search query of the Alta Vista search engine. Clicking on them will send the query off and display the results of the search (and a current word count) in the lower frame.

Most articles are cut up into a collection of webpages, featuring one leading title page and several successive text pages. Tables are used to create columns of fixed text in a readable format.

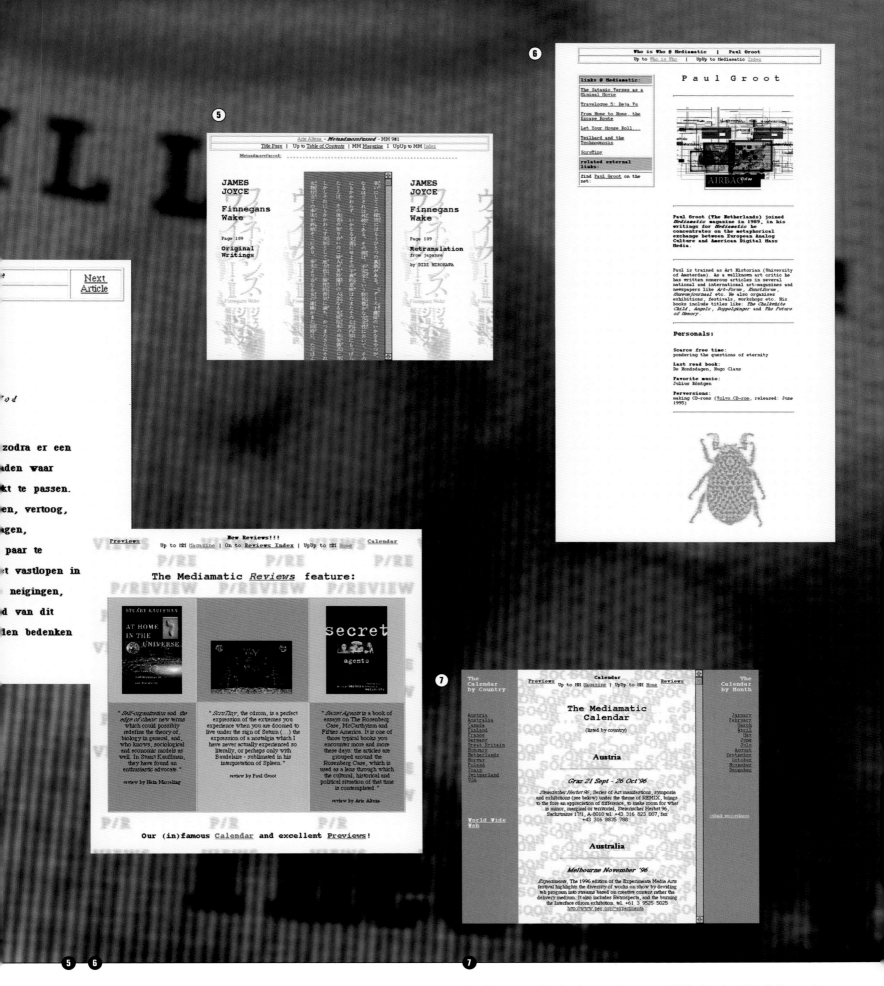

The Finnegan's Wake project, in the 'Secret Agents' issue, involved retranslating a page from the Japanese translation of Joyce's original. To present the three stages of the text side by side as well as an accompanying essay, a set-up of four frames was arranged. Triggered by Java script, various text fragments are revealed when the user 'feels' his/her way across the screen.

All writers for Mediamatic are represented by a biographical page, where links to other projects at Mediamatic or world-wide are also specified. A link to the Alta Vista search engine provides the option to search for the writer on the Web.

The Reviews section is where reviews are published and archived. New reviews are first featured on the page shown here, in a standard layout defined by tables and background colours. The section also contains an international calendar, listing and previewing events, conferences and exhibitions. The calendar page consists of three frames, and allows the user to access the calendar information (presented in the center frame) according to country (left frame) or month (right frame).

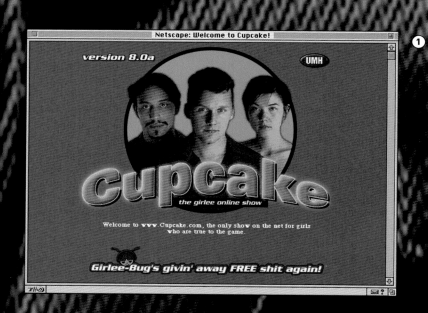

Cupcake: The Girlee On-line Show

http://www.cupcake.com

DESIGNER Urban Media House / CLIENT Publisher / YEAR OF DESIGN 1996 / PLACE OF DESIGN San Fransisco, USA / COPYRIGHT OWNER Urban Media House / DESIGN COMPANY Urban Media House / SCREEN DESIGN, ANIMATION/GRAPHICS Selino valdes / INTERACTION DESIGN Selino valdes, Martha Zee / PRODUCTION Selino valdes / EDITORS Brianna De Los Santos Pope / CONTRIBUTORS Cindy Zee, Janine Ashford, Dylan Chivian, Kira Talbot / SOFTWARE USED Mac: Adobe Photoshop, Nescape Navigator, Simple Text, Macintosh Program Launcher, sgi: Generic Java Compiler, Vi, Netscape; mpc: Ms Explorer, Netscape / DESIGN PLATFORMS mpc 20%; Mac 75%; sgi 5%

Cupcake is a brazen, straight-shooting girl's magazine – a 'girlee on-line show on the Web'. It has an almost entirely horizontal architecture. All of the contents items are represented by circular buttons, usually containing no text. These are arranged in a row, like beads on a string, in the lower frame of the main interface. The only order here is chronological: items are added one after another, right to left, and we can look at them nine at a time. Once published, they are not removed. The string of items is a complete archive in chronological order. The features themselves appear in the larger, top frame. They are brief, to-the-point and well illustrated, some with 'slide shows' and animations.

This open, maximally horizontal interaction design is perfectly suited to Cupcake's provocative, direct content. Hiding nothing in a hierarchy, the designers have placed everything right out front, like an old-fashioned vending machine with one knob per item, giving readers maximum choice about their own mise-en-scène in this 'girlee show', with only the visual design of the buttons as a guide. Readers' opinions form a prominent red thread – the string of items is a virtual fence where opinions from every corner are traded intensively (sometimes hurled vehemently) back and forth.

Within this simple and optimally navigable structure, there is no limit to the complexity or variety of the items, however concise. Wonder Woman's costume through the years or Granny's impatience with the clumsiness of the World Wide Web are presented in straightforward, simple formats; a plug for the 'virtual killer' heroine of a video game has visuals that can be admired at closer range; a girl's love affair with her scooter sparkles with animated gems. Readers can scroll along fashion panoramas, vote for their favourite hunk or even watch him strip in his own particular fashion. Typography reinforces the polemics in a more serious item about child labour in the flower fields of California.

A small row of buttons at the upper left of each screen gives continual access to the staff pages, chat space, photo collection, letters about love, news, links, a McDonald's advertisement, hot events, the Cupcake Super Chick, mail, software, the Urban Media House page (publisher of Cupcake) and, last but not least, an extremely well-written help page showing how to navigate the site.

The site provides Cupcake's girlee show with an ideal theater, unimpeded by labels and hierarchies.

James Boekbinder

1

Cupcake opens its on-line girlee revue in a typical out-front fashion. Only a few, rather minimal options accompany the dominant central entrance to the 'show'.

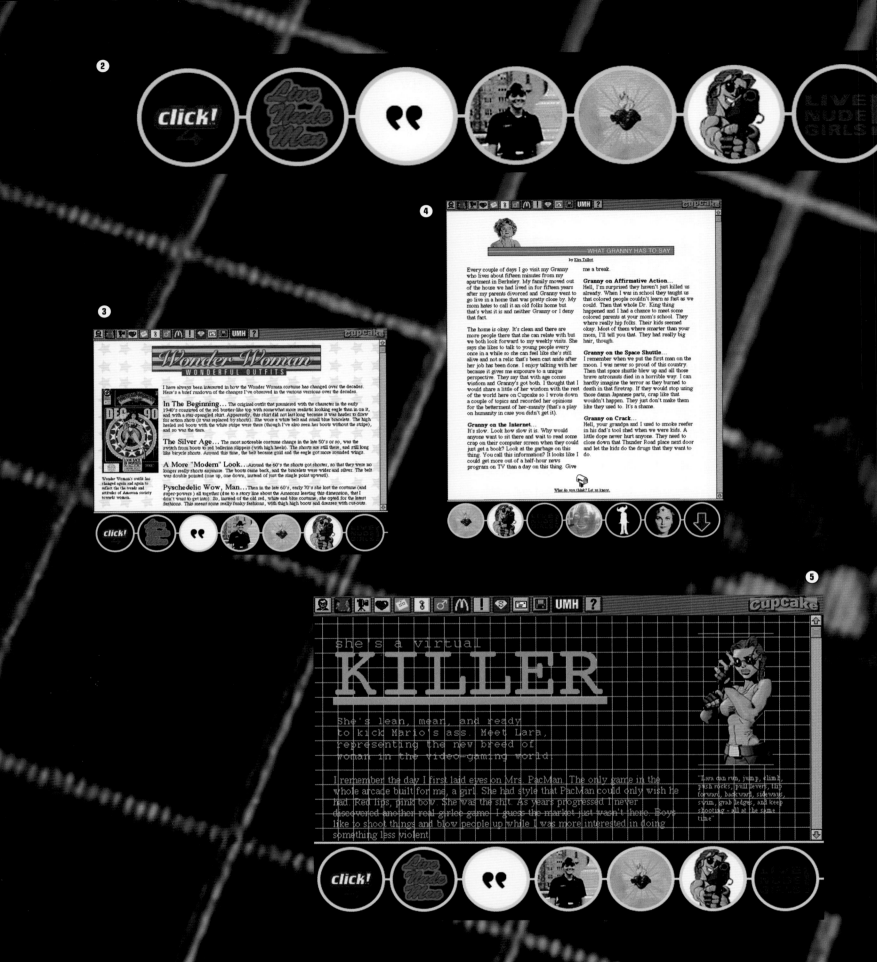

The main interface to Cupcake. Each item has a button on the string in the lower frame. They are added chronologically, never removed, and displayed nine at a time: the simplest of horizontal navigation devices.

The changes in Wonder Woman's costume are traced through the decades. In a window on the left, the comic book covers of Wonder Woman from various years scroll by.

As a kind of matron saint, Granny appears in a simple, old-fashioned 'column', where she discusses crack, the Internet, affirmative action and the space shuttle.

The text praises the merits of this rare creature, a fully fledged, female 'virtual killer' video game heroine. At closer range we can admire some images showing her in action.

154

Hell on Wheels. The animated scooters sparkle in the firmament of this tribute to a girl's old friend: her scooter.

This summer fashion panorama is typical of the site: a single, wide page which can be scrolled left to right, with no text apart from the credits at the end.

Tommy's slide show strip act, which appears when we click for a look at the readers' favourite hunk.

'The flower children' takes a serious look at the fate of child labourers in the fields of California. When scrolling down, critical responses, which are highlighted typographically, put the content into perspective.

The 'helpful hints' page is certainly one of the best-written help pages anywhere; a few seconds is all it takes to fully understand the background and workings of the site. The page breaks it down into five parts, which are explained in less than a few hundred words.

go2net

http://www.go2net.com

DESIGNER Those People / CLIENT go2net Inc. / YEAR OF DESIGN 1996 / PLACE OF DESIGN Seattle, USA / COPYRIGHT OWNER go2net Inc. / DESIGN COMPANY Those People / SCREEN DESIGN Bryan Rackleff, Rebeca Mendez, Kevin Bauer / ANIMATION/GRAPHICS Bryan Rackleff, Rebeca Mendez, Kevin Bauer, Ray Greenwell, Michael Bayne / INTERACTION DESIGN Claudia Anfuso, Bryan Rackleff, Rebeca Mendez, Kevin Bauer / PRODUCTION Claudia Anfuso, Kevin Bauer / EDITORS Stephen Rosen, Dino Christofilis, Jay Howard / CONTRIBUTORS Bill Russel, Joe Morgan, William Fleckenstein, Jennifer James, Martin Schoffstal, Paul Phillips / AWARDS Yahoo! Site of the Day, Netscape New Destinations / SOFTWARE USED Mac: Adobe Photoshop, Adobe Illustrator / DESIGN PLATFORMS Mac: 50%; unix: 50%

1

All you need to know to get started: in one flash of the eye, the homepage of go2net explains who they are, how their site works and presents the offerings of the day for the visitor. The colours given to respective sections form a navigational code throughout the site.

go2net sells itself as an interactive media network with 'a mission to provide sports, business and Internet content combining unique commentary with the latest technologies.' What they do is supply the sports fan, the edgy investor and the websurfer with facts and opinions about their respective fields of interest. The site is not only updated every day, but also every second. In a modest and intelligent way each section is equipped with a dedicated ticker keeping the latest news flowing in constantly. The user can customise the information towards his specific needs and even have a browser window — a Java applet called go2net vision — open at all times, thereby combining all the running tickers with a close-at-hand websearch function.

After the homepage the levels of information never go any deeper than three levels. This is expressed in the design of the site, which uses everyday travel symbols. The main page of the sports and business section holds an abstract image of air travel at the top of the page: you are airborne yet have minimal control. Clicking upon a topic takes you to a page with images of a freeway at the top: you have chosen a direction, but are still part of the system. When proceeding one step further pedestrian signs appear: now you have found the details you

were looking for. And all along it is a smooth and swift download. The Internet section has moon images as its main design metaphor, conveying the allusive character of cyberspace, which sparks the imagination just like outer space does.

Another remarkable feature in the images at the top of the pages is the advertisements, which are not boxed away in banners but integrated in the design. The Yahoo logo is a billboard on the side of a bus, the Converse logo a flying saucer in the sky. The advertiser has become fully part of this seductive on-line environment.

The navigation of the site is simple and easily intelligible. Although the sections are dense with information, the guidance offered by the specific icons and colours of each section, by invisible frames and conventional newspaper headlines soon makes you feel familiar and comfortable with the site. The substantial value of go2net's information delivery strategy lies not just in its savvy use of state-of-the-art web technology, but also in its smart and clear design. The result makes go2net the ideal intelligent agent for those who have an interest in these topics, whether general or specific.

Adam Eeuwens

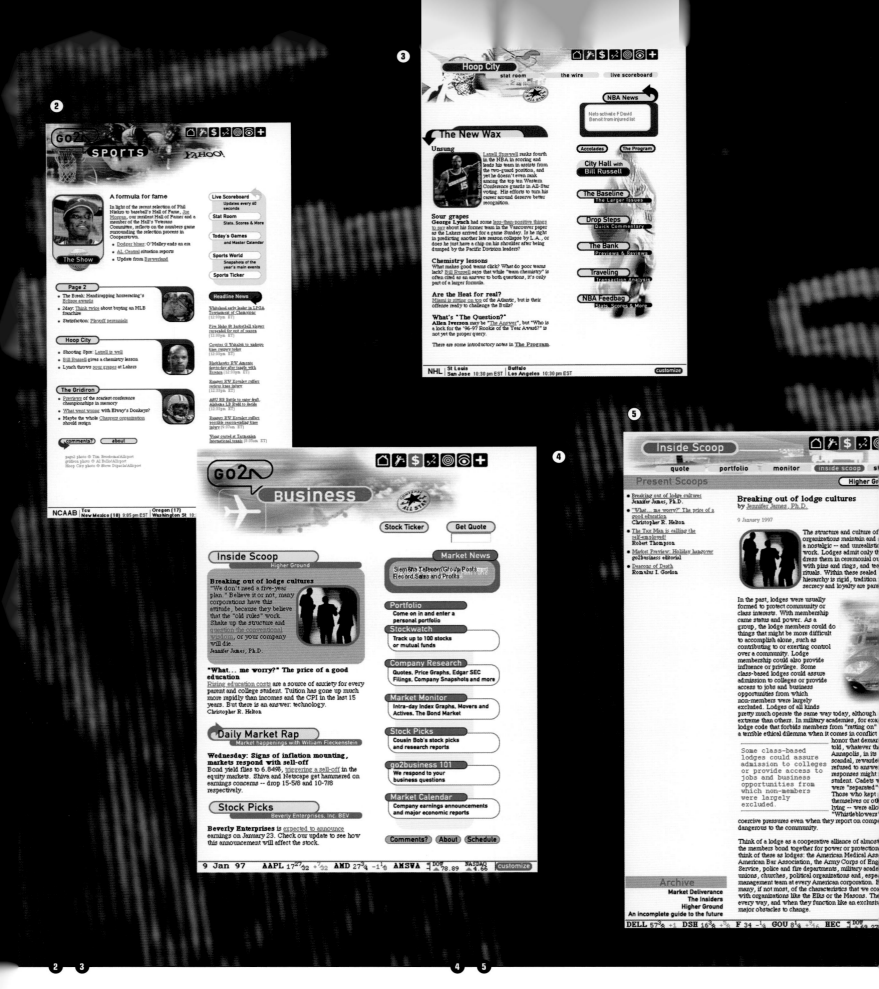

The main page of the Sports section. Headlines offer the main stories. Several active elements like the live scoreboard and the Headline News display the latest news, while the regular features of basketball, football and baseball have unmistakable icons to click on.

From the go2net logo to the subsubheads within a section, all relevant information is presented within rectangular shapes with softened edges that offer ubiquitous buttons to surf on through the information.

The main page of the Business section. The left side of the screen shows the news of the week. The main story of the day has its own introduction in a sidebar box, and the other features trail underneath. On the right the regular subsections are listed. Meanwhile two tickers — one in the upper right corner and the other at the foot of the page — keep the latest news rolling in.

The freeway runs overhead as we enter Inside Scoop, a subsection of Business. The frame to the left, occupying one third of the screen, archives past events. The article on the right has a traditional magazine layout, using pull-out quotes to make it more lively and draw you into the text.

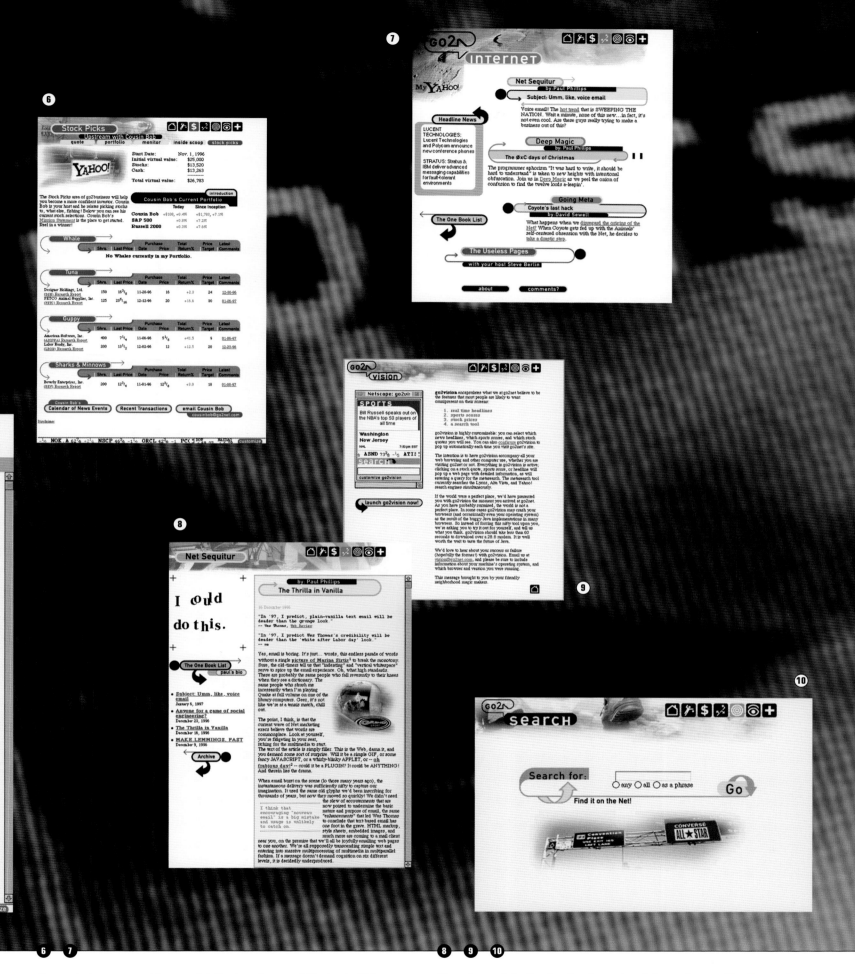

How to design a page with rows of daily changing stats? Maybe the Fish Market of go2net is the attractive solution. To get out of this statistical hell, just choose one of the seven icons always present at the top of the screen.

The main page of the Internet section. The animated black dot refers to the latest uploaded article. This section also incorporates the famous website 'Useless Pages'.

The column of the Net Sequitur is worthy of the top image of landing crafts on the moon. Underlined words in the body texts can be clicked, causing a comment or a Java joke to appear. Some serious steps into 'new journalism' can be found in this weekly updated column.

The pop-up menu of go2net vision encapsulates headlines, sports scores, stock prices and a search tool which can be customized by the user.

The search engine page of go2net, which includes their coolest incorporated advertisement: a freeway road sign with their own logo.

Netscape: dutch1.html

DUTCH

Dutch is a quarterly magazine of trends, fashion, models and lifestyle, with articles on subjects associated with these fields of interest. It is a glossy of sorts, but rather 'arty'. There is a lot of black and white on the pages of Dutch. The subdued glitter of the conventional version of Dutch has been adequately translated to the Web version of the magazine, where the Dutch logo, designed by Swip Stolk, functions as a button for indices. Although the editors state that Dutch On-line uses the characteristics of a hypermedium, the graphic design of the digital Dutch remains fairly close to the printed design. In both versions we find much white space around carefully chosen photos of models and famous people. In order to balance the image-only sections, the site contains long and sparsely illustrated articles in a stern typography.

The navigation in Dutch On-line is a little vague, because clearly different 'issues' of the magazine have been interlinked. This does enable you to browse the complete volume. Sometimes, however, it is rather difficult to return to a place once the 'index' button has brought you to another 'issue'.

Although the general feel of Dutch On-line is not that different from its printed counterpart, the Web version can – and does – benefit from the technical possibilities of the medium. The clickable time bar, introducing a trip to London, seems a rather linear way to structure material in a Web environment, but it allows you to browse the time scale in a non-linear way. In a Paris fashion update, you can see a quick follow-up of models in three frames on the same page. Furthermore, there is a page with QuickTime videos of a series of TV-ads made by Dutch for broadcasting on MTV. So now you can download advertisements at your own expense! Advertorials like these are consistent, though, with a magazine like Dutch, in which it is sometimes impossible to discern the boundaries between editorial content and ads. In the end it is all about 'elusive customers', as Dutch states in a five-point 'manifesto', who because of their nature drive marketers crazy. This manifesto reads as follows: '1: Spend time for Living 2: Accept everyone is a designer 3: Use your imagination 4: Mix Values 5: Enjoy the Results.'

Max Bruinsma

❶

A hollow-eyed model poses on Dutch's welcome page, just like the cover of an arty glossy on fashion and lifestyles. The crown, the Dutch logo, was designed by Swip Stolk.

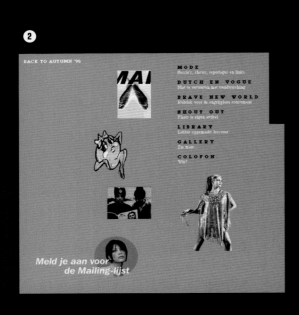

idee & uitvoering (in atomen)
Erik Kessels (29) en Johan Kramer (30)
werken in Londen als art-director en copywriter
bij GGT Advertising, regisseren via Spots
Films, doen freelance projecten zoals de nieuwe
CD-ROM voor de Raggende Mannen zijn
bereikbaar op erik@ggt.cityscape.co.uk.

fotografie Julian Germain het
veelzeggende boek 'In soccer geeft colleges aan
de Universiteit van Sunderland, heeft dit jaar
twee exposities in Nederland (Groningen en
Enschede) adoreert de Nederlandse voetbalclub
Go Ahead Eagels.

GALLERY | INDEX

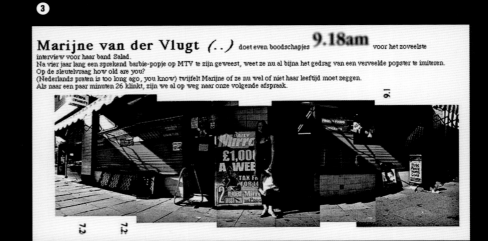

The index page, where various images link to special features and a table of contents gives access to sections like Dutch En Vogue, The Gallery and much more.

On a trip to London, Dutch visited resident Dutchfolk. The pictures are accessible from the long timeline on the opening page. As in most of Dutch On-line, the graphic design closely follows the aesthetics of the printed version of the magazine.

Dutch En Vogue is explicitly 'not trendwatching', but it does neatly sum up the ingredients with which you can compile your 'ego-mix' lifestyle. The default text in one extended column, combined with a modestly sized picture and the Dutch crown, create a classy feel.

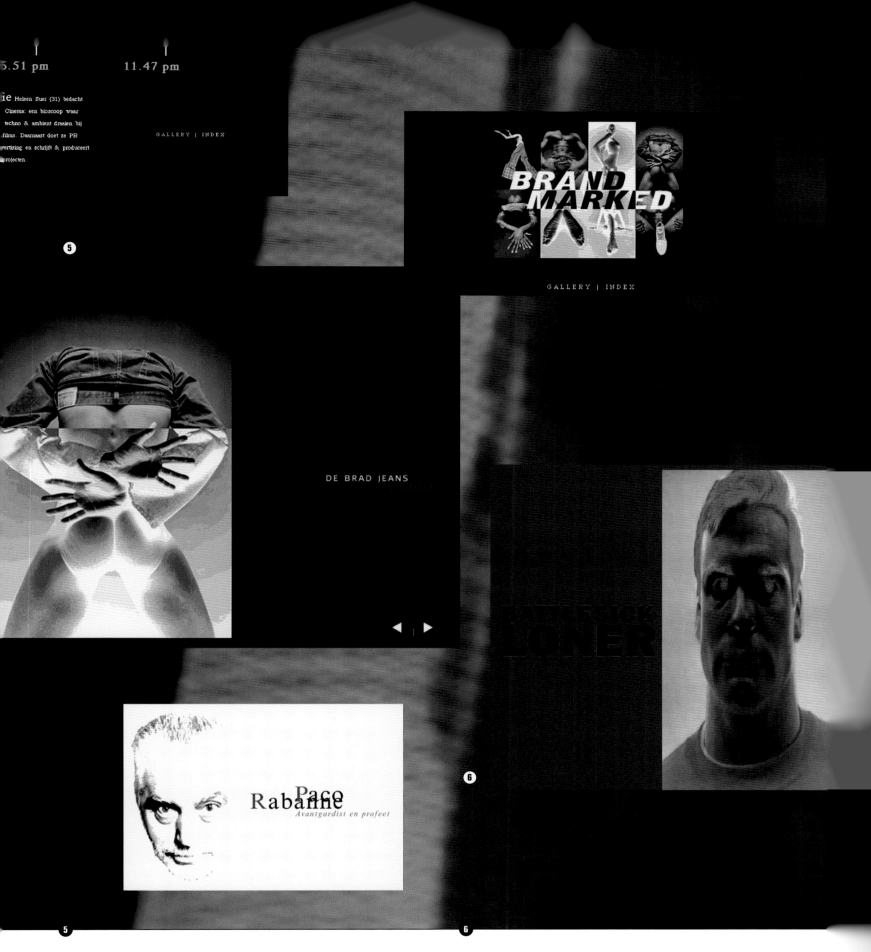

5.51 pm   11.47 pm

ie Heleen Suer (31) bedacht
Cinema: een bioscoop vaar
techno & ambient draaien bij
films. Daarnaast doet ze PR
vertising en schrijft & produceert
projecten.

❺

**BRAND
MARKED**

GALLERY | INDEX

DE BRAD JEANS

◄ ▌ ▶

❻

Paco
Rabanne
Avantgardist en profeet

❺   ❻

On the Brand Marked index page the thumbnail images of a fashion series flip between positive and negative. On the pages that follow these fashion photographs are enlarged. By loading a positive image over a negative one, a fascinating spectacle is created (the image shown here is half-way through the transformation process).

Two coverpages from the Library section introducing features on Paco Rabanne and Henry Rollins. Note the excellent use of transparent imagery, both in portraits and texts.

Word

http://www.word.com

DESIGNER ICon New media / YEAR OF DESIGN 1995 / PLACE OF DESIGN New York, USA / COPYRIGHT OWNER ICon CMT Corp. / DESIGN COMPANY ICon New Media / SCREEN DESIGN, ANIMATION/GRAPHICS, INTERACTION DESIGN Yoshi Sodeoka, Marisa Bowe, Stephen Fowler, Alix Stewart Lambert, Stephen Williams / EDITORS Marisa Bowe / CONTRIBUTORS Stephen Fowler, Alix Stewart Lambert, Stephen Williams / AWARDS Folio Award, I.D. magazine Design Annual / SOFTWARE USED Mac: Adobe Photoshop, Macromedia Director, BBEdit, Adobe Illustrator, Infini-D / DESIGN PLATFORMS Mac: 100%

1

The homepage of Word features a number of 'fresh' articles, presented by an image, an icon and a short text, and on the left-hand side a string of icons linking them to the main categories. The banner above contains two random-ised elements, adding a different mission statement and advertisement every time you log on.

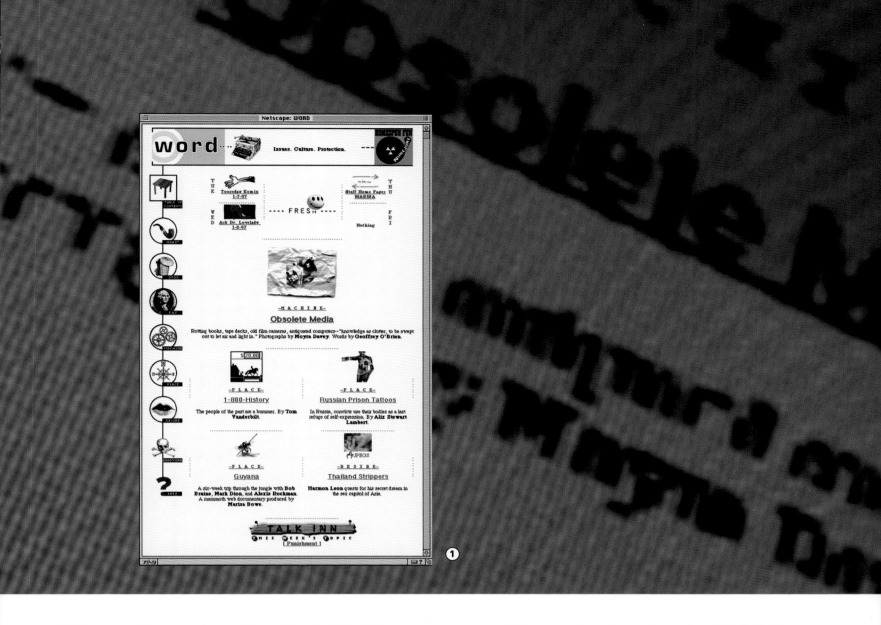

Unlike many other magazines on-line or in print, Word is not much concerned with presenting a unified style or design. Rather it is a growing collection of 'articles' on broad cultural issues, which try to create and explore writings and designs for the Web. This becomes apparent when you log on to the Word homepage. There is no coverpage presenting you with issue number so-and-so or a certain volume. Instead the main page offers a selection of 'fresh' articles, and a menu of categories or topics represented by icons along the side. This string of 'beads' provides the main interface of Word and leaves you to discover other articles for yourself.

Present as the general interface throughout the site, these icons only hint at what to expect from the individual articles. Even looking through the 'matrix' of articles on the page with the table of contents (yes, there is one) one may find it hard to deduce a fixed concept behind topics such as 'GIGO', 'Habit' or 'Machine'. However, this openness of the general concept of Word — also reflected in the ever-changing banner statement 'Word: Issues, Culture, ...?' — allows the designers to present innovative screen designs for each new project. If there is such a thing as a design strategy in Word, it lies in finding playful solutions to arranging and navigating through non-linear articles. Therefore discussing the visual design of the Word site

automatically means focusing on the variety of individual 'articles'.

For example, in the contribution by Stephen Williams on Rats the layout of the screen is the result of a continuously changing interplay of six frames. Slightly more low-key, Stephen Fowler's Salvage Culture gives a second life to old books found in a trash-can. It basically rearranges the old material into two visually attractive frames. In her production of Guyana Diary, a documentary report of the travels of three artists in Guyana, Marisa Bowe uses a set-up of five frames to combine three diaries, images and an overall navigation on one screen. The experience conveyed is that of reading through three diaries at the same time, offering multiple viewpoints on the same events. Guyana Diary is an excellently structured, and highly legible, personal account, allowing for many excursions and open ends.

The ingenious use of frames recurs in many Word articles. However in general the 'Word style' is devoid of high-tech fetishism. Real Audio and Shockwave are usually applied as a support. Generally relying on the appropriation of pre-existent visual material, Word is able to maintain a familiar feel in a very new context.

Geert J. Strengholt

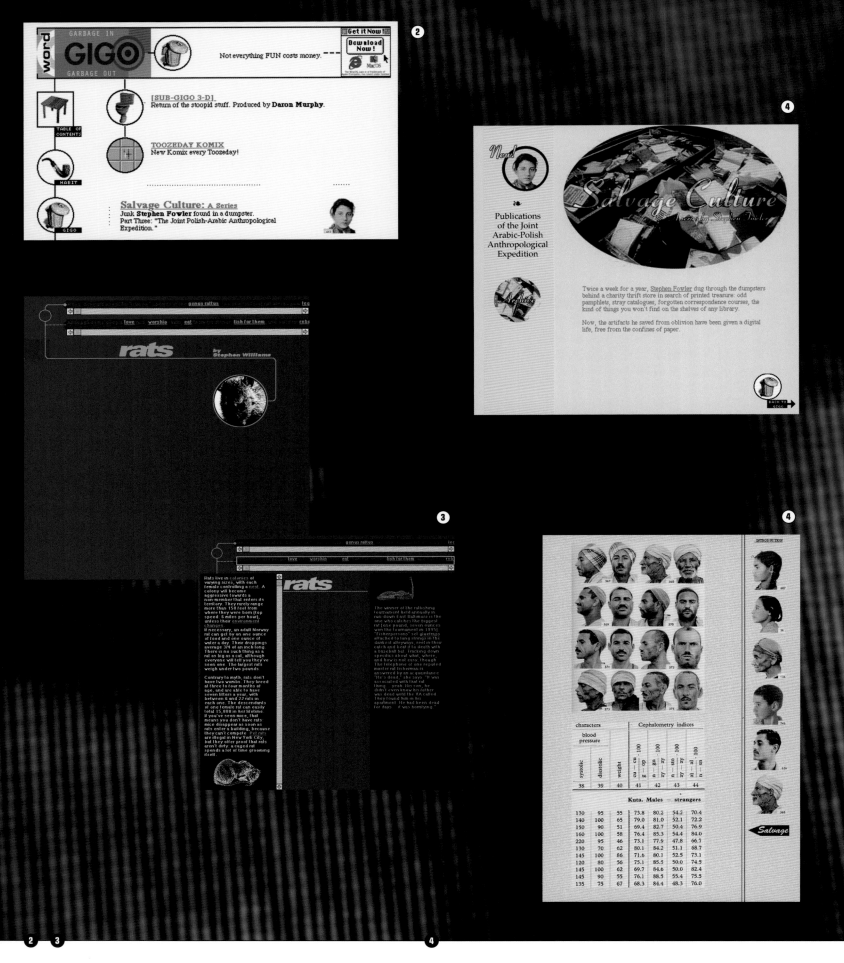

The index pages of topical categories — in this case GIGO (Garbage-in, Garbage-out) — reflect the same layout as the homepage; the icons for the other categories remain available on the left.

Watching 'Rats' build its first screen, loading bits and pieces in a construction of six invisible frames, is an amazing spectacle. The primary interface for the piece are the two panoramically scrolling lines of text. The links within these lines load other texts and images in the three frames on the lower side of the screen, which in turn also contain cross-reference links.

Salvaged from a dump store wastebin, this report from a Polish anthropological expedition to west Egypt has gained a second life in hypertext setting. Clicking the string of images on the right loads actual pages in the left-hand frame.

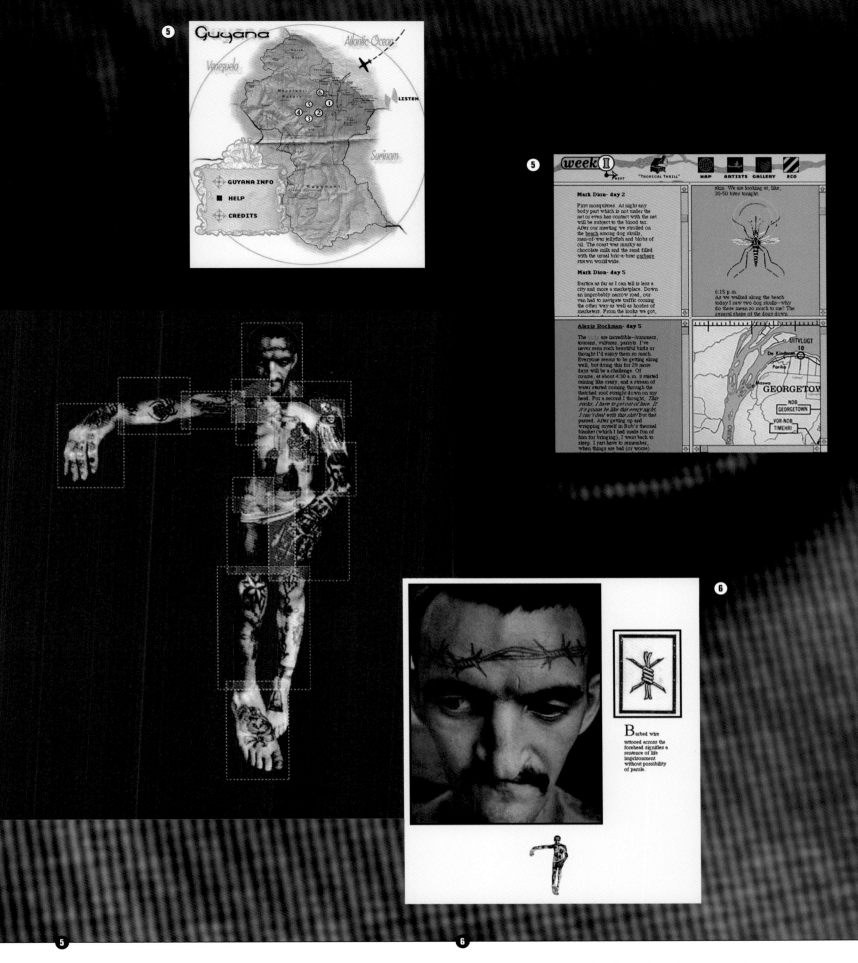

The main page for Guyana Diaries is this (image)map. An animated GIF projects the route of the incoming flight. The artists spent a week in each of the places marked 1 to 6, and clicking on them will take you to their weekly Diary reports. The Diary page is composed of five frames, a top-frame for general navigation, three for diary entries and the remaining frame for images available through links in the diaries.

In his exposé on tattoo practices in Russian prisons — an underground tradition in which tattoos symbolically proclaim the background and rank of the wearer — Alix Stewart Lambert presents this 'body map' to navigate through a collection of examples. Each tattoo is clearly illustrated and its meaning explained in detail.

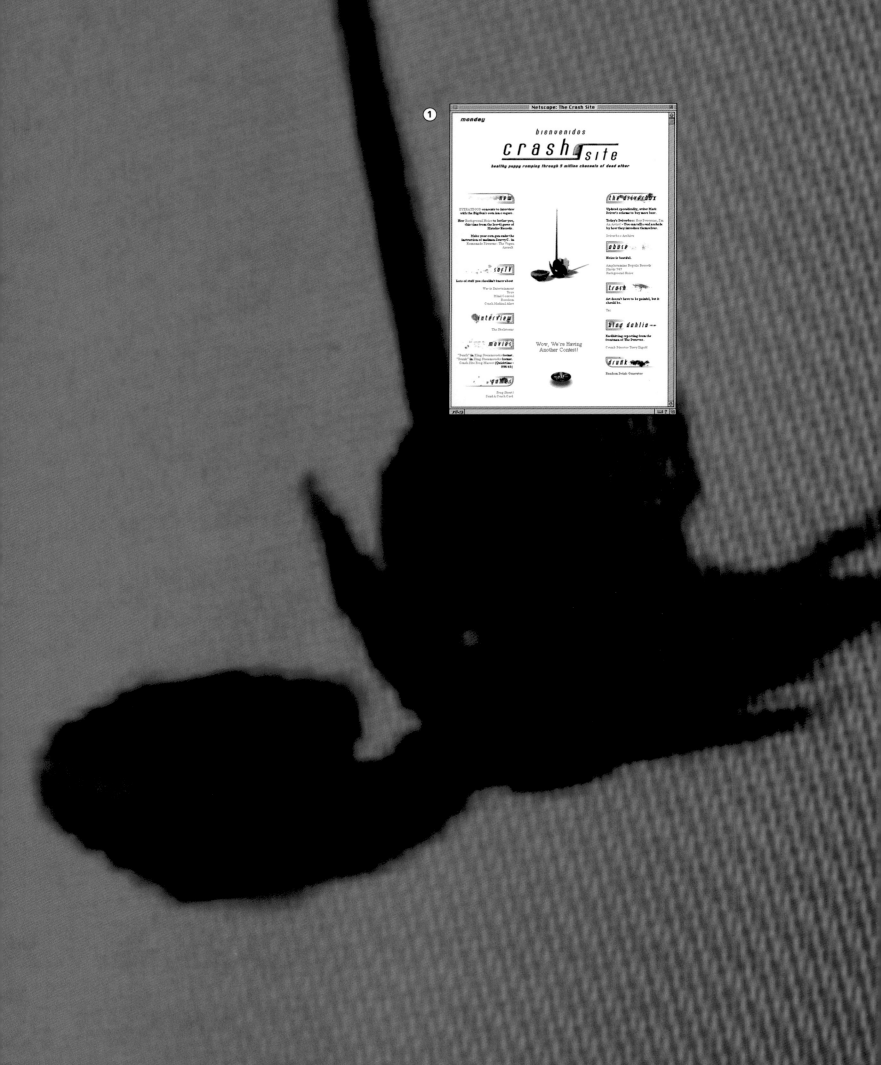

The Crash Site
http://www.crashsite.com

DESIGNER rNzone Inc. / YEAR OF DESIGN 1995 / PLACE OF DESIGN Santa Monica, USA / COPYRIGHT OWNER rNzone Inc. / DESIGN COMPANY rNzone Inc. / SCREEN DESIGN Gibron Evans, Jim Evans ANIMATION/GRAPHICS Gibron Evans / INTERACTION DESIGN Ian Rogers, Vince Koser / SOUND DESIGN Mark Driver / PRODUCTION Michael Siegel, Jim Evans, Gibron Evans, Ian Rogers, Mark Driver, Michael Blume / EDITORS Mark Tyson, Jim Evans / CONTRIBUTORS Patrick Delaney, Ray Robin, Jay Babcock, John Ulf / AWARDS Cool Site of the Day on April 18 1995, September 1995 Nominated for Cool Site of the Year, PC Magazine — Top 100 Web Sites, A Project Cool Sighting, Amsterdam Valley Banquet, Cyber-Toilet's Pick of the Week, Cool Central — Cool Site of the Hour / SOFTWARE USED Non-linear: Electric Image; Adobe After Effects, Adobe Photoshop, Adobe Illustrator, Wdf (Procustor Professional); sgi: Pearl; msg: Java Workshop / DESIGN PLATFORMS Mac: 80%; sgi: 10%; sgi: 10%

This is one of the weirdest e-zines around. It aims at what one might call a 'Verelendung' by overconsumption of filth, boredom, violence and immorality. The editors consider themselves to be 'Common Sense Hardliners', stating that 'America is sick (and) heading for a huge Crash.' The Crash Site was started in an attempt 'to accelerate the decline any way it can, and hopes to position itself somewhere in the middle of the New Republic once America is rebuilt.' The site must be the ultimate fanzine for the 'faces-of-death' generation, with information on how to construct homemade firearms, music from 'Cool Starving Bands', interviews with 'Total Freaks', and much RealAudio, Streaming Video and QuickTime Clips. With all this, The Crash Site takes a lot of time to download, but you can read the text while the pictures load.

The design reflects the target audience as closely as do the subjects and the lingo: many images with skulls, bodies cut open, bloodstains, distorted heads – in short, the usual post-modern-mannerist-youth-culture grotesqueness. The Crash Site has all these elements, and a lot more, in a graphic design that is as consistent as stainless steel. The logos, illustrations and navigation bars are all carefully designed and do not clutter the pages. Actually, it is rather amazing that a site of this kind has any white or empty space at all! This one does, and it makes the weird virtuosity of the designers stand out. Check their 'Masturbatory Graphical Interface', with the most ridiculously elaborate moving, turning and glistening buttons you have ever seen. For the 'monkeys' (those surfers with archaic web browsers) there is a text-based interface, which offers the choice of three different ways to access the huge stack of material on The Crash Site.

Underneath all the blatantly immoral stuff about Hot Supermodel Sniper Action one can detect a genuine concern regarding the state of the nation. Behind the smiling dictator portraits on the 'War is entertainment' page, for instance, there is concise but serious information about their demonic deeds and a clear condemnation. Although the editors explain how to make a 'Potato Gun', they make it clear that they would not be so infinitely stupid to use such a thing. Do not say that The Crash Site did not warn you: 'If you still have questions, you are very dumb. Turn off your computer and do something simple, like watching TV.'

Max Bruinsma

❶

The opening slogan, which changes daily, sets the tone for this e-zine for Generation X. An animated GIF shows a pendulum decapitating a small frog. This page is one of three interfaces to the wealth of material on the site.

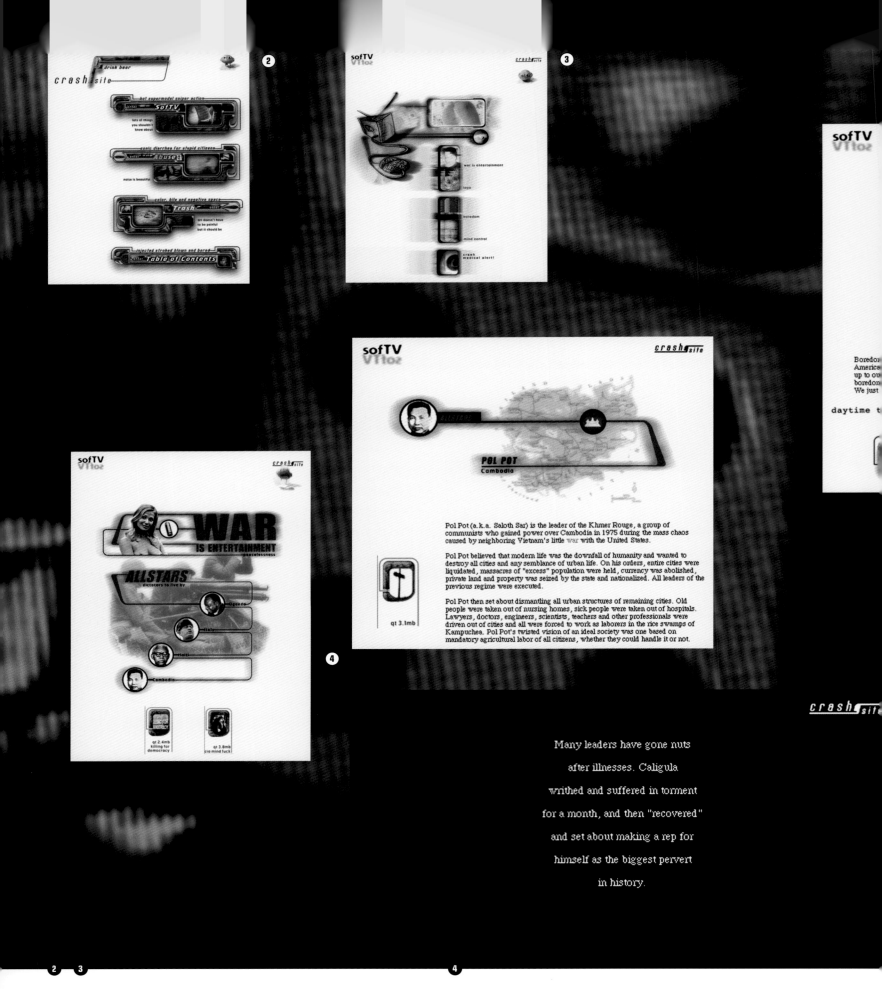

This stainless steel, machine-gun design prompts you with SofTV, Abuse and Trash when you click the 'Masturbatory Graphical Interface' button on the homepage. Shrapnel of imagery is intricately worked together to form entrance pieces to these sections.

The TV as a piece of fruitcake, wired to a disembodied brain. The associations with 'brain drain' are further worked out in the 'boredom' section. Behind this page there are also historical updates on the most cruel dictators ever, a 'how-to-make-your-own-bazooka' (with potatoes as ammunition) and a practical course in psychological torture.

4

Cynicism is the trademark of the 'faces-of-death' generation, and of The Crash Site. The 'entertainment' behind the portraits of the ultra-mass-murderers on these pages, however, consists of the raw facts of theirbelligerent careers. No more, no less.

boredom.

...tion that motivates. Fear of boredom is probably the biggest driver of the ...We arrange our lives so that we are entertained from the second we wake ...s until we fall asleep watching television. Not that this is a bad thing. If ...able state, nothing would ever get done and nothing would ever get created. ...reful that our antidotes for boredom aren't killing us.

...on

drunk-o-matic

Hello drunk, you are pathetic. It's OK, we are too. We're so pathetic, in fact, that we've grown beyond all our bar books and have created a bunch of our own drinks. Realizing that the taste of a drink becomes less and less important as the night (or afternoon) goes on, our alcohol soaked brains became clouded in apathy, and we programmed a random drink generator.

we play it this way

Roll a die (yes, you can use your 20 sided attack die, you geek). The number on the face is the number of times the "reload" button gets hit. The drink that sits on the page is what EVERYONE MUST DRINK! NO EXCEPTIONS!

disclaimer

This is not a game for the weak, if you are a wuss, go play the 90210 drinking game with wine coolers or something.

Misunderstood Bed Sheet

2 oz. Dark Rum
4 oz. Brandy
5 oz. Water
1 oz. Triple Sec
1 Pineapple Slices
3 shakes Ground Black Pepper

background noise

NOISE
AMPHETAMINE
SLAVIC 747
EYEHATEGOD

TRASH TAZ

A POSTER A DAY FROM T.A.Z.

THE "STORY"

Boredom as the American 'condition humaine' is analysed behind the link 'daytime television'. It is a lengthy report on a regular nine-to-five day of zapping through the available channels and staring at too much of nothing.

The introduction page of the music section of The Crash Site, with RealAudio clips to listen to while you read, and updates on the site's favourite 'cool starving bands' and record labels. File under: 'loud 'n raw'.

The visual arts section of The Crash Site, with a portfolio of works and a story by poster designer TAZ.

The 'drunk-o-matic' seems to be an effective way of getting drunk while still maintaining an appearance of 'savoir vivre'. Clicking the 'new drink' button reveals one exuberant drink after the other. For the really careless there is a game: roll a dice and drink the given amount of different drinks from the 'drunk-o-matic'.

You may remember the improbable scenes from futuristic movies of the fifties and sixties. A large screen in somebody's ultra high-tech apartment lights up and a soft voice croons: 'welcome, what can I do for you?'. Then the film character orders a bottle of champagne on ice, glasses, caviar — 'and oh yes, I'll be needing a car for tomorrow, what are your options?'

Today this scenario is very close to being realised in the average home. You still cannot talk to most computers, but you can do the rest. On-line shopping is the Next Big Thing, if we are to believe the marketers, and the only thing that prevents its total instant success is the problem of identification and payment on-line. Countless whizzkids are working on watertight theft-proof digital cash systems, so that minor bugs will probably be solved in the near future. Then we can all go shopping on the Net with a pocket full of cyberbucks. Right now you can purchase flowers, **PCs,** stock photos, clothes, domestic decorations and much more via the World Wide Web. You can browse the digital shops just like the floors of a department store, picking up things here and there, and at the end emptying your basket at the counter. At that point the illusion of walking a shop floor usually stops: there is nothing to take away, and you have to fill in lengthy forms with your name, address, telephone and fax numbers, credit card data, e-mail account... After that you have to wait for the shopkeeper to call you back for confirmation. Finally you pay by credit card or money order and wait for delivery. These are minor problems which only come to your attention at the end of your shopping experience. Before that, the sites do their very best to look like real shops. There is entertainment in the large warehouses, updates on trends and little games to please the children. Every screen tries to be a shop window, displaying glamorous products. The interfaces sometimes literally imitate the signposting of the physical sites. Then you see the elevator lights at the top of your screen, indicating which floor you are on, or the neon signs that tell you in which direction to go for the domestic department. Other sites look more like the advertisements on the pages of 'door-to-door' papers, embellished with many moving dots, flashy letters and rotating pictograms that approach you saying: 'order now for the holidays!' Like in the real world there's upmarket and downmarket shopping on the Web.

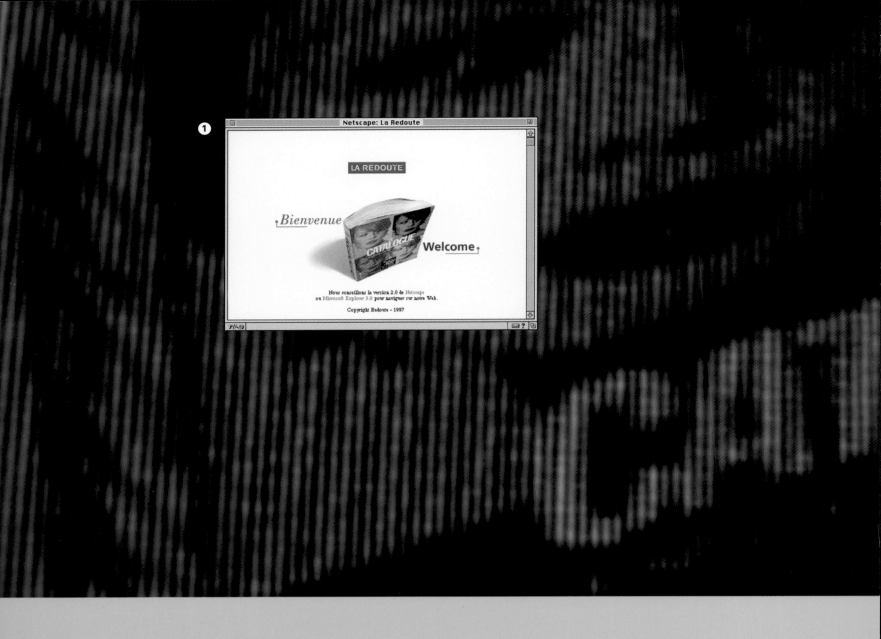

La Redoute

http://www.redoute.fr

DESIGNER Netforce / CLIENT La Redoute / YEAR OF DESIGN 1996 / PLACE OF DESIGN Roubaix, France / COPYRIGHT OWNER La Redoute / DESIGN COMPANY Netforce / SCREEN DESIGN Christophe Lombart / ANIMATION/GRAPHICS Christophe Lombart / INTERACTION DESIGN Christophe Lombart / PRODUCTION Henri Lenfant, Olivier Lombart / EDITORS Olivier Lombart, Catherine Paris / SOFTWARE USED Mac: Adobe After Effects, DeBabelizer, Claris Homepage 2.0, MPC: NET OBJECT FUSION, FRONT PAGE 97 / DESIGN PLATFORMS MAC: 50%, MPC: 50%

1

This clear and simple front door of the site welcomes you in to browse and shop. From the outset the aims of the site are clear. It acts as an on-line companion to the 1,200-page La Redoute catalog.

No hassles, no crowds, no endless search for a sales clerk... Welcome to the digital domain, where you can indulge in a care-free virtual shopping experience, provided you speak French. La Redoute is oriented towards a French consumer market, with a predominantly female audience in mind. It is a hybrid site, functioning as an on-line shopping mall, a women's consumer magazine and a corporate showcase. For those users still queasy about parting with their e-cash and purchasing goods on-line, this site offers additional light entertainment and information about the company.

A good deal of the graphic style of the printed La Redoute cata-log is echoed here. From the start the splash screen of the site features the printed catalog, and throughout there are plenty of crisp white pages with short paragraphs of description accom-panying the product photos. In fact, in the Miss Web magazine section it becomes apparent that the site functions as a com-panion to the printed catalog. In view of the fact that the catalog is printed biannually, the website is a valuable service that complements La Redoute's existing mail-order business, giving a range of special offers that refer to specific pages in the printed version.

The omnipresent navigation panel has a simple column of icons which take you either to the homepage, the catalog or the point where you can check the contents of your virtual shopping bag. When you select a product you wish to purchase, the shopping bag bulges, so you instantly know that it has registered your order. At the bottom of the navigation panel there is a small directional arrow. This comes to life once you have delved through sufficient levels of information away from the main menus. Three-dimensional cones allow you to travel between screens in a simple way until you reach another menu or a set of options within the main screen.

The corporate showcase offers a series of pages packed with facts and figures centering around the history and international development of this huge mail-order company. A more playful area of the site is the Miss Web magazine. Here the site produ-cers have included chatty questionnaires which, based on your answers, offer a range of responses which sum up your charac-ter. It also includes a selection of topical articles with a variety of links to other relevant sites. All these features allow for plenty of interplay between the user and the information on offer.

Sophie Greenfield

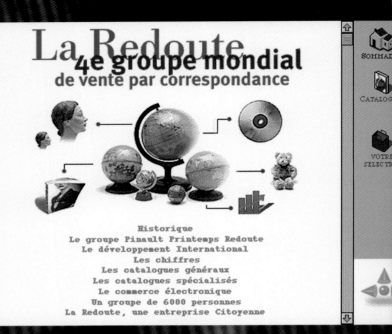

The centerpiece of the homepage is the animated, illustrative header composed of visual elements extrapolated from the La Redoute printed catalog. From the clear design it is immediately obvious how the information within the site is divided.

The main menu for the corporate showcase section of the site uses a graphic image map at the head of the page, which includes icons representing the global influence of its marketing and the diversity of its products. The tripartite navigation panel is introduced here.

The linear timeline acts as a concrete mapping device, condensing the history of the company into an easily digestible form. The icons along the line represent highlights and notable events in the history of the company, which are further explored by scrolling down the flowing paragraphs of the text.

Fun, informal, young... the top end of the Miss Web magazine presents a collage of snippets of gossip, cross-references to the printed catalog and a questionnaire to give the user a sense of involvement in the information.

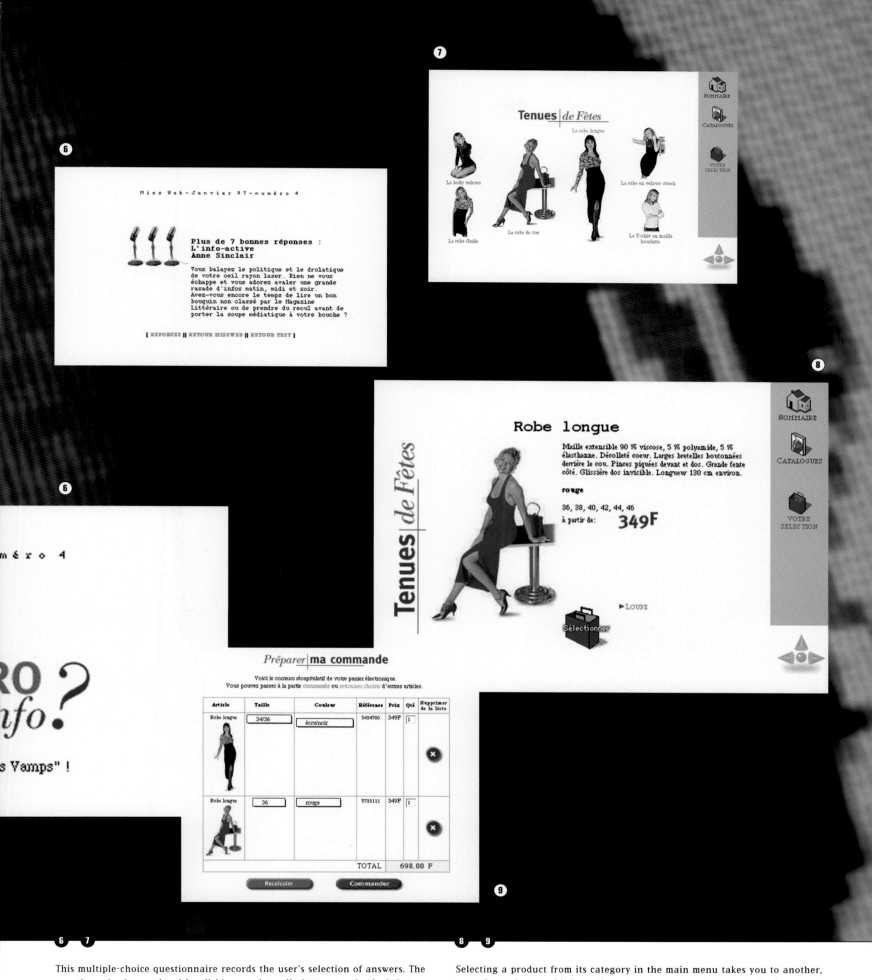

Miss Web-Janvier 97-numéro 4

**Plus de 7 bonnes réponses :
L'info-active
Anne Sinclair**

Vous balayez le politique et le drolatique
de votre oeil rayon laser. Rien ne vous
échappe et vous adorez avaler une grande
rasade d'infos matin, midi et soir.
Avez-vous encore le temps de lire un bon
bouquin non classé par le Magazine
Littéraire ou de prendre du recul avant de
porter la soupe médiatique à votre bouche ?

[REPONSES || RETOUR MISSWEB || RETOUR TEST]

Tenues | *de Fêtes*

La robe longue

Le body velours

La robe fluide

La robe de star

La robe en velours stretch

Le T-shirt en maille
bouclette

SOMMAIRE

CATALOGUES

VOTRE
SELECTION

Robe longue

Maille extensible 90 % viscose, 5 % polyamide, 5 %
élasthanne. Décolleté coeur. Larges bretelles boutonnées
derrière le cou. Pinces piquées devant et dos. Grande fente
côté. Glissière dos invisible. Longueur 130 cm environ.

rouge

36, 38, 40, 42, 44, 46

à partir de: **349F**

▶LOUPE

Sélectionner

Tenues | *de Fêtes*

SOMMAIRE

CATALOGUES

VOTRE
SELECTION

Préparer | **ma commande**

Voici le contenu récapitulatif de votre panier électronique.
Vous pouvez passer à la partie commande ou retourner choisir d'autres articles.

Article	Taille	Couleur	Référence	Prix	Qté	Supprimer de la liste
Robe longue	34/36	écru/noir	5434700	349F	1	✕
Robe longue	36	rouge	5733111	349F	1	✕
				TOTAL	698.00 F	

Recalculer   Commander

This multiple-choice questionnaire records the user's selection of answers. The
questionnaire is completed by clicking on the radio buttons and submitting
the set of answers at the end. A response is swiftly returned, correlating with
the user's input.

From the top level of the Catalogs section you can quickly survey the main
categories of merchandise on offer. They range from clothing for adults and
children to electronics and furniture. Selecting a category takes you to a
more detailed level of information where you can make your purchases.

Selecting a product from its category in the main menu takes you to another,
more focused page of information where you can order the goods. You can
also take a closer look by clicking on the magnifying button, allowing you to
double check the items before deciding to make a purchase.

This is the easy-to-read, easy-to-use order form. A concise oblong box is all
that is needed to finalise your on-line purchase. Small vignettes of the items
you have stored and selected along the way appear in the top left of the form.
If you want to change your mind, you can simply edit your selection.

PhotoDisc
http://www.photodisc.com

Some Web presences make more sense than others. PhotoDisc.com is a prime example of a service better provided through the medium of the Web, making life easier for all parties involved. Imagebroker PhotoDisc publishes over 50,000 images on-line for graphic designers, advertising agencies, desktop publishers and other communications professionals and enthusiasts. They offer digital stock photography available at a click of the mouse, easily beating the time-consuming process of having to order the CD-ROM, or worse: flicking through pounds of dusty catalogs, then calling a pushy representative who sends a delicate slide along with a cut-throat contract in which you are always screwed. Those days are over. 'Register, search & download', 'Right here. Right Now'. Who would want it any other way?

The PhotoDisc website is roughly divided into three topical areas. Each area focuses on different information needs. The first area is concerned with 'image (re)search' and 'download', the core functions of the site. A useful feature is the search function for an image, which accurately finds all the relevant pictures and lists them in a small, but still clear GIF format, making the choice swift and easy. In addition, you are not burdened with a download time of many minutes, waiting for the page to fill with hundreds of pictures from a subsection. You are only given a few, and have the choice to continue browsing.

Quite an accomplishment is the way in which the presented material gives all the information you need, with a too low re-solution to be copied and stolen. Elegant words, capturing the essence of a subsection, are highlighted in various ways, ranging from distorted type, as if in a whirlpool, to hazy words that gradually become clear. This offers a friendly, non-obtrusive touch to the core information.

The two other sections of the site contain information relevant to both designers and photographers and are best described as 'e-zines'. Photographers' portfolios along with interviews are presented here, enriching the value and feel of the particular stock. The PhotoDisc company is described in the final section. The aim of the makers is 'to maintain the leading role in the development and publication of innovative, high-quality material for the digital publishing and multimedia markets.' Their site does not have a glitzy state-of-the-art high-tech design, but a sober, to-the-point and user-friendly navigation design which will gratify its professional users. Sticking to functionality is the main principle of database design, while the focus of webdesign is entertainment and interaction. The PhotoDisc site manages to merge these two principles successfully.

Adam Eeuwens

①

The PhotoDisc homepage: a textbook example. The top banner states clearly what is to be found in this site. The picture is attractive and inviting, the headlines tell all and the subheaders list the current attractions. At the bottom the index bar is clearly designed.

One of the two e-zines to be found in PhotoDisc.com. This has a layout focusing on the index/contents page. Soft colours have been chosen to avoid imposing unnecessary information upon the visitor.

A small animation of photo-related images runs next to the title. Soft focus images represent sections of the second e-zine of the site, of which two features are raised to offer more exposure. The 'Wait, where am I' remark at the bottom is handy, reminding the visitor which link is being viewed.

No need to feel threatened by the prospect of accessing the 50,000 pictures in stock, as the opening page of the image library has been kept quiet and serene, with a concise reference bar in the left frame.

After selecting a field of interest three hyperlinks are available to access further information. If you leave the page untouched for a moment, samples of images run by like a slide show, while the words flow in like neon signs.

After following a hyperlink a second browser window opens to display the information. When the actual images are presented there is no need for embellishments, just a modest design.

The Image Finder leaves little room for misunderstanding to arise. However, if it does the central question mark cannot be missed.

After a search all available results are listed next to an order form which does not finalise the deal, but places the picture in the shopping cart. A pop-up menu allows you to opt for high or low resolution and decide about the kind of deal you wish to make.

A wide variety of background images from the collection appears as a slide show in the side bar to the left.

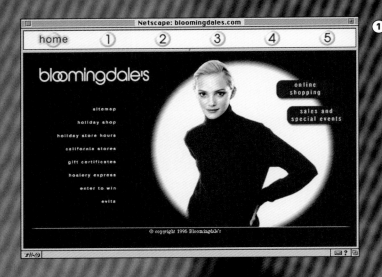

Bloomingdale's
http://www.bloomingdales.com

DESIGNER Think New Ideas Inc. / CLIENT Bloomingdale's / YEAR OF DESIGN 1996 / PLACE OF DESIGN New York, USA / COPYRIGHT OWNER Bloomingdale's / DESIGN COMPANY Think New Ideas Inc. / SCREEN DESIGN Noah Brown, Valerie Hallier, Joe Suarez, Fabian Tabiblan / ANIMATION/GRAPHICS, INTERACTION DESIGN Noah Brown, Valerie Hallier / PRODUCTION Noah Brown, Valerie Hallier / EDITORS Michael Petry, Doa Oliver, Valerie Hallier, Joe Suarez, Fabian Tabiblan / CONTRIBUTORS Jackie Natter, Lawrence Rubin, Helena Fogarty / SOFTWARE USED Mac: Adobe Illustrator, Adobe Photoshop, BBEdit, Netscape 3.0, WebMap, Transparency, Pixel Spy, Macromedia Director / DESIGN PLATFORMS Mac: 100%

1

The homepage introduces the general interface to the site in the top frame, which remains visible throughout. Mousing over the 'floor numbers' gives an indication of the 'floor contents', and clicking takes you there. In order to navigate further into each section (and for visitors whose browser does not support frames), there are carefully designed links on the pages which are loaded in the lower frame.

A 19th-century fad — the hoop-skirt — was the reason that the brothers Lyman and Joseph Bloomingdale started an enterprise that was to become a true department store by the turn of the century. In the spirit of Lyman Bloomingdale — who was never shy about creating a splash — Bloomingdale's is moving into new territory more than a century later.

The feel of Bloomingdale's site is a combination of tradition and innovation. Reminiscent of the elevators in the traditional stores, the main interface, present in the top-frame throughout the site, gives access to six main 'departments'. Almost like a real elevator display it clearly indicates, through a series of animations triggered by 'mouse-overs', what is to be found on each 'floor'. Further navigation is integrated into the pages that follow. Through the use of frames the site is very coherent and its structure extremely clear.

The main department here — what else could it be — is the on-line shopping facility. Like an on-line variation on the department store index, an image-map provides the necessary guide to divisions such as 'for him', 'for her', 'for kids', 'the home' or 'the fragrance shop'. Plain but graphically well-arranged links on a deeper level refer to the individual products. At present shopping is limited to ordering by fax or phone, but these pages offer some general product information and prices. Buttons provide links for ordering products or further navigation to other departments. The shopping section is expanded on level 3, where information on sales is to be found.

On the '5th floor' we are presented with a site map, which seems to indicate a much larger site than one might have expected upon entering. Links to corporate information are easiest to find here. The news department on the '6th floor' seems to be the playground for designers to experiment with new tricks. Links to news items currently consist of animations triggered by 'mouse-overs', which work fascinatingly well.

Overall, the design of the site is well balanced in its use of images and text (throughout fixed in Helvetica). Especially commendable is the fact that there is no noticeable doubling of navigation, thanks to the non-obtrusive design of buttons and links in the individual pages (necessary for people who have browsers without frames). The site creates an open and dynamic impression, and new additions (such as a search option) are currently being developed.

Geert J. Strengholt

The entrance to the main shopping section provides a kind of virtual 'floor plan', which as an image map leads the visitor to various departments.

This page, showing the fragrance department, displays a clear arrangement of the brands and products available. As in most other pages the general layout uses borderless and hence invisible tables.

The product pages come with images displaying the products and information about sizes and prices, and of course the order button. For an easy navigation backwards and forwards to other departments additional buttons are provided at the bottom of the page.

By taking a glance at the site map in the Explore section, an elaborate graphical representation of the entire site, the visitor is able to locate pages which could easily be passed by when using the general navigation tools.

Aside from corporate info and history, one of the things to be found through the site map is the information on the Bloomingdale's card. As on all other pages, the designers have chosen to fix the font in Helvetica, overriding the user's font settings.

The most frequently updated section of the site is News, which introduces the latest items in the Bloomingdale's collection in new and surprising ways. Mouse-overs trigger GIF animations in some of the icons linking to individual News features. Most of these features, like the cK Barbie, relate to new products and provide links back to the relevant department.

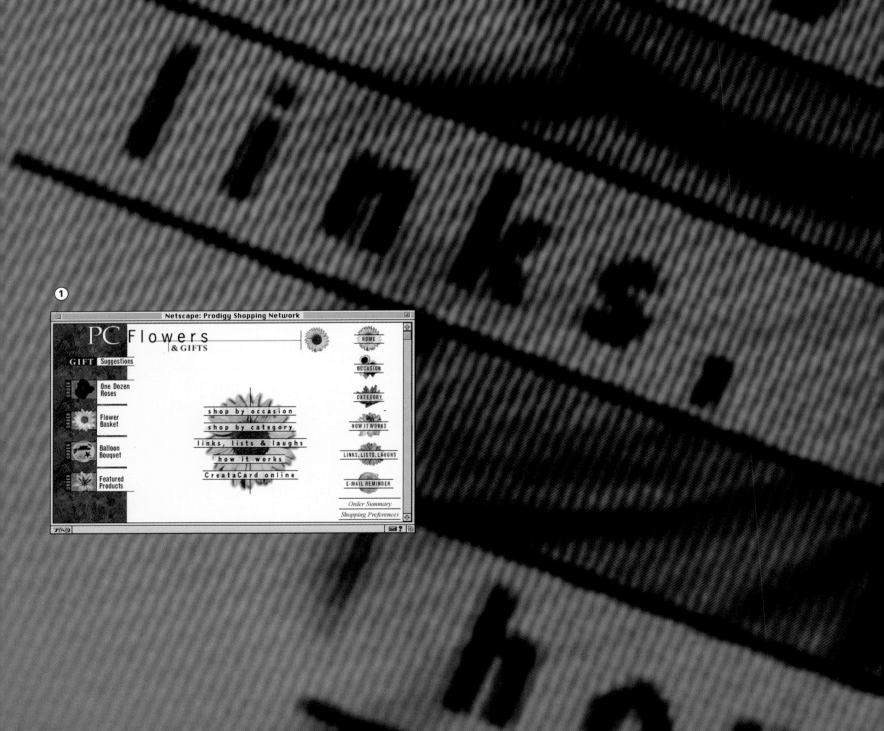

❶

PC Flowers & Gifts

http://www.pcflowers.com

DESIGNER Online Business Associates / CLIENT PC Flowers & Gifts Inc., / YEAR OF DESIGN 1994; site was redesigned by Online Business Associates in 1996 / PLACE OF DESIGN Stamford / COPYRIGHT OWNER PC Flowers & Gifts Inc., / DESIGN COMPANY Online Business Associates / SCREEN DESIGN Craig Spurrier / ANIMATION/GRAPHICS Craig Spurrier / INTERACTION DESIGN/PROGRAMMING Alfred Werner, Paul Delano / SOUND DESIGN Deborah Gilbert / PRODUCTION Online Business Associates / EDITORS Patti Ann McAdams / AWARDS 1993 Outstanding Achievement Award, 1996 Best Online Application Award / SOFTWARE USED Mac: Adobe Photoshop, Adobe Illustrator, WebMap, Alpha, design platforms, Mac: 20%, Sgi: 80%

Shopping on the Net can be a daunting experience. There are a tremendous number of on-line catalogs out there trying to get at your e-cash. After wading through a range of drab on-line catalogs or squinting at miniature pictures and meager product ranges, it is a joy to find a welcoming, organised site. PC Flowers & Gifts is a good example of the potential success of on-line marketing. It started as an on-line ordering service as far back as 1989. Today, it is a user-friendly cyber-flower shop where you can buy cuddly toys, order gift baskets and get present ideas.

This site presents you with clearly illustrated information about a concise collection of products. Right from the homepage, the site displays a right-hand column of six flowers on which it hangs its section signposts. Select a flower and an enlarged version appears in the main window, presenting a menu of gift options and further information. As you navigate from one visual, hierarchical menu to the next, you can explore the range of products and home in on the specific item you wish to purchase. For each teddy bear, gift basket or bouquet of flowers featured, there is a large photograph accompanied by an informative text description. This is vital when viewing merchandise for which you hardly have any physical clues to go by. In this case, however, slow modems are a drawback, because the majority of the product information comes to you as a collection of illustrative photography.

Finding and selecting the products you want from the site is a simple process. After all, you are in a medium-sized gift shop, not in a cavernous book shop like Amazon, which features 'a million books', and so requires a comprehensive search engine. At PC Flowers, you are only ever a couple of clicks away from your virtual shopping basket, where you can survey the goods you have selected. The purchase forms are clear and straightforward, although mostly geared toward the US market.

In many on-line shopping malls, the crunch comes when you have to pay. Many sites warn you that they do not have any specific security measures to protect your transactions. At this site you are reassured that the purchase and order forms are secure documents and are 'encrypted for privacy while in transit'. You also get ample assurance that the goods will be delivered on time to the destination you specify. PC Flowers even offers a gift reminder service so you do not forget your favourite aunt's birthday. All this flower shop needs is a scratch-and-sniff option.

Sophie Greenfield

❶

The style of the page headers mixes bold, roman, serif and sans-serif fonts. The yellow flower at the top signifies the homepage, while all the other flowers in the scrolling panel function as section identifiers and menu icons. This scrolling panel is consistently positioned at the right of the screen, allowing for simple, speedy navigation of the site.

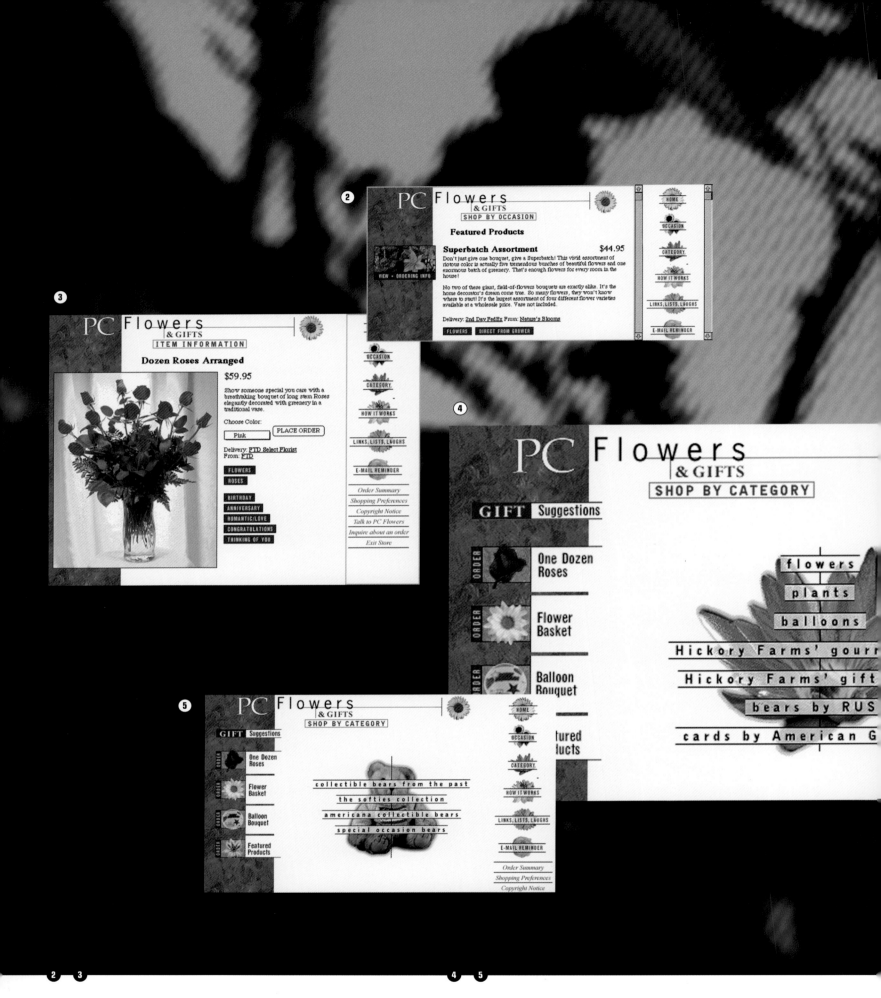

Selecting one of the quick reference icons to the left of the homepage takes you to a cross-section of items for sale, avoiding a lengthy selection process.

At this location you can place an order for either pink, red or white roses or go on to explore the other items on offer. Dispensing with the repeatedly used 'shopping basket or shopping trolley' metaphors, this site has simple 'order' buttons that take you to a page where you confirm the items you want to buy. From there you can either go on to the 'checkout' or return to the homepage to continue your shopping spree.

This page shows a list of gift categories. A clear, illustrative menu provides all the information required.

Sub-menus such as this one, featuring a collection of cuddly toys, help to condense and categorise information so that pages are not weighed down with long lists and descriptions.

The products are illustrated with clear photos. This is frustrating with a slow modem, but it helps to speed up the decision-making process for the potential customer, an important consideration for any catalog.

PC Flowers is part of the Prodigy Shopping Network. Once you have selected your goods, you can go to the checkout, accompanied by dialogue boxes with text assuring you that your transactions are secure. At this point you get a US-style billing form, which has an entry field for every conceivable detail of your purchase.

In the spirit of enhanced cyber-shopping, this section has suggestions and connections to coax you into adding more items to your shopping list.

Just to prove how many good excuses there really are for spending your e-cash, a simple page with wall-to-wall default text spills out a whole range of oddball occasions that demand your gift-purchasing attention. Did you know that July is National Hot Dog month in the US?

With the 'About PC Flowers', 'Supplier Information' and 'Delivery Information' options, this flower gives you all the answers.

Addresses

Glossary

Bandwidth: The spectrum of electrical frequencies that a device or communication line can handle. The term is mostly used in a broader perspective as a standard for the transferring capacity of a device or communication line.

Banner: Usually a combination of text and image that stays on display in the browser window when the page is scrolled through.

Browser: A client program (software) that is used to view various kinds of Internet resources. It downloads HTML files and displays them on the user's screen. Most commonly used browsers are Netscape Navigator and Microsoft's Internet Explorer.

Clickable map: See image map

E-zine: Electronic magazine. A magazine in an electronic medium (either on CD-ROM or Internet).

FAQ's: Frequently Asked Questions — FAQs are documents that list and answer the most common questions on a particular subject.

Form: An HTML-solution allowing user interaction based on filling out forms and sending the information across the Internet.

Frame: A divider that creates separate windows in a webpage. Each frame displays a separate HTML-document and has its own URL independent of the other frames. Frames allow the combination of different documents in a single browser window and the creation of pages where only sections of the page change.

GIF: Graphic Information File. One of the most used formats for graphical files (images, charts etc.) on the World Wide Web.

GIF animation or animated GIF: a form of animation created by arranging a series of GIF images as a sequence in one downloadable file. The sequence can be looped or run through in a single pass. It is a simple alternative to Director-based Shockwave animations.

Homepage: The main page in a website, to which most other pages are linked. Usually this is the first page you see upon entering a site.

HTML: HyperText Mark-up Language. The fundamental make-up language in which web documents are written.

HTML tag: A set of words or characters enclosed between the less than (") and greater than (") symbols in an HTML document, telling the web browser how to format and display a particular piece of the content.

Hyperlink/hypertext: A hyperlink consists of a direct link or reference from one document or piece of text to another, creating a web of (textual) references called hypertext.

Hypermedia: An expansion of the concept of hypertext, linking text with other forms of data such as graphics, motion video or sound — in short any form of information that can be displayed or stored in a computer.

Image map: A graphical element (image, chart, etc.) in an HTML document which, combined with a pixel co-ordinates file, links to several specified URLs. This construction makes the graphical element clickable and turns it into an interface for navigation.

Intelligent agent: A software application that performs certain actions or tasks (semi-) autonomously, often applied in search engines or other information gathering services.

Java: The programming language (developed by Sun Microsystems for downloadable applications), modelled after C++, required to create Java-applets.

Java applet: A downloadable application that runs inside an HTML page when displayed on a compatible browser.

Java-script: The descriptive language derived from Java, which, mixed with HTML-code, enhances the functionality and interactive possibilities of a simple HTML document.

Morphing: A software-based special effect that creates a seamless transition between two shapes or images.

Mouse-over: A Java-script that triggers an action, like loading a new document or a GIF-animation, when the mouse moves across it.

MUD(MOO): Multi User Dungeon (MUD Object Oriented). A multi-user virtual space where people can talk to each other on-line. Most are text-based, but recent versions (like The Palace) create visual environments as well.

QuickTime: An application made by Apple for playing video-files with .mov-extensions.

QuickTimeVR: QuickTime Virtual Reality. An application made by Apple for displaying and manipulating 3D images.

RealAudio: A software application which allows users to play real-time audio over the Internet.

Shockwave: A plug-in, based on Macromedia Director or Authorware, which allows users to interact with animations, digital video movies and sound.

Site map: A graphical representation giving an overview of a site, often allowing direct access to certain parts or individual pages.

Table: The tables, based on the HTML table-tag, allow a sophisticated arrangement of rows and columns of data in cells that can include text, images, and even form input elements

URL: Universal Resource Locator. The address that identifies the location of a site, its pages or documents on the Internet.

VRML: Virtual Reality Mark-up Language. A language like HTML that describes 3D shapes, environments and relationships. It enables the creation of virtual reality-style 'worlds' on the World Wide Web.